Your Dissertation in Education

Nicholas Walliman
& Scott Buckler

Los Angeles | London | New Delhi
Singapore | Washington DC

First Published 2008
Reprinted 2012

SAGE Publications Ltd
1 Oliver's Yard
55 City Road
London EC1Y 1SP

SAGE Publications Inc.
2455 Teller Road
Thousand Oaks, California 91320

SAGE Publications India Pvt Ltd
B 1/I 1 Mohan Cooperative Industrial Area
Mathura Road, Post Bag 7
New Delhi 110 044

SAGE Publications Asia-Pacific Pte Ltd
3 Church Street
#10-04 Samsung Hub
Singapore 049483

Library of Congress Control Number: 2007933815

British Library Cataloguing in Publication data

A catalogue record for this book is available from the British Library

ISBN 978-1-4129-4622-3
ISBN 978-1-4129-4623-0 (pbk)

Typeset by CEPHA Imaging Pvt. Ltd., Bangalore, India
Printed in Great Britain by the MPG Books Group
Printed on paper from sustainable resources

To my wife, Ursula.

N. Walliman

To Claire, Mum and Dad.

S. Buckler

Your
Dissertation
in Education

Summary of Contents

Contents

Acknowledgements

The authors would like to thank the many people who have provided their support in bringing this book together. Indeed, this book would only be an idea floating in the ether if not for the discussions with colleagues and students, past and present, at our respective institutions of Oxford Brookes University, the Open University and University of Worcester. Their discussions and determination have helped inspire this book and indirectly will benefit students to come.

We would also like to acknowledge the support and guidance from everyone at SAGE Publications, especially the editorial team of Claire Lipscomb, Claire Reeves, Patrick Brindle and Vanessa Harwood alongside Lyn Taylor and Aravind Kannankara from the Keyword Group.

Furthermore, this book could not have been written without consulting the expertise of many other authors who are cited in the list of references and reading lists. Although most of the anonymous artists of the copyright-free illustrations used in this book must have passed on by now, we salute their skill and artistry, and often also their humour.

Finally, we would particularly like to acknowledge the support of our wives, Ursula Walliman and Claire Buckler, who have provided the much needed impetus and encouragement at crucial times. Thank you!

Introduction

Don't panic!

These are the words inscribed in large friendly letters on the cover of Douglas Adam's *The Hitchhiker's Guide to the Galaxy* (HHGTTG). Alas, at some point (if not already experienced), panic may well saunter unabashed into your reality during the dissertation process. Such panic may be minor apprehension ('Should I use Arial or Times New Roman?'; 'Should I list the cat in the acknowledgements?') to earth-shattering distress ('It is due in three weeks and I haven't started!', 'I wondered why you kept telling me to ensure my files were backed up on the computer ...!'). Indeed, I have heard these among many others since supervising my first dissertation and nothing now comes as a surprise. Yet, the mantra that preserves my sanity (oh yes, ... and that of my students) are the two distinct, if not rather humble, words at the top of this page.

In keeping with the HHGTTG, use this humble book you are now holding in your hands as a guide. Extract what you find useful (which I hope is most of it), and leave aside the parts that are not relevant. Although this book will not tell you the best drink to numb your senses after a stimulating day of studying (a Pan-Galactic Gargle Blaster according to the HHGTTG), it is offered to you as a handbook to the dissertation process, a handbook which will lead you gently by the hand as we meander through the chapters in order to enable you to achieve a completed masterpiece.

Talking of masterpieces, this is an update of the original book authored by Nicholas Walliman, a book I have recommended to many students as the core text for helping to structure and complete their dissertations. Indeed it is my honour to be able to work with Nicholas on producing a specifically tailored guide for education students, whether you are in teacher training, education studies, early childhood or any other educationally-related degree programme.

Although it may seem that ploughing through another book may distract you from actually getting on with your dissertation, reading this book should enable you to complete your dissertation more quickly and more easily, and is more likely to result in you obtaining a good grade (alas, no money-back guarantee, however). The main consideration is that you will be conducting a research-based written exercise of this scale for the first time, resulting in a lot to learn and implement over a relatively short duration. Furthermore, there will be little room for making errors with this process as the deadline cannot be postponed indefinitely. This is where this book will be of invaluable use in helping you plan, organize and conduct your work; it may even reduce the number of other textbooks you will need to consult to glean necessary information from here and there.

Research methods textbooks do not come with a health warning, but they are generally a heavy read. With this in mind, it would be worth defining what this book is ... and what this book is not:

- It is ...
  - A guide to completing a dissertation, looking at the whole process from start to finish.
- It is not ...
  - A research methodology book, although research methods are discussed. There are numerous books on the market that could, however, be recommended.

This book has been structured by grouping various chapters into different sections which relate to the different phases of your dissertation. The chapters have been kept short (that is why there are so many of them) in order to focus on answering one particular question at a time. You should easily be able to pick out whichever question interests you at the moment. It is therefore not necessary to read through from the beginning to the end. However, I have tried to put the questions into the same general sequence as they appear when you progress through your research project, so you should find navigating the process easy enough. This also results in some elaboration later on in the book of topics that were raised earlier, consistent with your growing understanding of the issues.

- **Section 1** introduces the dissertation and the structure, while also discussing key aspects of educational research and preliminary issues to consider before embarking on the process.
- **Section 2** is based on establishing a focus for your work, structuring a proposal and writing an introduction.
- **Section 3** discusses how to explore the background of your topic, specifically focussing on literature and forming sound arguments.
- **Section 4** explores different aspects of practically conducting your research, focussing on specific research methods.
- **Section 5** provides suggestions on how to make sense of the data you have collected and discusses the implications of this.
- **Section 6** concludes the book by looking at practical suggestions for surviving the process, for example using tutorials effectively, time management and presenting work.

It appears to be a growing trend that textbooks provide a lot of exercises to complete in order to practise what you have read and to test yourself on whether you have understood the main points raised. In general, it could be questioned whether these are completed as they may seem remote from your specific focus, and that the reason for reading a book is to gain information, not to be asked 'what do you think?' Instead, I would urge you to constantly reflect on what you are reading, how this influences your thoughts in relation to your dissertation, what you will do and how you will do it. In this way, you will be able to decide what is relevant to your own work and where you will need to follow-up on issues in more detail in other literature. In order to prompt you to make some decisions at the end of each chapter, there is a section on 'what to do next'. Again, what you will do will be directly linked to your own research focus, so you will not waste any time completing these generalized academic exercises. Furthermore, at the end of each chapter are a number of references where you can find more information on the topics discussed if you need to.

This book has been written in order to give a basic introduction to the main factors in writing an undergraduate dissertation in education. What this book will also help you to do is decide just what further information you require. Of course, background and specific information about your subject will need to be gathered independently by you, irrespective of the research approach you take.

Ultimately, I hope that you find your dissertation a useful experience, where you learn a lot about a subject in which you are interested and end up getting the good marks you deserve.

A word about language

Education covers a variety of contexts. Throughout this book, examples have been provided across different educational settings. For brevity, however, please note that where I use 'pupil' or 'child', this could stand for any learner aged 0–99. Furthermore, where 'school' has been mentioned, this could refer to any institution, whether formal (college, pre-school, organization) or informal (the home, outside, etc.).

SECTION 1

This first section looks specifically at what an educational dissertation consists of and provides a background to the rest of this book.

Chapter 1 specifically provides the structure for this book, discussing what a dissertation is, the key elements and how these thread together. As such it sets the scene for how this book develops: whereas subsequent chapters may be 'dipped into' when your need arises, I would recommend that this chapter is read initially.

Chapter 2 discusses educational research. What do we mean by 'education'? What do we mean by research? How do these two words interconnect?

As the likelihood of your dissertation will focus on human participants, particularly children or young adults, Chapter 3 is concerned with ethical issues. It would be a shame if you had prepared a wonderful focus through your reading, established a detailed methodology to enable your research to be conducted, for your work to come to a stand-still as you had not considered the ethical concerns as paramount importance. Although this would be unlikely, this chapter will ensure that you consider the implications of your research intentions.

1 What Is a Dissertation?

1.1 Why do I have to do a dissertation?

The dissertation is commonly the last component of a degree course, or a module taken towards the end of the undergraduate course. Over your years of study you have been guided step-by-step and fed with lots of information, yet consumed more through your own research for assignments. The dissertation however, is an exercise in independent study. Indeed the term 'independent study' is increasingly being used across institutions in place of dissertation, either way they mean more or less the same thing. Whatever term is used at your institution, the dissertation/independent study tests your abilities to educate yourself, to demonstrate your expertise in collecting and analysing information and to come to conclusions based on solid argument. It also gives you an opportunity to show how well informed you are, how well organized you can be and how you can make a clear presentation of your work for effective communication.

The big difference between this and your previous work is that you will be doing the dissertation on your own. You will probably receive some general guidance on the process, and a supervisor to oversee your work, but most of the decisions about what you do and how you do it will be yours. This not only gives you a lot of freedom to pursue a particular interest but also enables you to put your own individual talents to their best use. This will inevitably require some soul-searching and evaluation of where your strongest talents lie. It is really up to you to make yourself shine in your best light!

What you are required to do can be termed 'research', as it is about finding out new things (even if they are only new to you), making sense of these and presenting your

FIGURE 1.1   You will be doing this on your own.

findings in an organized and well-argued way. As with any research project, there must be stated aims at the outset, and some kind of achievement of these by the end.

This type of work obviously presents lots of opportunities but also some dangers. The point of this book is to guide you through the process of doing a dissertation, and to explain and discuss the options you might have at each stage. It will help you to make informed decisions that you can build on in order to produce a successful outcome. It should not be all hard slog, but it will present some serious challenges in terms of your knowledge and understanding of your subject matter and of your abilities to organize and

FIGURE 1.2   Lots of opportunities, but also some dangers.

motivate yourself. In fact it can be one of the most satisfying processes to go through – and come out of at the other side.

1.2 What skills does the dissertation demonstrate?

Ultimately the dissertation demonstrates your ability to work independently, utilizing a number of personal skills, something employers are only too eager to look for within their employees. Remember that a degree is a sheet of paper given to you at graduation … and what an expensive piece of A4 it is! The time, effort and financial sacrifice you have made over the years is condensed into, albeit a rather intricately designed certificate. The only thing differentiating your certificate from that of the person sitting next to you, or any of your cohort for that matter, is your name and degree classification. When compared with fellow students with similar degrees across the country, what enables an employer to ensure that you are the right person for the job?

No doubt over the duration of your degree you have meticulously tracked and recorded how you have developed your developing graduate skills. Although there are specific frameworks of skills depending on your actual subject and the way your institution implements these, your skills will be a combination of attributes that employers want. An example of such skills is demonstrated in Illustration 1.1 where different areas of mechanical, personal and academic skills unite through research. This in turn demonstrates that if you can conduct independent work to a good standard, this implicitly demonstrates your ability to perform a number of tasks expected from a graduate.

I would argue that every graduate career has an element of research and that education is no different. Such research may include day-to-day tasks of assessing performance of learners, through to reflecting on how you could develop and progress your learners through trialling and implementing a new method. This research process has been summarized in Illustration 1.2, where the different aspects commonly associated with research link from one to another. At the centre of this diagram is research. Research skills may be listed as:

- Acquire: obtaining information through one of many processes, for example, interview, observation or questionnaire.
- Record: noting the information down in a usable format, for example comments a person says, frequencies of an observed behaviour, etc.
- Organize: once the information has been noted, it needs to be structured into a useable format.
- Analyse: the information needs to be reviewed and analysed in order to establish if there are trends, etc.
- Synthesize: more than one source of information may have been collected, for example a person's views may have been recorded from an interview and a questionnaire. This information then needs to be compared to other information, for example, existing theories from literature, or compared to other results collected to establish new theories.

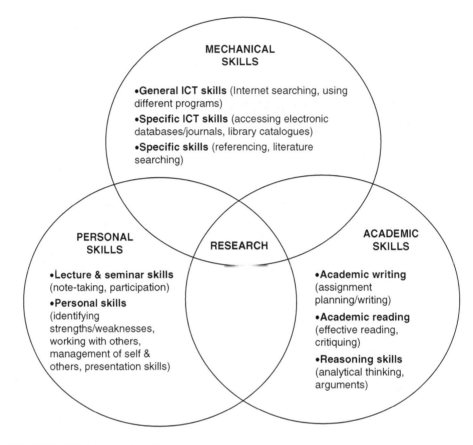

ILLUSTRATION 1.1   Study skills.

- Apply: the information once collected and analysed needs to be put into practice in some format, otherwise there is little point in having conducted the research in the first place!
- Evaluate: once the information has been applied, it is necessary to assess how effective this was in achieving a desired result.
- Reflect: finally, depending on the evaluation, what worked? What didn't? What would be the next logical step to take?

Consequently being aware of the skills you are developing and demonstrating through your dissertation will put you at an advantage when confronted by an interview panel. Such research skills demonstrate that you are a true professional, one who continually questions what they do on a day-to-day basis.

1.3   How is a dissertation structured?

The dissertation should be a journey both for you and for the reader. In relation to yourself, the final product could be related to a series of holiday snaps. As such, other people can get a snapshot of where you have been and what it was like, however, they will never be able to sense all that you have – all of the sights, sounds, smells, feelings,

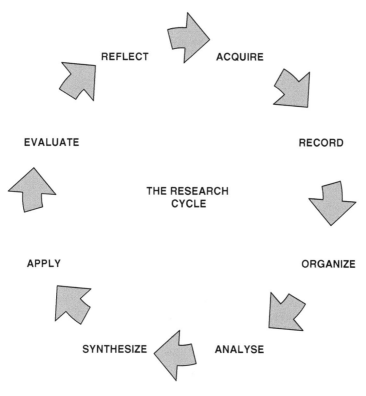

ILLUSTRATION 1.2   The research cycle.

etc. in full. In relation to the reader, the snaps should be in order and illustrate the story of your holiday: it would look out of synchronization if your snapshots started with you arriving back at your home before you had been anywhere. Indeed, would anyone really be interested in seeing you loaded up with your suitcases, or would they prefer to spend more time looking at photos of the actual place you went?

It must be noted however, that the dissertation is not likely to be completed in one smooth transition, where you write your chapters in order. Research is a messy process and you may be engaged with the actual research before you have written your methodology. This is common with nearly all the students I have worked with however, the key to a successful dissertation is to ensure that eventually the final product makes logical sense in how it unfolds without making erratic jumps.

Consequently there has to be a logical sense of ordering and progression, with additional weighting given to some parts and less to others. This is the secret of success for your dissertation! However, it is easier said than done ... how can this realistically be achieved?

An analogy of the dissertation journey was once shared with me by Dr John Hockey of the University of Gloucestershire: he was the person who made the whole research process make sense through a simple diagram (so my gratitude will always go to you John!). This analogy was quite simple and related to an hourglass. It is this model that

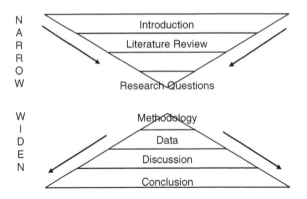

ILLUSTRATION 1.3   'Hourglass' research approach.

I have elaborated on further within this book and which will serve as a model for the various stages.

The basic idea behind the hourglass model is that you need to narrow a focus initially to a series of research aims/objectives or research questions. These then are broadened through your actual research activity, with generalizations made towards the end of your research. Illustration 1.3 illustrates the hourglass approach and the key chapters of the dissertation (which will be discussed next).

There are a number of chapters that are generally expected in any education dissertation. These may have different terms depending on your institution, however they are generally applicable to the headings used throughout this book. Put imply these are:

- Introduction
- Literature review
- Methodology
- Results
- Discussion and conclusion

This five chapter dissertation structure is perhaps one of the most common, however there are different variations, for example the conclusion may be written as a separate chapter taking the dissertation to a total of six chapters. For this book, we have adopted the five chapter model.

The chapters will be discussed in greater detail as you progress through this book, however for the moment, a brief overview of the content of each chapter has been provided.

Introduction (refer to Chapter 7)

- Define the focus of your research
  - A short summary of the context of the study.
  - The main problems or issues to be investigated.
  - The overall approach to the project.

- The environmental issues of your research
- Research aim and objectives
- Signposting your research

Literature review (refer to Chapter 12)

- Introduction
- Development
  - Aspects of the subject investigated
  - Historical and current context
  - Evidence of problems or contentious issues
  - Current debate – comparison of different opinions or approaches
- Conclusion
  - Shortcomings in the level of knowledge

Methodology (refer to Chapter 18)

- General approach to your research (your research stance/philosophy)
- Selection and description of methods related to your objectives
- Selection of samples
- Ethical statement
- Discussion of how your research adheres to validity and reliability
- Method(s) of analysis and presentation of results (e.g. charts, graphs, diagrams, spreadsheets, statistics, coding systems, models, commentaries, etc.).

Results (refer to Chapters 19 and 20)

- Charts, graphs, diagrams, etc. with annotation and interpretation

Discussion (refer to Chapter 21)

- Introduction
- Impact of findings
- Impact on practice
- Recommendations for action
- Impact of methodology
- Impact on you
- Conclusions (although this may be a separate chapter)
  - Conclusions drawn from sets of data in relation to the main issues (this can be separated into sections for each aim/objective
  - Overall conclusions of the dissertation

Additional information

At the end are sections that provide important information on aspects of the work.

- A list of references – fuller details about all the publications and other sources that you have cited in the text.

FIGURE 1.3   Some kind of illustrations or diagrams.

- Appendices – supplementary information such as questionnaires, letters, related information, pictures, etc.) These give examples of your methods of working and/or further
  background information about issues that are important to your work, but not so central
  as to warrant being included in the main text.

I don't know about you, but I always like to see some kind of illustrations or diagrams
in things that I read. Not only do these enliven the appearance of the page, but they also
can encapsulate ideas or issues in an incredibly compact manner.

1.4   What will impress? Seeing it from the examiner's perspective

In order to be awarded a really good grade, it is obviously useful to understand exactly
what the examiner will be looking for when marking. The following list will indicate the
main areas that gain marks in any dissertation. These areas will be discussed in detail in
the following chapters of the book, with many handy hints to help you achieve the best
possible result. The list is not presented in any order or priority and is separated into
three areas. These areas are likely to be the way the examiner marks your dissertation,
from the first impression of the work, through to a quick review in order to ascertain
the focus and main findings of your work, finally a detailed reading to assess how your
dissertation is threaded.

First impressions count

Presentation   Although your dissertation will be marked according to academic content, creating a favourable first impression to start with can only be of benefit. A neat

FIGURE 1.4   On the pile with all the rest.

cover, practical binding and well-deigned page layout all contribute to creating such an impression. Furthermore, ensure that the font is easily readable, for example using a basic font (Arial, Times New Roman, etc.) that is of a clear size (size 12) with at least 1.5 line spacing. Your institution may detail specifically how they want your work to be submitted: take note! Remember that your dissertation will be on a pile with all of the others to be marked, and your examiner will be naturally better disposed to the more attractive submissions.

Organization   A brief scan through the dissertation should give an immediate impression of how the work is organized. This means clearly headed sections, easily spotted chapter divisions and a logical arrangement of the sections of the study. The examiner will feel much more comfortable with work that is easy to navigate. A clear structure is a strong indication of clear thinking – a markable aspect of the work.

Length   Should conform to the requirements. A report that looks too thin or too thick immediately rings alarm bells for the marker. The former will be difficult to award sufficient marks and the latter will be a daunting task to wade through.

Quick review

Abstract   Although this is not always a requirement, this is useful as a brief introduction for the reader. Summarize your whole dissertation in 150–200 words, including the main conclusions. Not an easy task but good practice, and again demonstrates clear thinking.

List of contents   Situated near the front of the dissertation, this gives a simple overview of not only what is in the text, but how it is organized. It will also provide a useful navigation tool for later on to find the page numbers of the different sections.

Main conclusions   One of the main points of doing a dissertation is to come to some conclusions based on the research. The final chapter should spell out the conclusions extremely clearly so that they can be picked out by the examiner by simply scanning through the pages. He/she will check that the conclusions relate exactly to the research problem or question.

Reference list   This will be a measure of your background reading, both in depth and in scope. You will impress your examiner if the relevant books are cited, but won't if your list is padded with numerous extraneous references.

Detailed reading

Relevance and quality of background study   You will not be reinventing the wheel. Whatever the subject you are tackling, there will be numerous other writers and experts who have worked in the same area. The examiner will look to see if you have discovered the main ones relevant to your study and have understood what they have written. This will provide the context for your own research and will enable you to pinpoint the particular issue that you will tackle in your study. It will also provide precedents of how the research might be carried out.

Clarity of research problem or question   It is essential to be clear, not only in your own mind but also in your writing, about the exact problem or question that you are tackling. This is the foundation stone of your dissertation and produces the main aims of the research. The research problem or question will be elaborated

FIGURE 1.5 The foundation stone of your dissertation.

and dissected during the course of your study, but it remains the linchpin of all your research efforts. It should be possible throughout the dissertation for the examiner to relate the writing to the stated aims derived from the research problem or question.

Selection of methods for data collection and analysis   One of the main aims of doing a dissertation is to discover and implement basic research methods. The choice of methods is huge, so you will be marked both on the discussion about possible methods and on the appropriateness of your choice.

Use of research methods   Each method has its own rules and procedures, so you need to demonstrate that you have understood these and implemented them correctly.

Solidity of argument to support findings and conclusions   You could see the whole dissertation as a piece of detective work, with the report being the evidence and argument that leads to your conclusions. Do you have a watertight case? The examiner will dissect the logic of your argument and weigh the strength of your conclusions based on the evidence you bring forward.

Quality of referencing   Your work will inevitably be based on the research and writings of others; after all, that is how we learn about most things. It is therefore essential that you acknowledge the source of your information and ideas by consistent use of a citing and referencing system. Marks are specifically allotted to this aspect of the work.

Quality of writing   The main form of your communication is the written word. Correct spelling and grammar are basic requirements (your word processor will help to some extent). Proper sentence and paragraph construction are also essential; these will be partly dependent on your personal style. You should aim at clarity throughout. The examiner will have limited time to read your work, so make it easy for him or her: you will be rewarded for this. If you are not writing in your first language, it is a good idea to find a native English speaker to read through your work and correct it as necessary.

Marking criteria

It is also important that you refer to any student course handbooks in order to see the explicit criteria used for marking. This may mean that you will have to dig out the handbooks provided to you in induction week of your first year! Institutions are increasingly placing handbooks online, so again it may be worth locating these. If in any doubt, ask your supervisor for a copy of the marking criteria.

The criteria are likely to be subdivided into a number of different areas correlating with respective grades. These areas are unlikely to hold equal weighting but it should be clear which areas are of paramount importance: again, if in doubt, ask your supervisor. Remember these criteria are there to ensure markers grade dissertations fairly and are not a state secret!

Check your degree regulations

It is also worth remembering that the dissertation can significantly alter your grade profile. The final classification of your degree is generally worked out on either an aggregate score of your second and third year grades, or solely your third year grades, depending on which gives the higher grade. Your dissertation may be worth one-quarter of the grade weighting for your final year, perhaps more (you will be aware of the relative grades used within your institution). Some institutions place such significance on the overall grade, that even if you have averaged a high overall pass mark for most of your work, a poor dissertation can reduce this significantly. By this, some institutions have regulations on degree awards where the overall classification of a degree has to be in line with the dissertation. For example, if you average an A grade, yet your dissertation is awarded a D, the highest award you may possibly earn is a C.

1.5   A word of warning

The dissertation process should come with a health warning ... you are likely to endure many variations of psychological states from elation to severe frustration. I do not have the intention of scaring you from attempting and completing the process this early on in the book however, if you know what to expect, you can be prepared for it. In other words, take it as advice from one who has gone through and continually goes through the 'research rollercoaster'.

If you like rollercoaster rides, then you will love research! The research rollercoaster has many highs, a few lows, is both exhilarating and nerve-wracking at the same time. Indeed you may loose all sense of direction as you appear to go back on yourself and turn upside down. This is demonstrated by Illustration 1.4.

From this illustration, you are unlikely to end up where you originally intended. As new information is acquired, whether through literature or through your research activities, you may head along a different route. If you ever find a person who says that they ended up exactly where they intended, they are either (a) extremely insightful and a rare researcher, or (b) not telling the whole truth!

1.6   One of the most important tips in this book is ...

This next bit may make you think I am slightly insane – thank heavens I am writing a book for education students and not psychology students as they may have a lengthy-named condition for me!

I have a number of thought fairies who come to me when I least expect them. (I am in good company – Richard Bach originally noted such creatures in his writings!) The garden fairy and the supermarket fairy are the most active with the car fairy trailing slightly behind. These folk come to me with their greatest ideas at the most inopportune times, no more so than when pondering which toothpaste may help prevent the most cavities.

You could spend two weeks thinking about an important area on your dissertation and not be able to make sense of it, then when you least expect it *BANG* the thought explodes into your mind with such clarity that is knocks you senseless. However, this

GET A NOTEPAD AND PEN AND KEEP THESE WITH YOU AT ALL TIMES!
You will get your best ideas at the most inopportune moments!

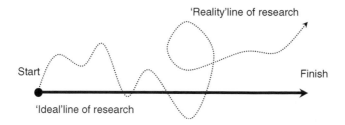

ILLUSTRATION 1.4   The research rollercoaster.

only lasts for a fleeting moment so you need to try and capture this muse at that moment before it flees.

So in order to maximize the potential of these inspirational moments, a notepad and pen are your key research tools that prevent you accruing a pile of supermarket receipts, bus tickets, chewing gum wrapper, etc., with your key ideas penned in a scrawl you can barely read.

Nowadays I have a digital voice recorder I keep with me for these inspirational moments, although I must warn you that if you suddenly start talking to yourself in the middle of the supermarket, you will get funny stares! Thankfully with technological advances, most mobile phones have some voice record mechanism and it would be worth getting to know where this is on yours.

Indeed, if there are any readers versed in psychology, you may be able to explain how and why these ideas come at inopportune times. It may be that the subconscious is actively working on the problem and can only surface when you are engaged with more mundane tasks.

Whether you use modern technology or trusted pen and paper, develop the habit of keeping these to hand and writing up your notes from the outset. This will make the dissertation process easier and when you come to write up your closing chapters, you will already have a stock-pile of notes on which you can draw.

1.7   What should I do now?

Even if you do not know yet exactly what you are going to choose as a subject for your dissertation, it is a good idea to go and look at the work of students from previous years. Your department or your university/college library should keep copies of all the dissertations. Find out where they are. You will probably be impressed by the sheer number of them, so how do you start looking to find something useful? Here is a good way to do it.

Find out what order they are in on the shelves. If they are in some kind of subject order, then choose four or five on the subject area that you are interested in. If not, any recent dissertations from your course will do. If you can only get them by request from the library catalogue, then choose some from the list. Ideally, choose dissertations that have been completed according to the regulations and instructions that you have to follow.

Don't sit down and try to read them. First, compare the following features:

- format (size and shape)
- design of cover
- type of binding
- design of page layouts
- printing fonts and styles and text layout
- number and type of illustrations.

Now that you have got a general impression of a range of designs (note how important these are in the initial impact), it is time to look more carefully at the components and structure of the dissertations. Check each for the following:

- Title – length and clarity. Can you understand what it is about just by reading the title? Is it too long and complicated? Is it too short and general?
- Preambles – are these clearly labelled and set out? Check what they consist of: title page, acknowledgements, abstract, list of contents with page numbers, lists of figures and tables, anything else (e.g. statement of individual work, dedication, etc.). Look at the layout and design of each of these.
- Chapters or sections – how many, how long and in what sequence. Does the sequence of chapter titles show you how the dissertation is structured? One example might be: introduction, background, research problem, research methods used, data collection, data analysis, conclusions. There are, however, several different ways of structuring dissertations, depending on the type of research undertaken. Compare those that you have selected.

Now go to the end of each and compare the add-on sections. Note:

- length and format of the list of references
- number and type of appendices.

Now if you want to, you can read a few sections of the text to see what the written style is like. Note the use of technical words, the method of citing references and the style of the writing. Check the length of paragraphs and sentence construction. Are they short and precise, or long and complex? Explore how the illustrations are used to complement the text. Whatever you do, don't try to read all the way through. Rather if you have the time, pick a few more examples of dissertations and repeat the exercise. You will soon get a feel of the difference in quality and style, which will help you to form your preferences on which to base your own work.

The length and complexity of the dissertations might be rather daunting, particularly when you consider that you will have to produce something similar within a few months or even weeks. Don't get too worried. Although there will be a lot to learn and plenty to write, if you can choose a subject in which you are really interested, despite the hard work it should be a pleasurable and rewarding exercise, and something to be proud of when you have finished.

1.8   References to more information

As mentioned above, a good place to start is to look at previously completed dissertations. This will not provide you with instructions on how to proceed, but will give you plenty of food for thought, and help to stimulate your own critical faculties about the quality of the work presented. This will be important when it comes to reviewing your own work later on.

Most books on this subject cover the whole sequence of preparing and writing essays and dissertations, much like this one. But hardly any actually discuss why you should do a dissertation, and what the examiners will be looking for. Despite this it is interesting, if you have time, to compare the advice given at this stage of the process. The approaches vary, depending on the level of essay or dissertation aimed at, and in some, the specific subject area catered for. Only look at the preliminary advice given in the first few pages of the books and scan the contents page to see if there is anything else of interest further on. You can probably do this in the library without even taking the books out on loan.

Here are a few books that I have found, and I have given notes on what to look for in them. Each gives a slightly different view of the issues, so refer to as many as possible. Consult your own library catalogue for these and any similar ones that are available. When you locate them on the shelves, look at the contents list of promising books for relevant chapters.

Blaxter, L., Hughes, C. and Tight, M. (1996) *How to Research*, 2nd edn. Buckingham: Open University Press.

Cottrell, S. (2003) *The Study Skills Handbook*, 2nd edn. Basingstoke: Palgrave Macmillan.

> This book is one of the best on study skills. It is easy to read and written in a very friendly style with numerous checklists, hints and tips to help survive. Although your dissertation is your final piece of work, this book would be worth referring to in order to ensure your other academic skills are in check.

Hart, C. (2004) *Doing Your Masters Dissertation (Essential Study Skills)*. London: Sage.

> A useful, generic book especially for those working at post-graduate level.

Mounsey, C. (2002) *Essays and Dissertations*. Oxford: Oxford University Press.

> See Chapters 1 and 10.

Redman, P. (2005) *Good Essay Writing*. London: Sage.

> Chapter 2 discusses what tutors look for when marking essays.

Rudestam, K.E. and Newton, R.R. (2001) *Surviving your Dissertation: A Comprehensive Guide to Content and Process*, 2nd edn. Thousand Oaks: Sage.

Swetnam, D. (2000) *Writing Your Dissertation: How to Plan, Prepare and Present Successful Work*. Oxford: How To Books.

2 What Is Educational Research?

2.1 Introduction

There are four words in the title of this chapter. Out of the four words, the two predominant ones will be discussed individually before the holistic term 'educational research' is defined. You may well have completed a module on educational research which would have provided you with considerable depth into this topic. This chapter will therefore look briefly at the terms 'education' and 'research' before progressing to discuss the overarching themes within educational research.

2.2 What is education?

A book could be written on this question alone … and many have! Thankfully, you should have a good knowledge of the term at this stage of your degree, which makes my task easier. Indeed this question may have been discussed in your induction session many moons ago. But have you stopped and considered this question recently? Your degree is centred on 'education' yet if some interested friend/family member asks what you have been studying for the best part of three years, how would you respond? 'Education', obviously! However, the follow-up question may subsequently be asked … 'but what is education?' And there we are, back at the start of this paragraph!

We could explore a few definitions of education to see how other people have defined the term. Clark (2005: 295) notes that 'education is not a phenomenon at all – its presence of absence is relative to the values of the observer'. Indeed, this places the interpretation on the observer. Matheson (2004) similarly places the onus on the observer, describing education as a slippery concept with a vast range of definitions, meaning precisely what the speaker wants it to mean. Annoyingly this doesn't bring us any closer to a definition!

To the opposite extent, Bartlett, Burton and Peim (2001: 3) define education quite simply, noting that education is 'normally thought to be about acquiring and being able to use knowledge, and developing skills and understanding'. Such simplicity in this definition should be the foundation from which deeper concerns of education are developed. Consequently, between Bartlett et al.'s definition and Clark and Matherson's comment, a more specific definition of education may be reached. In the true style of a tutor, I would like you to consider the term 'education' before progressing any further. Spend a few minutes considering as many ideas as possible on the following questions about education:

- What is 'education'?
- Where does 'education' take place?
- When does 'education' take place?
- Who is involved with the process of 'education'?
- How is 'education' structured?
- Why do we have 'education'?

Of course the answers to the above questions will vary considerably on your perspective: if you are based in the early years, your answers may well differ from a professional police trainer, yet both are concerned with 'education'. Indeed how you personally interpret and view education affects your philosophy of education: your philosophy of education is central to how you progress with your dissertation. (This will be discussed in greater depth as we proceed with the book.)

If we return to Matherson, he actually highlights four key aspects of education:

1 Intentionality and 'something'
2 The notion of transmission
3 The criteria for ascertaining whether the 'something' is worthwhile
4 The basis upon which moral acceptability is to be judged.

Intentionality and 'something'

This could be referred to as the 'What' of education. What is it that needs to be taught?

There is an intention behind education, a motive for educating others. The 'something' is the actual content of education – the knowledge, skills, etc. to be passed on. This takes us to …

The notion of transmission

This could be referred to as the 'How' of education and more specifically the 'Who', 'Where' and 'When' of education.

Education is passed to another in some way. This is through the interaction of teacher to learner: teacher could be a class teacher, parent, colleague, computer program, etc.

The criteria for ascertaining whether the 'something' is worthwhile

This could be referred to as the 'Why' of education. Why is education important?

What is the value of the 'something' that has been transmitted? If it is valuable, then great; if not, what is the point on transferring it? So how can this 'something' be judged? Assessment, OfSTED, etc.

The basis upon which moral acceptability is to be judged

Again, this could be referred to as the 'Why' of education. Why educate others?

Moral acceptability is concerned with the ethics of education: what is acceptable to teach and why? What will be the repercussions of such education, etc?

From this succinct overview of education, we will now progress into discussing research.

2.3   What is research?

In essence research is generally translated about finding out something you didn't know beforehand (although I would like to add that at times, you research something you may have known but forgotten. I may have taken a train on a number of occasions, yet I still check the timetable to ensure it is the right one – this surely employs research skills?) Consequently, a better definition posited by MacNaughton, Rolfe and Siraj-Blatchford (2006: 3) states that 'Research is about discovery. Research creates knowledge'.

There are however, more specific aspects relating to research, for example how to actually ensure that what you find out is genuine, whether the information is actually what you require, what the best method is to find the information, etc. Ultimately, how can we ensure that research is efficient and effective in finding what we want? Consequently, research can get quite involved in a short amount of time. Although Section 4 of this book will discuss research in greater depth, for now the issue is in defining research and its place within education.

There are, however, a number of specific elements in discussing research as an academic activity. Although looking up information on a timetable or checking the weather forecast could be called 'research', how does this compare with completing a dissertation as a sustained piece of academic research? Is time necessarily a factor? Perhaps complex arguments are a contributing factor to academic research?

The notion of research can seem quite troubling from the outset due to the expanse of research issues to consider, the required depth of the research and whether you have completed enough research. It is worth noting that your dissertation is unlikely to demand that you use skills that you have never put into practice before, although it may demand that you combine such skills in different ways in order to research an issue you would like to know more about (you may want to refer back to Illustration 1.1).

Fundamentally, research is conducted daily with your senses: as humans, we continue to process information for our survival through touch, taste, sight, hearing, smell. Generally, research in education limits this to eyes – what we observe, and the ears – what we hear; indeed I am hard pressed to think of examples where the other senses may come into operation!

Furthermore, if you consider how and where you have utilized research previously (perhaps through finding information for assignments) the only difference with the dissertation is that it is multifaceted, a collection of smaller research issues that relate and interrelate to your focus.

Research can thus take different formats for different purposes. Verma and Mallick (1999: 11) propose that research can be either:

- Pure or basic research: development of theory and discovery of fundamental facts to extend the boundaries of knowledge.
- Applied or field research: application of new knowledge to everyday problems.
- Action research: research on specific practical situations carried out by practitioners. Its purpose is to solve clearly identified problems and is continuous and cyclic.
- Evaluation research: carried out to assess the effectiveness of specific projects to see if the original aims have been achieved.

Ultimately, we come to conclude that educational research is derived of two words: the adjective, 'educational' (something related to or involving education) and the intransitive verb 'research' (a methodical investigation on something specific). Yet the sum of these two parts is far more convoluted.

2.4   What is educational research?

From the last two sections of this chapter, you may have gathered that education and research have been problematic to define ... this does not help in actually defining the term 'educational research'. However, various authors have had some success in defining this term. Opie (2004: 3) defines educational research as 'the collection and analysis of information on the world of education so as to understand and explain it better', whereas Clark (2005: 289) defines educational research as 'the scientific construction of the causes of "effective" teaching'. Clark also notes that the subject of education consists of separate disciplines, something Bartlett et al. (2001) also comment on, whereby education consists of philosophy, sociology, psychology and history. Indeed Clark and Bartlett et al. suggest that the disciplines contributing to education can be studied separately or combined.

One often-cited author on educational research is Bassey (1990: 39), who defined educational research as entailing 'systematic, critical and self-critical enquiry which aims to contribute to the advancement of knowledge'. Furthermore, Bassey provides details of what this term means, noting:

- Enquiry: Research is conducted for a purpose in order to get answers to questions, however, this is an attempt and one that may not be achieved.
- Systematic: The importance of collecting and analysing data in a regular pattern has at its foundation, a theoretical rationalized basis.
- Critical: The research ensures that the data presented is as accurate as possible, for example by being a representative sample.
- Self-critical: The importance of the researcher needing to be critical of their methods of collecting, analysing and presenting data.
- Advancement of knowledge: Research should aim to increase the individual's knowledge through informing them of something they didn't know beforehand. This knowledge may in turn be shared with others should it be beneficial through publication.
- Knowledge: Knowledge is the understanding about events, things and processes. Such knowledge includes descriptions, explanations, interpretations and value orientations.

The elusive term 'educational research' could perhaps be illustrated by previous examples of research within education. Such use of examples may help crystallize your ideas on what could be achieved within the classroom.

Nisbet (2005: 6) provides some interesting research findings from the past. In 1908, Binet (synonymous with intelligence and IQ scales) investigated the effect of eating bread on a child's intelligence. His research consisted of analysing housekeeping records of boarding schools, specifically the amount of bread consumed over the school year. His research indicated that the consumption of bread decreased over the year thus concluding that 'intense intellectual work injures the appetite'. Could there really be such correlation? Perhaps you have considered alternate suggestions: the school budget may be diminishing as the year progresses, so that there is less food to go around. Perhaps the children are literally 'fed up' with the same bread and opt for other provisions.

Binet's work, although interesting, does not compare with that of Lorenz, however. Nisbet (2005: 29) outlines the research, whereby Lorenz noted that due to fatigue, children's work was poorer as the school day progressed. From this, he sprayed a class with 'antikenotoxin' (a nerve gas) in order to assess the impact on their work, concluding that their mental processing skills increased by 50 per cent and lowered the number of mistakes made.

Alas on second thought, this last example of educational research may be problematic in obtaining ethical permission, therefore such examples may not help you define an area for your dissertation! Hopefully however, this discussion indicates that the term educational research is very broad, encompassing many areas. You may have been provided with a limited focus for your dissertation (perhaps being constrained to analysing an aspect of learning within a curriculum subject), although it is likely that you can pursue almost any direction you wish. This scope can be far more problematic than being provided with a limited focus as you may well have too many areas that you wish to research. Consequently, Section 2 of this book provides guidance on establishing such a focus.

2.5   What should I do now?

This discussion of educational research has hopefully given you an overview of what you can and cannot do for your dissertation. Instead of limiting the options for what you can study for your dissertation, hopefully this brief chapter would have provided you with a blossoming view of what you could conduct for your research, as long as the parameters of 'education' are met. By this, as long as you can argue that your dissertation is based on education (however, you wish to interpret this), then your research options are limitless.

It would therefore be worth revisiting your understanding of 'education' and consider potential areas of interest for you to pursue with your dissertation. Can you argue that your focus is 'educational'? If someone was to ask you to defend that your dissertation was based on education, could you? You may want to use the who, what, how, why, where, when framework to help structure your thoughts.

2.6   References to more information

There are a number of sources in which you could obtain further information, in fact these can sometimes be overwhelming! Using an effective search strategy should help limit these to a useful number. It would be worth checking previous reading lists for the modules you have completed, especially those on the theoretical and practical aspects of your subject. Your library catalogue is another source, and a quick search of 'educational research' should provide a thorough list. The problem then occurs in identifying those useful for your purposes. As a rule, look for the most recent additions first (those within the past five years), also see whether the title is appealing. Does the title provide a good indication of the contents? Once you have limited your search, read the back cover of the book and the chapter contents to assess whether the information would be beneficial.

The books provided here are indicative of those available:

Theoretical aspects of educational research

Aubrey, C., David, T., Godfrey, R. and Thompson, L. (2000) *Early Childhood Educational Research*. London: Routledge.

Bartlett, S., Burton, D. and Peim, N. (2001) *Introduction to Education Studies*. London: Sage.

Bartlett, S. and Burton, D. (2003) *Education Studies: Essential Issues*. London: Paul Chapman.

Briggs, A.R.J. and Coleman, M., eds (2007) *Research Methods in Educational Leadership and Management*, 2nd edn. London: Sage.

   Part A of the book and specifically Chapter 2.

Carr, W. and Kemmis, S. (1986) *Becoming Critical: Education, Knowledge and Action Research*. Brighton: Falmer.

Christensen, P. and James, A., eds (2000) *Research with Children: Perspectives and Practices*. London: Falmer.

Hopkins, D. (2002) *A Teacher's Guide to Classroom Research*, 3rd edn. Buckingham: Open University Press.

MacNaughton, G., Rolfe, S.A. and Siraj-Blatchford, I. (2006) *Doing Early Childhood Research: International Perspectives on Theory and Practice*. Maidenhead: Open University Press.

Matheson, D., ed. (2004) *An Introduction to the Study of Education*, 2nd edn. London: David Fulton.

McNiff, J. Lomax, P. and Whitehead, J. (1996) *You and Your Action Research Project*. London: Routledge.

See particularly Chapter 2.

Rudduck, J. and McIntyre, D., eds (1998) *Challenges for Educational Research*. London: BERA/Paul Chapman.

Sharp, J., Ward, S. and Hankin, L. (2006) *Education Studies: An Issues Based Approach*. Exeter: Learning Matters.

Ward, S. (2004) *Education Studies: A Student's Guide*. London: Routledge Falmer.

Practical aspects of educational research

Clarke, A. and Erickson, G., eds (2003) *Teacher Inquiry: Living the Research in Everyday Practice*. London: Routledge Falmer.

Cohen, L., Manion, L. and Morrison, K. (2007) *Research Methods in Education*, 6th edn. Abingdon: Routledge.

Denscombe, M. (2003) *The Good Research Guide for Small-Scale Social Research Projects*. Buckingham: Open University Press.

MacNaughton, G., Rolfe, S.A. and Siraj-Blatchfor, I. (2006) *Doing Early Childhood Research: International Perspectives on Theory and Practice*. Maidenhead: Open University Press.

Nutbrown, C., ed. (2002) *Research Studies in Early Childhood Education*. Stoke-on-Trent: Trentham Books.

Opie, C., ed. (2004) *Doing Educational Research: A Guide to First Time Researchers*. London: Sage.

Robson, C. (2002) *Real World Research: A Resource for Social Scientists and Practitioner-Researchers*, 2nd edn. Oxford: Blackwell Publishing.

A resource book, and should be used as such. Good for getting more detailed information on most aspects of data collection and analysis. Read the recommendations at the beginning, on how to use the book.

Verma, G.K. and Mallick, K. (1999) *Researching Education: Perspectives and Techniques*. London: Falmer Press.

It would also be worth asking your tutors for advice on current journals within your area. The following list indicates journals that may be appropriate for your research: this list is not extensive, furthermore the journals may provide too much depth than you actually need. Further information on literature searching will be discussed in Chapter 8.

Early childhood studies

Child Development
Children and Society
Contemporary Issues in Early Childhood
Early Childhood Practice
Early Childhood Research and Practice

Early Years
Education 3–13
European Early Childhood Education Research Journal
International Journal of Early Years Education
Journal of Early Childhood Research
Nursery World

Education studies

American Journal of Education Studies
British Educational Research Journal
British Journal of Educational Psychology
British Journal of Special Education
Comparative Education
Educational Action Research
Educational Management, Administration and Leadership
Educational Studies
Educational Theory
Harvard Educational Review
Journal of Further and Higher Education
Journal of In-service Education
London Review of Education
Pedagogy, Culture and Society
Professional Development Today
Research in Education
Research in Post-compulsory Education
School Leadership and Management

3 What's All This About Ethics?

3.1 What are ethics?

You may well have heard about medical ethics, for example should euthanasia be legalized? Hopefully, you will also have heard about ethics in educational research … after all, you will be working within an ethical framework as you conduct your research and may well have signed an 'official' institutional document relating to this. However, what actually are ethics?

Although there is a branch of philosophy devoted on the area of ethics (or the interchangeable word, morals), as you have a dissertation to write I will only discuss the practical aspects related to educational research. On a simplistic level, ethics is concerned with 'right' and 'wrong', yet who defines these? Is it ever 'right' to stop a person from speaking freely? Is it always 'wrong' to impose your will on someone else? Consequently, these issues of right and wrong and how these apply to your work are paramount.

Ethics is about moral principles and rules of conduct. What have these got to do with writing a dissertation? Quite a lot actually; they focus on your behaviour towards other people and their work. You are not producing your dissertation in a vacuum. You definitely will be basing your information and ideas on work done by other people, and you will be interacting with other people in a more personal way during your study. It is therefore important to avoid unfairly usurping other people's work and knowledge, invading their privacy or hurting their feelings.

3.2   Why are ethics important?

Ensuring that you work within an ethical framework offers security to those you will be researching and also yourself. Let's consider an example: a few years ago, it was claimed that blue 'Smarties' led to hyperactivity in children, due to an artificial colouring used. How could this actually be tested? Perhaps you could go into a classroom and provide only orange Smarties to one table, green to another, yellow to another and blue (the colour at the centre of the furore) to another table... then stand back and observe the consequences. Consider what could go wrong with this research situation.

- Are any of the children on a strict diet?
- Are there any allergies within the class?
- What happens if a child starts to choke on a Smartie?
- What would happen if any of the blue Smartie group injured themselves or another? How would you explain this to their parent/s?

(Alas, for those considering conducting such a Smartie experiment, blue Smarties have now been replaced with white ones!)

Perhaps, opposed to testing the effect of food colouring on behaviour, you were investigating the activity levels and eating habits of children due to the raised concerns of childhood obesity. You have selected a sample group you will focus on, those defined as overweight or obese, and for three weeks you work with this group, monitoring what they eat and leading them through a series of physical activities. Again consider what could go wrong with this research situation.

- The sample group who have been 'labelled' as overweight/obese.
- The parent/s who complain to your headteacher that you are investigating their child's eating habits.
- The parent/s who confront you about 'snooping' on their child.
- The child who has a physical problem, which has been exacerbated through your physical activity programme.

The first scenario is unlikely ever to be conducted in school, yet the second scenario is certainly more likely. As such, how can the 'risks' be reduced or eliminated so that your research does not come to a complete standstill. This is where working within an ethical framework will not only protect your participants but also yourself.

3.3   How can I ensure that I work within an ethical framework?

There are four aspects to consider within any research:

1 Proposal – what are your intentions?
2 Potential – what are the benefits of your research? What are the risks?

3 Permission – who do you need to gain access from? How?
4 Protection – how will you ensure research participants and/or the organization will be protected? How will you ensure that you are protected?

Proposal

This is where you may well have prepared and submitted a dissertation proposal for scrutiny by your supervisor, possibly also completing an ethics form. In some institutions, a research method's module may culminate in the production of a research proposal. The research proposal will be discussed in greater depth in Chapter 6.

Along with your proposal, it is likely that you will need to complete an ethics form. This is a series of questions based on your intended research activities: three of the most likely listed which may well affect your proposal are:

1 If your research involves human participants who may not be able to give fully informed consent
2 If there is a risk to the participant/s (physical, social, psychological or emotional)
3 If the research involves access to sensitive or confidential data.

If for example, your proposal indicates any of these, you may well be asked to provide further details to your supervisor or department in order to limit the risks. The ethics form is then signed by both you and your supervisor and sent to a panel for scrutiny.

Potential

If I were a headteacher at a local school, why would I let you come in to conduct research when it may disrupt the learning experience of the pupils? In other words, what is in it for the school or the children? Furthermore what are the risks? Can you ensure that nobody will be harmed physically, mentally or emotionally due to the intervention of your research? As a headteacher, I offer a duty of care to the pupils, so should it be my concern to question each research proposal, or should it be that of the researcher? If you can demonstrate that you have considered specific risks and how you propose to limit these, then I am more likely to allow you to conduct your research as you would appear a conscientious researcher.

A further consideration is the potential offered to the research participants. What is in it for them? Why should they help you? If for example you wanted to trial two different methods for learning spellings to see which method was the best, children could be encouraged to take part if the benefits resulted in less time being used to learn spellings.

Permission

Who actually needs to give their permission for research to be conducted and why? The chair of governors, headteacher, teacher, parent/s, pupils can all be considered for gaining permission. Have they been informed of your research intentions, the benefits and potential risks? Although your research may not necessarily warrant asking the headteacher or governors questions, these people are the 'gatekeepers' to the research participants and without their permission, you will not get far!

Perhaps you do not want people to know that you are conducting research. If your research was based on the topics of conversation in a staffroom, if staff knew that you were recording their conversations, they are likely to alter their topics. Indeed, is there ever a place for covert research … is this 'right' or 'wrong'?

It would be worth discussing with your supervisor who they feel should be considered for permission depending on your research intentions. Predominantly this will consist of the headteacher (or equivalent), although it may well include any of those mentioned above. The school may have previously asked prospective parents to sign a disclosure allowing permission for out-of-school activities (for example, visiting the local library, or going to swimming lessons during school time), furthermore asking their permission for small-scale research to be conducted with their child. This cannot be guaranteed, so it would be worth asking the headteacher whether they feel further permission needs to be granted.

In general, if your research is based on a curriculum intervention, for example gaining views on favourite genres of story, such research is unlikely to warrant gaining parental permission as the research focus is an everyday activity. If however, you wanted children to complete a food diary for a week, recording their breakfast, lunch and evening meal, parental permission is likely to be sought, whereby you would need to explain why this research was taking place. Similarly you may be relying on parental support to help complete the diary. Furthermore, let's say that you had an interest in bullying: how could you tactfully raise this with the relevant gatekeepers? For example, would you just go up to a headteacher and say 'I'm interested in conducting a study into bullying. Please can I have permission to come into your school?' Would any headteacher acknowledge that their school had a bullying problem? Of those who do, how many would want you to come in and research it? This is not to say that you cannot conduct a study on bullying but that you need to be very careful in what your intentions are and how you gain relevant permission.

There is no hard and fast rule on whose permission you need to seek: this is why it is an ethical consideration. One person may think it is not necessary to seek permission, yet you may feel it is.

There are two main ways of seeking permission: in person and in writing. With the former, you may be in a position where you can approach the place directly, for example, you may currently work there or be on school experience. As such, it would be easy to approach the headteacher and outline your research proposal. If however, you are not in such a position, your first contact may be through a letter. Either way, the following advice will be of benefit to ensure your research can go ahead.

Written permission

It would be great to think that your letter will take precedence on the headteacher's post pile. You are passionate about your dissertation, so they surely must equally be so. Although I cannot talk for all headteachers, generally such letters may end up in the in-tray of 'things-to-do-when-I-have-a-minute' and may well sit there for some time. Consequently, it is worth ensuring that the letter is direct, outlines specifically your intentions and what you require, and finishes with a 'hook', something that will either (a) get them to respond to you, or (b) allows you to approach them again in person.

Ideally the letter should be one side of A4: if it is any longer, they are unlikely to read your letter in depth. The letter should contain the following information:

- Your name/address/date
- The headteacher's name (there is nothing worse than a letter being addressed impersonally, i.e. 'To Whom It May Concern', 'Dear Headteacher'. If you are unsure about their name, look up the website for the school and failing that, the OfSTED report from www.ofsted.gov.uk, although the report may be dated)
- Some detail about who you are (you could be anybody!)
- An overview of your research intentions (what you actually intend to do)
- Why the research is important (it may be stating the obvious to the reader but at least it demonstrates something they are secure with and therefore non-threatening)
- How the research will be conducted (what are the 'costs' in terms of time and effort to the school/organization?)
- The benefits (will these outweigh the 'costs' – if so, you should seek a career in marketing!)
- Potential risks (and how these will be negated)
- Ethical considerations (the framework in which you will be operating)
- What will happen with the data (will they appear as an exposé in some suspect newspaper?)
- Additional questions (your opportunity to 'get your foot in the door').

The following is an example of the main components of a consent-seeking letter based on the above points:

Dear Mr Lawrence,
I am a third year student studying Education at the University of XXX. I am specifically interested in the development of children's spelling and am proposing to conduct research into this area for my dissertation. As I am sure you are aware, effective spelling strategies are fundamental to success in literacy.
Through my research I am hoping to evaluate a couple of spelling strategies that have recently been posited in 'Spelling Today' and assess which may be of most use for Year 5 children. This would entail working with two groups of Year 5 children for 20 min each week for half a term. As these strategies have been demonstrated to raise children's spelling success, I would be happy to share my findings with your staff at a later stage.
This research is unlikely to put anyone at risk, as I would be conducting the research within the class, hopefully during a time when other children may be working on their

spellings. Furthermore, I would be happy to work with other groups in the class so that all of the children had an equal opportunity to develop these strategies. It is unlikely that these strategies will conflict with the methods they are familiar with, if anything it will provide the children with an additional approach to implement. Furthermore, this research will adhere to the British Educational Research Association and University ethical guidelines.

The data I will gather will ensure anonymity of participants and the school but will be used in the completion of my dissertation. Confidentiality will be ensured at all times.

I am sure that you have questions relating to my proposed research and as such I would welcome the opportunity to discuss this further. Please may I ask you to complete the attached form and return in the pre-paid envelope.

Or

I will telephone on … at … to discuss my proposed research and whether you would allow me to conduct my research at your school.

Yours sincerely,

Dear Scott

I am available to see you to discuss your research intentions further on ………………
at … a.m./p.m.

I am sorry but I do not wish to partake of this research.

(Please delete as appropriate)

Signed …………………………

There are some points to keep in mind when preparing your letter. The first is when your letter is likely to reach them. If it lands on their desk first thing on a Monday morning, it is unlikely to get read immediately and filed to one side (no doubt the latest educational update, or most recent government policy will be more pressing). If your letter reaches them on a Friday, it may be filed away to deal with the following week. Try to keep in mind the busy times of the school year (the start and end of terms in general), thus ensure that you have plenty of time to seek permission before you actually need to start your data gathering.

Your letter needs to make a good impression! A sheet of quality paper and matching envelope will ensure that your letter is not binned with all of the other marketing leaflets distributed on a daily basis. Similarly, ensuring that your letter is easy to read (visually and grammatically) will be of benefit.

Protection

Although this has been covered through discussing the risks, other factors also need to be considered, for example the rights of the individual. If a respondent mentions something derogatory about another person and I record this, what could happen if I carelessly left my notes lying about? As a rule of thumb, if your research (or some part of it) was dropped on the street, could it find its way back to the individual or school being researched? If it was dropped in the school, could it find its way to the child or their parent?

Not only do you need to protect the rights of the individual but you also need to protect yourself through not exposing yourself to unnecessary risks. No doubt if your degree involves work placements, you are likely to have previously completed a Criminal Records Bureau check, however, in this day of litigation, could you be at risk if researching with a group of children when alone in an unsupervised room? What happens if somebody takes offence at your research, whether a member of staff, a child or a parent? Needless to say, the aforementioned section on risk assessment should cover this, however. If in doubt, ask your supervisor or someone within the research setting for advice.

3.4   What are the rights of the individual?

Many dissertation subjects require the getting of information from people and in particular with education, this may well involve children. This data collection may predominantly be in the form of interviews or questionnaires, but could also be types of experiments. Whenever dealing with other people, specifically children, you must be sensitive to issues of privacy, fairness, consent, safety, confidentiality of information, impartiality, etc. This is actually quite a complex subject, and it requires real thought about how your plans for getting information or opinions from people can be carried out in a way that complies with all these ethical issues.

Here are some of the main aspects to check.

Inform people

Participants have a right to know why you are asking them questions and to what use you will put the information that they give you. Explain briefly before interviewing and add an explanatory introduction to questionnaires. If you will be conducting some kind of test or experiment, you should explain what methods you will use.

> *Example:*   You want to find out how much time children spend in various clubs or activities after school. You may have written a questionnaire to parents with a covering letter explaining that you are conducting a study for your degree to gain an insight into the range of activities available in the locality.

Ask permission and allow refusal to participate

Do not assume that everyone is willing to help you in your research. Once they are informed about the project they should be clearly given the choice to take part or not. A more formal agreement like the one suggested in the previous section will be appropriate for extended projects or those of a sensitive or intimate nature.

> *Example:*   You may want to identify a specific group of learners and assess their physical coordination skills. You will need to explain exactly what you wish them to do, safety implications, clothing and footwear required, what your role will be and how information

FIGURE 3.1   Getting information from other people.

will be collected. This will enable the possible participants to judge if they want to take part.

Respect privacy through anonymity

Most surveys rely on the collection of data, the sources of which do not need to be personally identified. In fact, people are far more likely to give honest replies to questions if they remain anonymous. You should check that the way data are collected and stored ensures anonymity – omit names and addresses, etc. Treat data as numbers wherever possible.

Example: You are distributing a questionnaire to parents about the television viewing habits of their children. To ensure anonymity, the questionnaires must not contain anything that may identify the respondent, for example even a family profile might do this. Delivery and collection of the questionnaires should also be considered to ensure that the information cannot get into the wrong hands.

Attribution

If anonymity is not desired or even possible, for example when obtaining particular views of named influential people, the information collected must be accurately attributed to the source. Agreement must be obtained that the opinions/information given can be used in your dissertation.

Example: You are interviewing teachers and the headteacher about the implementation of a new behaviour policy. There must be no confusion in your account of the interviews about who said what. Ask before the interviews if you will be allowed to quote them in your dissertation.

Obtain authorization

It is good practice to send a draft of the parts of your work containing the views or information given by named sources to those concerned, asking them to check that your statements are accurate and that they are allowed to be included in your dissertation.

Example: In the above example, if the interviews are lengthy, and the opinions are contentious in what is probably a sensitive situation, you will gain respect and cover yourself against problems if you get a signed copy of the drafts of your accounts of the individual interviews from the respective people. This is absolutely necessary if you quote people directly. If you say you will do this in advance, you will be likely to get a less cautious response during the interview, as there is an opportunity for the interviewee to check for accuracy.

Fairness

In any tests or experiments, thought should be given to ensure that they are fair, and can be seen to be so. Participants will feel cheated if they feel that they are not treated equally or are put at some kind of disadvantage.

Example: You have devised a simple test to gauge people's manual dexterity on equipment that can only be used by the right hand. Left-handed people will feel justifiably disadvantaged.

Avoid sexism

The way language is used can often lead to sexism, particularly the use of masculine labels when the text should actually refer to both men and women. Bias, usually towards the male, is also to be avoided in your research.

Example: The use of words such as 'manpower' rather than 'labour power', 'one-man show' rather than 'one-person show', and the generic 'he' or 'his' when you are referring to a person of either sex. Research bias can occur when you devise a study that assumes the boss is a man, or that all primary school teachers are women.

Be punctual, convenient and brief

Punctuality, brevity and courteousness are essential qualities to help your efforts to gain information. Appointments should be made and kept. Time is a valuable commodity for almost everybody, so it will be appreciated if you regard it as such.

Example: You need to get expert information on the intricacies of life as a pre-school leader. You turn up three-quarters of an hour late, just at a time when a large crowd of parents have accumulated to collect their children. You have missed your 'slot' and will cause real inconvenience if you start asking questions now.

Be diplomatic and avoid offence

On the whole, people are willing to help students in their studies. However, do not abuse this willingness by being arrogant and insensitive. You might be dealing with delicate issues, so try and get informed about the sensitivities and feelings of the participants. Above all, do not make people appear ridiculous or stupid!

FIGURE 3.2   Avoid causing offence.

Example: Do not regard yourself as the host of a chat show when, say, interviewing a group of parents about their past educational experiences. They may have very different views on what is proper to talk about, so avoid the pressure tactics and 'clever' questions used to prise out information not willingly given.

Give thanks

Any help should be acknowledged with thanks, whether verbal or, in the case of questionnaires or letters asking for information, written.

Example: Adding a short paragraph at the end of the questionnaire thanking the person for answering the questions is simply done, as is a simple expression of thanks before leaving after an interview.

Professional ethical frameworks

Most professions have an ethical framework governing research in the field. Your institution may also have a similar framework which all students conducting research need to adhere. Within education it is worth working through the British Educational Research Association (BERA) 'Revised Ethical Guidelines for Educational Research (2004)'. For the full set of guidelines, visit: www.bera.ac.uk. The guidelines are listed under 'Publications', however, it may be worth typing in the title into the search box.

Other professional associations may need to be consulted if relevant to your field, for example, if taking a combined education degree. Ultimately the advice provided in this chapter should ensure you are aware of ethical issues and how to proceed with your research ethically under the guidance of your supervisor.

Listening to the child's voice

One particular aspect, thankfully of increasing concern within research, is that of the participant being central to the research process, opposed to being viewed as laboratory rats. One fundamental aspect is that of listening to 'the child's voice'. The United Nations Conventions on the Rights of the Child provides an internationally guiding framework and a set of standards for children's rights. Some of these are obvious, for example, the protection and development of children, however, of specific note also is in obtaining their voluntary participation. Indeed if you have covered any aspect of 'Every Child Matters', you may well be aware that this important document was based on the views of children: this goes contrary to the Victorian notion of 'Children should be seen and not heard!'.

Consequently does your research actually engage with the participants? Do they actually have a 'voice' and how much precedence is this given? Does your research develop with the participants as a mutually beneficial exercise, or are they detached from the research process? Are you a detached investigator?

Despite your research intentions, there are further considerations to take note of when working with children. Fundamental to this discussion on ethics are the following Articles of the UN Conventions:

- Article 2 (1): Respect the rights of the child without discrimination of any kind irrespective of the child's race, colour, sex, language, religion, political or other opinion, national, ethnic or social origin, property, disability, birth or other status.
- Article 3 (1): In all actions concerning children, the best interests of the child shall be a primary consideration.
- Article 3 (3): The care and protection of children shall conform to standards particular in the areas of health and safety with suitably qualified and competent supervision.
- Article 12 (1): The child should be capable of forming their own views and given the right to express those views freely in all matters affecting them.
- Article 19 (1): The appropriate educational measures to protect the child from all forms of physical or mental violence, injury or abuse, neglect, maltreatment or exploitation,

while in the care of parent(s), legal guardian(s) or any other person who has the care of the child.

As a result of the various Articles listed, your research must not be discriminative (unless of course you are comparing specific views from a certain group: an example of this would be comparing boys and girls views on reading preferences). Your research must have the child's best interests are paramount (seeing how many times they can run around the playground before collapsing in a heap is not in the child's best interests!). Needless to say, the child's health and safety must also be paramount. Furthermore, the child should be able to provide their consent to taking part in your research. I would hope that these were common sense!

3.5 Scientific honesty and subjectivity

This refers back to some of the issues raised in Chapter 5 about philosophy. The main point I want to make here is that of being scrupulously honest about the nature of your findings, even (and especially) if they tend to contradict the main thrust of your argument. Good quality research is not achieved by using the techniques of a spin doctor. Politicians might want to put the right kind of gloss on data collected for them in order to bolster their arguments, but this is not tolerated in academic work. Data should speak for themselves. Your analysis should reveal the message behind the data, and not be used to select only the results that are convenient for you.

As with most things, this kind of honesty can be more complicated than at first glance. Consider the following scenario. A study is being carried out on improving behaviour through assessing positive reinforcement strategies and the use of punishment. The results of the measurements and observations are inconclusive. The researcher conducting the study feels that positive reinforcement are fundamental in improving behaviour and that this is fundamental to their personal educational philosophy.

How will the researcher present the data in an honest and balanced way?

It would be easy to present one side of the argument and stress the benefits of positive reinforcement while also discussing the negative aspects of punishment. But such certainty is not inherent in this situation. Much better, i.e. more honest, if the researcher discussed the issues driving the research, and the difficulty of gauging the level of suffering of the animals, and concentrated on assessing the strengths of the opposing arguments, taking into account the uncertainties of the data and of the eventual properties of the product.

If you can achieve a balanced view, it is probably not necessary to specifically state your personal attitude to the issues. However, there are situations where it is impossible to rise above the events and be a detached observer. For example, if you are passionate about the role of music in stimulating creative thinking and are a keen musician, you should declare your interest from the outset. Your arguments may well be valid and based on good evidence, but you are unlikely to seek supporting evidence for the other side!

FIGURE 3.3   A balanced view?

Another way to ensure that you will avoid being accused of spin or false interpretation of the evidence is to present all the data you have collected as fully and clearly as possible. This may be the results of a questionnaire, measurements of activities or any other records relevant to your study. You can then base your analysis on these data, and it is open to the reader to judge whether your analysis is correct and whether your conclusions are valid. All arguments are open to challenge, but if you present the raw materials on which your arguments are based then at least the discussion has a firm foundation.

Ethics of the writing process

A final element of increasing importance is in ensuring that your final work is ethically presented. Whereas this chapter has looked at the practical issues researching ethically and reporting your results ethically, the actual written process also needs to be addressed. By this, have you been open and honest about the information and arguments within your dissertation, i.e. have you acknowledged resources correctly? As you may be aware, avoiding plagiarism is an increasingly important issue. Plagiarism is where you claiming or implying that ideas presented in your work are your own, whereas they have originally been cited elsewhere. For example, I could suggest that humans are motivated by a series of needs, from base physiological needs through to higher psychological needs, yet this was originally discussed by Abraham Maslow. As such, it is of paramount importance that you support any such 'claims' with appropriate acknowledgement by referencing correctly. This will be discussed further in Chapter 10.

3.6   What should I do now?

The issues of ethics in academic work pervade almost all aspects. Some of these issues are based on simple common sense and civilized behaviour, such as one's relationships with colleagues and other people. Others are more formal in character and require real organizational effort in order to fulfil the requirements, such as gaining permission for use of information and activities. You should therefore:

- Consider in detail your intended research, considering the proposal, potential, permission and protection issues. Make a note of these in your research journal.
- Consider the participants central to your research. This may be the 'gatekeepers' of the setting, the participants, parental permission, etc. Consider the procedures for obtaining consent.

3.7   References to more information

Although ethical behaviour should underlie all academic work, it is in the social sciences (as well as medicine, etc.) that the really difficult issues arise. Researching people and society raises many ethical questions that are discussed in the books below. The first book has two sections that are short and useful. The other books in this list are far more detailed and really aimed at professional researchers – though the issues remain the same whoever is doing the research.

Cohen, L., Manion, L. and Morrison, K. (2007) *Research Methods in Education,* 6th edn. Abingdon: Routledge.

    See Chapter 2. This chapter provides a very detailed discussion on ethics within educational research.

de Laine, M. (2000) *Fieldwork, Participation and Practice: Ethics and Dilemmas in Qualitative Research.* London: Sage.

    The main purposes of this book are to promote an understanding of the harmful possibilities of fieldwork; and to provide ways of dealing with ethical problems and dilemmas. Examples of actual fieldwork are provided that address ethical problems and dilemmas, and show ways of dealing with them.

Graue, M.E. and Walsh, D.J. (1998) *Studying Children in Context: Theories, Methods, and Ethics.* London: Sage.

Haplin, D. and Tropyna, B. (1994) *Researching Education Policy: Ethical and Methodological Issues.* London: Falmer.

MacNaughton, G., Rolfe, S.A. and Siraj-Blatchford, I. (2006) *Doing Early Childhood Research: International Perspectives on Theory and Practice.* Maidenhead: Open University Press.

    See Chapter 5.

Mauthner, M., Birch, M., Jessop, J. and Miller, T., eds (2002) *Ethics in Qualitative Research.* London: Sage.

    This book explores ethical issues in research from a range of angles, including: access and informed consent, negotiating participation, rapport, the intentions of feminist research, epistemology and data analysis, tensions between being a professional researcher and a 'caring' professional. The book includes practical guidelines to aid ethical decision-making rooted in feminist ethics of care.

McNamee, M. and Burgess, R.G., eds (2002) *The Ethics of Educational Research*. Oxford: Blackwell.

Oliver, P. (2003) *The Student's Guide to Research Ethics*. Maidenhead: Open University Press.

Roberts-Holmes, G. (2005) *Doing Your Early Years Research Project: A Step by Step Guide*. London: Paul Chapman.

See Chapter 4.

Robson, C. (2002) *Real World Research: A Resource for Social Scientists and Practitioner-Researchers*, 2nd edn. Oxford: Blackwell.

SECTION 2

This section will help you to identify a focus: indeed, you may already have in mind what you want to focus your dissertation on; however, there are a number of issues and resolutions in Section 2 to ensure that you establish your own condensed and secure framework on which to develop your work.

Chapter 4 helps you to identify an area if you are unsure of what would be relevant or what you may be able to do over your allocated time. Chapter 5 develops this further by ensuring that your area is sufficiently focussed through defining a research issue. This issue will become the key structure to your dissertation framework, specifically as you develop a coherent set of research objectives indicating how you will address your research issue.

Chapter 6 discusses the development of a research proposal. You will probably be required to submit a proposal before you start your dissertation and increasingly, the proposal may be part of an assessed research methods module. With this in mind, having developed an effective research proposal, you will not only achieve a good grade for a module but also be well on the way to ensure your dissertation is of a similar quality.

Chapter 7 outlines how the first chapter of your dissertation could be structured with the elements that need to be incorporated to ensure the reader fully understands your intentions and why your dissertation is of importance.

4   What Will It Be About?

4.1   What really interests you?

Generally within education, you will have a choice about the subject that they will write about for their dissertation. Sometimes this amounts to so much freedom that it is really difficult to know where to begin. If you are in this situation, or if you don't know how to make a choice between suggested titles or themes, the following thoughts will help.

As previously mentioned, it is always easier to write an extended piece of work if you are interested in the subject and when the research involves activities that you enjoy doing. Moreover, greater interest inevitably means a greater thirst for knowledge, and this enthusiasm is bound to show in the final product. So how can you weave your favourite topic into the dissertation? You might need to indulge in some creative thinking to achieve this, depending on the focus of your study.

Most dissertation subjects are a combination of the background subject discipline, for example education, early childhood studies, etc. and a particular situation, activity or phenomenon, for example an area of the curriculum, play, friendship groups. You will have to take the subject discipline you are studying as a given, as that is presumably the label of what you are studying for your degree. The freedom lies in what you choose to investigate within this context.

A few examples of subjects and study title will be useful here, some pretty obvious, some less so. The following examples detail the subject discipline, an area of interest and a working title:

- Education studies and the development of the curriculum – '150 years of curriculum reform: how far have we come?'

- Professional education and new police recruits – 'The classroom versus reality: virtual reality computer simulations as a way forwards?'
- Primary and science – 'Misunderstanding children's misunderstandings on physical processes'
- Secondary and sport – 'Competition versus cooperation: what should we be promoting?'
- Early childhood studies and forest schools – 'But there's no tree in our playground! Adapting forest school principles within the city landscape'
- Any education course and residential trips – 'What is the educational value of spending a week on Dartmoor in the rain?'

As opposed to trying to consider a title immediately, make a list of several interests and from this, how you could approach them. Try to devise a connection between each interest and your main study subject and to formulate titles such as provided above. You will need to be aware of the diversity inherent in your main subject in order to spot promising connections: for example, primary education not only covers the entire National Curriculum, but also aspects affecting health, welfare, behaviour, psychology of learning, sociology of learning, etc.

If you find it difficult to pin down what your main interests are, you could try answering the following questions:

- What do you do when you are not 'working'? You may be doing something very useful, but you regard it as an enjoyable activity rather than 'work'. If it is something as general as watching the television, what programmes do you watch most? Wherein lies this fascination?
- If you are together with like-minded friends or colleagues, what do you enjoy talking about most professionally?
- Is there any activity, subject or skill that you have always wanted to find out more about, but have never had the time or incentive? This may just be the opportunity to get to grips with it.
- What modules have previously interested you so far on your course?
- Why were you originally interested in selecting your degree? What was the motivator behind this?

When you have devised one or perhaps several promising dissertation subjects, it is time to look more carefully at the practical implications of these. At this stage, you will not be able to go into details, but you will definitely be able to make a preliminary assessment so that really impractical ideas are rejected. Several issues need to be examined.

4.2   The scope of the subject

You will need to limit the 'width' and 'depth' of your study to keep it manageable. One of the most common problems encountered by a supervisor is probably when a student says that they are interested in a researching an area without setting any limitations. It can take considerable time and effort to take an initial idea and reduce this to a feasible investigation for the dissertation.

There is so much information on every subject, and so many implications can be followed up that link to a wider field, that it is easy to lose your direction and end up with an unfocused piece of work. Think about where you will draw the line, where you will say 'this goes beyond my field of study'. If we take a specific subject which is currently of prime importance, the subject of 'childhood obesity', how could this actually be refined? The following strategy may help to narrow your focus.

Consider your proposed topic as a forest. Visualize this forest of information and in particular, one solitary tree. Look at this tree in detail, the branches and how each branch leads to a number of twigs, each twig to a number of leaves. Identify one specific leaf … this is your specific focus for your dissertation. If this is related to developing an investigation on childhood obesity, we could establish a focus by narrowing the following:

Forest The entire wealth of information and potential areas to explore with a topic (childhood obesity).

Within this forest there are many associated aspects, each represented by individual trees, for example:

- Policy – 'Healthy Schools', 'Every Child Matters'
- History – Has this trend increased in recent years?
- Sociology – What will be the impact if this trend continues?
- Psychology – How does obesity affect self-concept?
- Intervention strategies – Increase in exercise levels; decrease in energy input (calories).

Tree One specific area (childhood obesity as a result of a decrease in exercise levels).

Branch A specific aspect relating to exercise. The variations could be in different strategies to get children more active. This may include exercise programmes, sponsored walk-to-school campaigns, providing children with pedometers to measure the steps they take each day, etc.

Leaf A specific focus relating to the branch. This may be where you decide specifically what group you are working with due to the location, age, gender of your sample group.

In summary, the aspects selected could be:

- FOREST – childhood obesity
- TREE – increase of exercise levels
- BRANCH – use of pedometers
- LEAF – mixed Year-8 class at an inner-city school

Consequently, delineation can be achieved by stipulating aspects such as a timeframe, location, size of group, type of group and level of detail. This would lead to a working title, which although somewhat wordy, is specific:

An investigation into increasing energy output through the use of pedometers with a mixed Year 8 class at an inner-city school to combat potential obesity.

Individuality

Is what you are planning just a repeat of what has been done before, or is there something different or new that can be learned from the outcomes? You do not have to achieve a scientific breakthrough or a new direction in thought. What is needed is an individual stamp on the work, some personal contribution that makes your project unique. This is gained by adding your own perspective to the study, your own collection of data (perhaps surveys or observations) and your own interpretation of some data, yours or from elsewhere. At this stage it is worth assessing your own capabilities in relation to the task: can you see yourself being able to do it?

Timing

You will only have a limited time in which to complete your work. How fast a worker are you, and how much do you already know about the topic, and how much time will you be able to dedicate to the project? If you are planning time within the research setting, or need to observe particular events, make sure that these can be reliably programmed into your allotted time. At this stage it will be difficult to devise a reliable programme of work, but you will be able to get a feel for how much time might be involved in getting prepared, collecting information, sorting and analysing it, and writing it all up and presenting it.

Resources

Many dissertation projects involve getting specific information and/or using particular pieces of equipment, or even meeting certain people. Does your subject imply the necessity for these? If so, what is the likelihood of you gaining the required access? You will need to establish alternatives if things do not work out as expected. There is also the question of cost. Calculate the likely cost implications (time, effort, money) of pursuing your topic(s), and whether you can afford it. You will incur basic financial costs anyway in the production of your dissertation (printing, photocopying, binding, etc.).

Important aspects of your dissertation are bound to be governed by the regulations of your institution, and also by more detailed instructions issued by your course administration. The principal matters covered are the maximum and minimum length (word count), format and presentation, quality of work, marking criteria and expected outcomes, approvals for subject choice, supervision arrangements, deadlines, extent of group or individual working and so forth.

It is essential that you are fully informed about these issues, so if you do not have a copy of both the general regulations issued by the university or college, and the course-specific instructions, get hold of them now and read them carefully. Your work will be judged on the basis of compliance with these, so you can save yourself a lot of time and grief by getting it right from the beginning!

Although the point of doing a dissertation is to challenge you to produce a piece of work devised and organized by yourself, you are not really expected to do this without any help. You should be allocated a tutor or director of studies whose duty is to guide and advise you during the project. Do make use of him or her, both to check on your progress and as a source of ideas and advice. Ask what format has been arranged for consultations: is there a weekly prearranged meeting, or do you have to book a slot when they become available? The onus will probably be on you to ensure that you get regular tutorials. Further advice on utilizing your supervisor effectively may be found in Chapter 21.

FIGURE 4.1   Regulations.

The regulations are likely to be quite specific about the approval required for the choice of your dissertation topic, so early consultation with your tutor is essential. Even if you have previously submitted a research proposal, it is likely that this will evolve. He/she will quickly be able to comment on the suitability of your title or titles. It is best if you can give a short explanation of how your topic relates to your main area of study (your tutor might not be familiar with your particular interest) and how it will develop your knowledge and skills in the subject. Once you get the initial approval of the title and subject, you will be able to start to develop a greater understanding of the tasks ahead. A good way to get a feel for the requirements of the whole project is to look at examples of completed dissertations.

4.3   Previous examples

Most courses will keep copies of all their previous dissertations and they should be available for you to consult. They might be held in the central library or in your own department: you should know by now where they are! You should look at them rather differently now from the last time. One of the really useful aspects of looking at completed dissertations is to be able to gauge the size and content of the finished works. The danger however, is that you become intimidated by the scale and detail provided, especially if they deal with subjects unfamiliar to you. Don't worry, they managed and so will you!

It is best to look at several dissertations. Perhaps you will find one or two that deal with subjects near to your own. What should you look for when reviewing these dissertations? Just as the last time, you will certainly not want to read them all. Here are a few points to consider:

- Visually compare the different styles of presentation, i.e. the use of fonts, illustrations and graphs, colour, chapters and headings, indexes and lists of references, etc. Which do you find more attractive and immediately informative?
- Look to see how the subject title is broken down into different aspects to make it easier to investigate. A clue to how this is done is to look at the chapter headings.
- Scan through the whole collection to get an idea of the range of topics covered. Are there any similar to your chosen title? If so, have a quick look at them to get an idea of the approach and content. Again, chapter headings will reveal a lot quickly. Spot the differences and similarities to your own thoughts about your approach. Again, make a note of those that might serve as a model. If there are no titles anything like the one you have devised, you might be either way off the mark or brilliantly innovative.
- Compare the scope of the work of several examples. Some will look at a wide subject but not in much depth; others will concentrate on one narrow aspect but delve deeply; and others will fall somewhere in between. Observe how the styles differ. Reflect on where your subject lies within this spectrum.
- Examine how the work was done. Did it involve careful measurement and calculation on a scientific basis, or was it more an interpretation of events or opinions that could not be accurately measured? Consider your own subject and ponder what sort of approach might be suitable. Sometimes a combination of both is required.
- You will probably want to refer to previous examples later in your work, when you are faced with specific problems of method, organization or presentation. So do make a note of those that you think could serve as good examples so that you will easily be able to find them again.

4.4 Getting background information

A title is only a germ of an idea. In order to really understand the implications of it, you need to investigate what has been done on the subject already, what information is available to inform your study and what gaps in your knowledge need to be filled. This is called doing a background study.

The main aim of doing this background study is to make sure that your subject idea is not just 'pie in the sky'. I am sure that you based your selection on some considerable knowledge of both your main subject and your enthusiasm. But what you probably are not so informed about is what other people have done in this field and how they have done it. When you devise the research proposal that gives a rationale for your project, you will need to argue that the subject is relevant to your studies and fits within the remit of the main subject. There is no better way of doing this than to cite work that has already been done in this field and to identify the gaps that still need to be filled.

FIGURE 4.2   Your title.

Your title will give indications of where to look for information. Take, for example a previously cited title 'Misunderstanding children's misunderstandings on physical processes'. Information will be required on the scientific area of physical processes: which particular process are we discussing: electricity, forces and motion, light and sound, the Earth and beyond? If we take forces and motion, we could then select: pushing and pulling, friction, measuring forces, gravity, attraction and repulsion. Taking friction, why may children get confused over this concept? Can we assume that if five children from a group all get an answer wrong on a test paper, that they actually got it wrong for the same reason? Could they have different reasons, or misconceptions, for getting the question wrong? How could we find out what their misconceptions are ... and how can we structure appropriate learning situations in order to ensure that they get them right? What is it they need to learn, how best could this be structured in terms of providing a variety of experiences.

Every title will have a series of connections to related information and research. Greater familiarity with the issues will in turn lead on to further relevant fields. There is a danger here of getting overwhelmed by the amount of information available and there is the problem of sorting out what is useful. A quick way to check that you have not missed anything important after you have done some initial investigation is to talk with experts in the field – those in your department or in other parts of the institution. Just a few words will suffice, so don't be shy to contact them by e-mail or letter.

Where will you find the required information? The first step is your institution's library. You should be pretty good at doing searches by now. Try using some selected key words to search for books on the main library catalogue. For more specialist issues, a search through the relevant databases of journal articles should be productive. Ask your librarian for help if you get stuck or do not seem to be finding the right kind of information. Then there is the Internet, again doing a search using key words; try not to get bogged down or waylaid by the sheer volume of material. More advice on searching for secondary (published and stored) information is given in Chapter 8, and on how to organize your note taking in Chapter 9. The secret is to know when to stop. At this stage, you are only testing the feasibility of your suggested title and getting a feel of the nature of the project.

These first steps in collecting information will form a useful foundation for your work, and help you to decide on the nature and scope of your study. Now is the time to change your mind if you see that things are not working out how you wish. Explore alternative approaches; or if you develop a real distaste for the prospect of work in that subject, abandon it and choose an alternative. In the latter case, you will have to move quickly to establish a new direction and get approval for your new subject; it is important not to lose too much time at the outset of the project.

Just remember that your best work will be done when you are really interested in what you are doing. But also remember that learning new things is always tough: there is no really easy way.

4.5   What should I do now?

If you have followed the advice above, you will already have done a lot! If you are still dithering, now is the time to examine your options and to make decisions. If you do not make your mind up about your subject, it is impossible to make any real progress in your work, as you cannot know where to focus your research.

Here is a checklist of things that have been suggested so far in this chapter:

- List your interests
- Combine your subject with an interest
- Explore the scope of the topic, using the forest analogy
- Check individuality, timing and resources required
- Read the regulations and instructions
- Look up previous examples of dissertations
- Get more background information.

If you are really lost for ideas, or have got hopelessly bogged down, make an appointment with your tutor and explain what you have done so far and ask for advice. If you have taken any of the steps recommended above, you will be some way to getting started, and will probably be aware of where your problem lies. This may be because, for instance, you are daunted by the complexity of the task, or you cannot decide between several options, or you are not confident that your choice is feasible, etc. It will be best if you can identify specific problems before seeing your tutor, rather than turning up and saying simply 'I don't know what to do!'

To get yourself well organized, make a list of the sources of background material that you have found useful. Then write a short text in the form of bullet points indicating the main issues that this material has raised. This text should indicate:

- The sort of information that you will be likely to need, and where you might obtain it
- The sort of techniques you might need to use or to learn in order to obtain the information and to analyse it
- The equipment that might be needed

- The people and places you might need to see
- Any timing considerations that need to be taken into account (e.g. waiting for special events).

When you are clear about these, and they seem achievable, it will give you confidence that the project is 'doable' and free you to proceed with defining and planning the project in greater detail.

4.6   References to more information

The guidance given above should be sufficient to put you on the right road (your road) to working out what your dissertation will be about. However, if you have time and want to compare advice, or need further inspiration, there are other books like this one that have a section with advice on how to decide what to do as a dissertation, or in many cases, a postgraduate thesis. It may help you to compare the different approaches. As mentioned in the previous chapter, specific guidance on topics in a particular subject can be gained from books dedicated to one particular discipline. Explore your own library catalogue for both general and subject-related guides to dissertation writing. But do be careful not to get bogged down in technicalities: peck like a bird at the juicy pieces of use to you now, and leave the rest.

Ajuga, G. (2002) *The Student Assignment and Dissertation Survival Guide: Answering the Question Behind the Question!* Thornton Heath: GKA.

See pp. 46–55. Do you want to become the teacher's pet?

Bell, J. (2005) *Doing Your Research Project: A Guide for First-Time Researchers in Education, Health and Social Science*, 4th edn. Maidenhead: Open University Press.

de Vaus, D. (2001) *Research Design in Social Research*. London: Sage.

Hopkins, D. (2002) *A Teacher's Guide to Classroom Research*, 3rd edn. Buckingham: Open University Press.

See Chapter 5.

Mounsey, C. (2002) *Essays and Dissertations*. Oxford: Oxford University Press.

Swetnam, D. (2000) *Writing Your Dissertation: How to Plan, Prepare and Present Successful Work*. Oxford: How To Books.

See Chapter 1 for simple guidance on how to get started.

The following books are aimed more at postgraduate research, but again, selective reading of the preliminary chapters will provide further hints about getting started.

Hart, C. (2004) *Doing Your Masters Dissertation (Essential Study Skills)*. London: Sage.

See Chapter 3 'Finding and formulating your topic'.

Murray, R. (2002) *How to Write a Thesis*. Buckingham: Open University Press.

Rudestam, K.E. and Newton, R. (2001) *Surviving Your Dissertation: A Comprehensive Guide to Content and Process*, 2nd edn. Thousand Oaks: Sage.

5   How Do I Get Started?

5.1   What's the problem?

Writing a dissertation is not like writing a novel: you cannot just sit down and start writing from out of your head. You need to do some preparation work first; you have already begun this if you have followed the book to this stage. By now you will have decided the subject area and done some background reading to get information and explore aspects of the subject. Now it is time to build on this and to focus more clearly on the direction of your intended study. To start with, it is best to define your research problem as clearly as possible in order to provide a focus for all your subsequent work. It sounds easier than it actually is, so don't worry if you agonize over it for a few days and alter your ideas several times over. Only by grappling with the issues can you forge some clarity in your thinking.

The purpose of the dissertation task is to get you to do some individual research. To do research you need to identify a problem or an issue that you will focus on in your investigations. After selecting your subject area and deciding on the issues that are of the greatest interest to you, the next step is to define the research more closely so that it can be expressed as a specific research problem. You will get to the point, when you are clear and decided, that you can explain the nature of your research problem in one or two sentences. Within educational research, this research problem is generally called your 'aim', the overall issue you are focussing on.

FIGURE 5.1   It is not as if problems are hard to find.

It can be quite difficult to decide on and to define your research problem, or aim. So what should you look for in your subject in order to generate a focus for your dissertation? It is not as if problems are hard to find: in fact, we are surrounded by problems. Take for example social problems such as poverty, crime, unsuitable housing and uncomfortable workplaces and the impact on education; or technical problems such as design deficiencies; or organizational problems that impact on education such as the inception of new policies and methods for teaching. In many subjects there may be a lack of knowledge that prevents improvements being made, for example, the influence of parents on a child's progress at school, or attitudes in the relationship to policy implementation between the government and teachers.

But don't think that real-life problems are the only subjects to choose. Many issues are worthy of investigation but present no threat to anyone. How about investigating the little known works of a key educationalist, a historical study of an aspect like playground games, or the use of language in particular contexts? The possibilities are endless. The difficulty lies more in devising a specific research problem that will be suitable in scale and character as the subject of a dissertation.

So, what are the necessary features of a dissertation research problem?

- It should be of great interest to you. You will have to spend many weeks or even months investigating the problem. A real interest in the subject is a great incentive to keep you going. If you have some choice in the subject you choose, then do yourself a favour and investigate something you wanted to find out about anyway.
- The problem should be significant. It is a waste of time and effort investigating a trivial problem or repeating work that someone has already done. Although you are not obliged to break new ground and extend the boundaries of knowledge, you will at least be expected to throw some new light on existing knowledge.

- It should be delineated. You do not have much time, even if it seems that you do at first. As you have to learn so many things in order to complete a good dissertation, you will take longer than you might think to do the necessary tasks. Hence the topic must be kept manageable, with restricted aims. Work out how much time you have got to complete the study, taking into account all the other commitments you have. How much detail do you need to go into? You can cover a wide field only superficially, and the more you restrict the field, the more detailed the study can be. Also consider the cost of necessary travel and other expenses.
- You should be able to obtain the information required. Obviously, you cannot carry out research if you cannot collect the relevant information needed to address your problem. Can you get access to relevant documents or other sources, and/or can you obtain the co-operation of individuals or organizations essential to your project?
- You should be able to draw conclusions related to the problem. The point of asking a question is to find an answer. The problem should be one to which the research can offer some solution, or at least the elimination of some false 'solutions'.
- You chould be able to state the problem clearly and concisely. A precise, well-thought-out and fully articulated sentence, understandable by anyone, should normally clearly be able to explain just what the problem is.

For this search you need to have an enquiring mind, an eye for inconsistencies and inadequacies in current ideas and practice, and also a measure of imagination. It often helps to pose a simple question, for example, 'Does playing classical music help develop creative writing?', or 'Does exercise help improve behaviour?', or 'What makes a successful young children's play area?' At this stage, the nature of the question will give some indication of the type of research approach (or approaches) that could be appropriate. Will it be a historical study, a descriptive inquiry, an analysis of correlations or an experimental exercise, or a combination of more than one of these?

Note though that seemingly simple questions are riddled with ambiguities that must be cleared up by careful definition. For example, in the above questions, how can creativity within 'creative writing' be assessed, what sort of 'behaviour' is envisaged, and are all types of 'young children's play area' included? It is likely that the problem is too broad if you can state it in less than half a dozen words: refer back to forest analogy of identifying an area.

A few additional questions posed against each word can help to delineate the problem: where, who, what, which, when, why? Break the problem down into short sentences, not worrying at this stage about the overall length of the problem statement. It is a useful trick to put each sentence on a separate slip of paper, so that they can be ordered in different sequences. When the best logical progression from sentence to sentence is achieved, the statement can be edited into a more elegant form.

Most research problems are difficult, or even impossible, to solve without breaking them down into smaller problems. The words used during the problem formulation period can give a clue to the presence of objectives. Does one aspect have to be researched before another aspect can be begun? For example, in one of the research questions asked above, 'Does exercise improve behaviour?', what exercise programme needs to be considered – one that is competitive or cooperative? Perhaps exercise which increases the heart rate above a certain level? What is meant by 'behaviour' and how is this measured? By defining the subproblems, you will be able to delineate the scope of the work.

Once you have defined the problem, you can then set about formulating your research aim and objectives which define how you will actually deal with the problem. This will be discussed in greater detail later in this chapter.

5.2   Second review of literature

Once you have defined a research problem, you will be able to make a much more focused review of the literature. You will be able to learn more about existing research on aspects of your research problem, and how it has been carried out. You will also be able to make more in-depth investigations into the factors that are important in your subject. Look for the following information in order to help you get started on your own research:

- Results of previous research, which can form a springboard for your own investigations
- Concepts, indicators and variables used (see below for details of these)
- Ideas on how to gather data
- Data presentation techniques
- Methods of data analysis
- Instrumentation which has been used
- Methods of argument and the drawing of conclusions
- Success of the various research designs of the studies already undertaken.

This exercise should not take too long, as you will be able to home in on the relevant research quite quickly using the key words from your research problem and question(s). Do reference everything relevant that you find, and make notes with comments about how the information relates to what you are intending to do (see Chapter 9 for specific instructions on note taking and referencing). This will be really useful stuff to put into your research proposal and the introduction and background section of your dissertation, to demonstrate that you have really investigated the present situation of research into your particular topic.

The words you use in your problem statement are loaded with meaning. You must have carefully chosen them from many other words to precisely indicate the main components of your investigation. Let us now look more closely at these words, or concepts, and how they are used.

5.3   What are the main concepts?

First what is a concept? It is a general expression of a particular phenomenon, for example cat, human, anger, speed, alienation, socialism, etc. Each one of these represents an idea, and the word is a label for this idea.

FIGURE 5.2   A particular phenomenon – cat.

We use concepts all the time as they are an essential part of understanding the world and communicating with other people. Many common concepts are shared by everyone in a society, though there are variations in meaning between different cultures and languages. For example, the concept 'respect' will mean something different to a streetwise rapper than to a noble lord. There are other concepts that are only understood by certain people such as experts, professionals and specialists, for example dermatoglyphics, milfoil, parachronism, anticipatory socialization, etc. Sometimes common phenomena can be labelled in an exotic fashion, often in order to impress or confuse, for example, a 'domestic feline mammal' instead of a 'cat'. This is called jargon, and should be avoided.

Any kind of enquiry requires a set of concepts that communicate the elements being studied. It is important to define concepts in such a way that everyone reading the work has got the same idea of what is meant. This is relatively easy in the natural sciences where precise definition is usually possible, for example acceleration, radio waves, elements. In education this may be much more difficult. Human concepts such as behaviour, learning, play, enthusiasm, etc. are difficult to pin down accurately, as their meanings are often based on opinions, emotions, values, traditions, etc. Hence the importance of carefully formulated definitions when using concepts that are not precise in normal usage.

You will be able to find definitions of the concepts that you are planning to use in your investigations from your background reading. Because definitions for non-scientific and non-technical concepts can vary in different contexts, you may have to decide on which meaning you want to give to those concepts. Rarely, you might even have to devise your own definition for a particular word.

5.4   What about indicators?

As you can see, many concepts are rather abstract in nature, and difficult or even impossible to evaluate or measure. Take 'anger' as an example, considering the link between

FIGURE 5.3   Signs that might indicate anger.

learning something and the resultant success or failure. How will you detect this in a child? The answer is to look for indicators – those perceivable phenomena that give an indication that the concept is present. What might these be? Think of the signs that might indicate anger: agitated demeanour, spluttering, shouting, wide-open eyes, stamping, reddened face, increased heartbeat, increased adrenaline production, and many others. Again, you can see what indicators are used in previous studies – which is much easier and more reliable than trying to work them out for yourself.

5.5   What are the main variables and values?

If you want to gauge the extent or degree of an indicator, you will need to find a measurable component. In the case of anger as above, it would be very difficult to measure the redness of a face or the degree of stamping, but you could measure a person's heartbeat, yet how would this be conducted within a class setting? You could even ask the subject how frustrated he or she feels. The values used are the units of measurement. In the case of heartbeat, it would be beats per minute; level of anger felt could be declared on a scale from 1 to 10. Obviously the precision possible will be different depending on the nature of the variable and the type of values that can possibly be used.

To summarize then, there is a hierarchy of expressions, going from the general to the particular, from abstract to concrete, that make it possible to investigate research problems. The briefest statement of the research problem will be the most general and abstract, while the detailed analysis of components of the research will be particular and concrete. The terms introduced are linked as follows:

- Concepts – the building blocks of the research problem which are usually abstract and cannot be directly measured
- Indicators – the phenomena which point to the existence of the concepts
- Variables – the components of the indicators which can be measured
- Values – the actual units or methods of measurement of the variables.

Note that each concept may have several indicators, each indicator several variables, and each variable several values. To clarify these terms consider the following, which gives only one example of each term:

- Concept – learning
- Indicator achievement
- Variable – success or failure on a task
- Values – instances of success over time.

Try to think of more indicators, variables and values related to the concept of learning.

Being aware of these levels of expression will help you to break down your investigations into manageable tasks. This will enable you to come to overall conclusions about the abstract concepts in your research problem based on evidence rooted in detailed data at a more concrete level.

5.6   Ways of stating your research problem

Once you have defined and narrowed the scope of your research problem, you can then formulate specific and succinct statements specifying how the problem will be investigated. These statements are referred to as your aims and objectives, and are the central spine to your dissertation. It must be noted that there are other terms that could be used to specifically phrase what you will actually do with your dissertation and these will be discussed at the end of this section. For this book however, the term aims and objectives are used throughout.

Definition of the research aim and objectives

When you have successfully formulated the various detailed research problems, you will need to indicate what measures you will take to do the investigation. You can do this by defining the research aim and objectives, and indicating how the research objectives will be achieved. This is a first step to planning your project and will enable you to check back to see if the objectives fall in line with your preferences for the type of research that you were interested in doing. Guidance provided by some institutions may only require you to state your aim and objectives; some may only ask you to specify your research questions, or your hypothesis, or the proposition or the statement of intent.

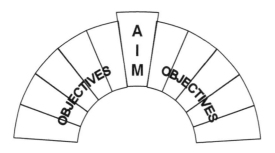

ILLUSTRATION 5.1   Aims and objectives.

Personally, I see that the aim and objectives provide a structured framework that keeps the research focussed. As such the difference between the aim and objectives are:

* The aim of the study is the overarching purpose of the research
* The objectives are precise statements of intent, indicating exactly how the aim will be addressed.

This could be viewed as an archway: the aim is the 'keystone', the central stone which keeps the arch together. The objectives are the 'voussoirs', the other wedged-shape stones on either side of the keystone. This may be demonstrated by the following example, which takes one of the previously cited areas on after-school provision.

* Aim
    * An investigation of the problems of offering after-school provision at a large rural secondary school
* Objectives
    * To systematically explore the issue of after-school provision through conducting an extensive literature review
    * To critically analyse the needs of children and parents through structuring a series of questionnaires
    * To examine the resource implications of after-school provision through interviewing key members of staff
    * To synthesize differing perspectives from staff, children and parents, on after-school provision in an attempt to propose feasible solutions.

Notice how there is an argument behind the build-up of the research problem and the definition of objectives. Briefly, it goes like this:

* According to the background research there is a problem, an issue, a lack of information, or an unanswered question about such-and-such. This provides the necessary motive for defining the aim
* The important aspects to be studied are this, this, and this, etc. (objectives)
* In order to investigate these it is necessary to do such-and-such, for example, noting the method of data collection you will use and with whom (objectives).

The objectives develop in a systematic manner, stemming from the literature review, furthermore each objective has two clear parts to it: the first indicates *what* needs to be completed to help answer the question, the second part indicates *how* this is to be completed.

There are a number of key verbs you can use to help structure your aim or objectives as highlighted by Oliver (2004: 105):

*   To discuss (an idea)
*   To examine (a proposal)
*   To analyse (some data)
*   To synthesize (several ideas or propositions)
*   To explore (an issue)
*   To reflect on (a theoretical model)
*   To investigate (a range of concepts)
*   To propose (a possible explanation)
*   To systematize (some initial idea)
*   To test (a hypothesis)

The important thing to keep in mind is that the objectives are clear and make logical sense. In fact, there is usually a choice of things you could do, so it may be necessary to limit the scope of the problem/question to make the necessary investigations more inevitable. It is important to keep in mind that the aim and objectives are central to your dissertation, providing the framework on which to base your work. If you can spend some quality time on refining these, perhaps bouncing them back and forwards to your supervisor in order to ensure they are just right, your dissertation will unfold gracefully. This is paramount to the structure of your dissertation as you are really setting your own criteria for what you will be assessed against. By this, if you have stated that you would investigate a specific issue yet end up exploring something on the periphery of this, your work would appear unfocussed. Furthermore, in order to thread together into a coherent discussion of an issue, if your objectives do not develop in such a way, neither will your dissertation! Consequently these are crucial to the spine of your dissertation, from which everything else hangs (Illustration 5.2).

Once you have got this far, you will have a good idea of what you are planning to undertake. Do you think you will be able to manage it?

5.7   Alternatives

As noted above, there are however, a variety of other ways in how to state your research problem and this will depend on how you will go about your investigation. Over the following pages are some other ways of presenting the research problem with examples to show how they work. These are:

*   Research questions
*   Hypothesis

- Proposition
- Statement of intent

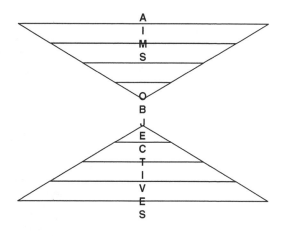

ILLUSTRATION 5.2   The spine of the dissertation.

Research questions

The method of investigating the problem may be expressed through asking a question or a series of questions, the answers to which require scrutiny of the problem from one or more directions. This is a very direct and open-ended way of formulating your investigations. Your aim is to provide some answers to the questions. It is your judgement, and that of the examiner's, whether your answers are sufficient and based on enough evidence. Here is an example of this form of presentation:

- The subject of this dissertation is 'Learning styles in mathematics'.
- The main research question is 'How are different learning styles incorporated in mathematics lessons?'
- Three interrelated research subquestions are raised:
  - What are the predominant learning styles displayed by children in mathematics?
  - How do teachers account for the variety of learning styles when teaching mathematics?
  - How do different published mathematics schemes account for the variety of learning styles?

Obviously, the question or questions should be derived directly from the research problem, give a clear indication of the subject to be investigated and imply the methods that will be used. As above, the form of the questions can be a main question, divided into subquestions that explore aspects of the main question. The main question is very general: you could probably devise other subquestions to explore different aspects of this question. But by being so specific in your choice, you can limit your research to only those issues that you think are important, or that you have interest in pursuing.

Hypothesis

The use of hypotheses is the foundation of the hypothetico-deductive approach to research, so it is important to know what makes good hypotheses and how they can be formulated. When used in a rigorous scientific fashion, there are quite strict rules to follow. Important qualities distinguish hypotheses from other forms of statement.

According to Kerlinger (1970), a hypothesis:

- Is an assertion (not a suggestion)
- Is limited in scope
- Is a statement about the relationships between certain variables
- Contains clear implications for testing the relationships
- Is compatible with current knowledge
- Is expressed as economically as possible using correct terminology.

FIGURE 5.4   Limit your research to only those issues that you think are important.

The objective of the method is either to reject the hypothesis by finding evidence that contradicts it, or to support it (you will not be able to prove it) by presenting evidence that underlines it. It might also be possible to modify the hypothesis in the light of what you have found out.

Actually, hypotheses are nothing unusual: we make them all the time. They are hunches or reasonable guesses made in the form of statements about a cause or situation. If something happens in our everyday life, we tend to suggest a reason for its occurrence by making rational guesses. For example, if the car does not start in the morning, we might hypothesize that the petrol tank was empty, or that the battery was flat. For each hypothesis, a particular action taken could support or reject it. If the petrol gauge indicated 'full', then the hypothesis of an empty petrol tank could be rejected, and so on. When a particular hypothesis is found to be supported, we have got a good chance that we can take the right action to remedy the situation. If, for example, we hypothesized that a wire to the starter motor had become loose, and then we find such a loose wire, fixing the wire back might result in the car starting again. If this was not the result, further hypotheses would be needed to suggest additional faults. Although these examples may seem banal, many of the greatest discoveries in science were based on hypotheses: Newton's theory of gravity, Einstein's general theory of relativity and a host of others.

In order to formulate a useful researchable hypothesis, you need to have a good knowledge of the background to the subject and the nature of the problem or issue that you are addressing. A good hypothesis is a very useful aid to organizing the research effort.

It specifically limits the enquiry to the interaction of certain variables; it suggests the methods appropriate for collecting, analysing and interpreting the data; and the resultant confirmation or rejection of the hypothesis through empirical or experimental testing gives a clear indication of the extent of knowledge gained.

You need to formulate the general hypothesis on a conceptual level, in order to enable the results of the research to be generalized beyond the specific conditions of the particular study. This is equivalent to the general research question. Then, you normally need to break down the main hypothesis into two or more subhypotheses. These represent components or aspects of the main hypothesis and together should add up to its totality and are equivalent to the subquestions. It is one of the fundamental criteria of a hypothesis that it is testable. However, a hypothesis formulated on a conceptual level cannot be directly tested: it is too abstract. It is therefore necessary to convert it to an operational level. This is called operationalization. The operationalization of the subhypotheses follows four steps in the progression from the most abstract to the most concrete expressions by defining in turn the concepts, indicators, variables, values. Each subhypothesis will suggest a different method of testing and therefore implies different research methods that might be appropriate. The various research methods for collecting and analysing data are explained in some detail later in this book.

Although the term 'hypothesis' is used with many different meanings in everyday and even academic situations, it is advisable to use it in your research only in its strictest scientific sense. This will avoid you being criticized for sloppy, imprecise use of terminology. If your research problem does not lend itself to being formulated in a hypothesis, do not worry: there are plenty of alternatives, many of which involve a completely different research approach to that of the hypothetico-deductive method.

Proposition

Focusing a research study on a proposition, rather than on a hypothesis, allows the study to concentrate on particular relationships between events, without having to comply with the rigorous characteristics required of hypotheses. Consider this example:

- The title of the research is 'Outdoor play in the Foundation Stage'.
- The main research problem is formulated in the form of three interrelated propositions:
  - Outdoor play for pre-school children has been increasingly recognized as a fundamental part of their education and development.
  - Provision for outdoor play is seldom given the priority due to a lack of resources.
  - From these two propositions follows the third: there is a mismatch between the intentions of suitable provision for outdoor play due to a lack of resources.

Statement of intent to critically investigate and evaluate

Not all research needs to answer a question or to test a hypothesis. Especially in undergraduate dissertations or in smaller research studies, a more exploratory approach may be used.

FIGURE 5.5   A more exploratory approach may be used.

You can express the subject and scope of the exploration in a statement of intent. Again, this must be derived from the research problem, imply a method of approach and indicate the outcome. Here are four examples of this form of research definition:

- The intention of this study is to identify contributing factors in developing user-friendly distance-learning ICT activities for post-compulsory students.
- This study examines the problems in offering effective after-school provision, assessing the needs of children and parents compared to the resourcing implications.
- In this study it is intended to consider the implications of individualized learning, through comparing and contrasting the teacher and pupil perspectives.
- This dissertation provides a reassessment of the effectiveness of incorporating 'Brain Gym' activities. It aims to explore whether such use of 'Brain Gym' increases children's ability to maintain concentration over a period of time.

5.8   What should I do now?

Now is the time to make some decisions about how you will formulate your research problem(s) so that you can make the first steps in embarking on planning your dissertation. If you take the following steps, you will form a good foundation for all the work ahead:

- Once you have decided on the particular research problem you will focus on, test it against the list of necessary features given in Section 5.1 (pp. 57–8). If it conforms to all of these you can be assured that you have got a good one!

- Consult the notes you have made during your background reading, or delve back into the books that are relevant to your research focus. Now search for what has already been done in this field, how it was carried out, and what were the main components of the work. Look at what terminology has been used, what factors have been studied and what methods have been used. This will help you enormously in deciding on what you could do, and in expressing your intentions in the appropriate language.
- In order to do this you should decide how you will state your research problem. Will you pose a question, formulate a hypothesis, suggest a proposition or make a statement of intent? Perhaps try out more than one way to see which works the best. Formulate it as succinctly as possible.

Now you should be in the situation where you will be able to put down in writing just how you will tackle the research problem. Break it down into 'do-able' components, and clarify just what your objectives will be. Check that you will actually be able to reach the objectives; be practical, as it is you that has to do it! Check also, when you have written it down, that the argument you make is sound (read more about argument in Chapter 11).

5.9   References to more information

Again, most books that provide an introduction to research and advise how to do dissertations have a section on how you get started. Apart from the ones that have been listed in the previous chapters, here are a few more in case you want to check them out. Which ones are the most important to you really depends on what aspects you are particularly interested in; so again, just look at the relevant bits, finding them with the help of the contents list and perhaps the index at the end of the book.

Allison, B. and Race, P. (2004) *The Student's Guide to Preparing Dissertations and Theses*. Milton Park: Routledge Falmer.

Bell, J. (2005) *Doing Your Research Project: A Guide for First-Time Researchers in Education, Health and Social Science*, 4th edn. Maidenhead: Open University Press.

McNiff, J., Lomax, P. and Whitehead, J. (1996) *You and Your Action Research Project*. London: Routledge.

See Chapter 2.

Moore, N. (2000) *How to do Research: The Complete Guide to Designing and Managing Research Projects*, 3rd edn. London: Library Association Publishing.

Mounsey, C. (2002) *Essays and Dissertations*. Oxford: Oxford University Press.

Redman, P. (2005) *Good Essay Writing*. London: Sage.

Chapter 2 discusses what tutors look for when marking essays.

Rudestam, K.E. and Newton, R.R. (2001) *Surviving Your Dissertation: A Comprehensive Guide to Content and Process*, 2nd edn. Thousand Oaks: Sage.

Swetnam, D. (2000) *Writing Your Dissertation: How to Plan, Prepare and Present Successful Work*. Oxford: How To Books.

See Chapter 3.

6 How Do I Write a Proposal?

CHAPTER CONTENTS

6.1 What is a proposal?

A proposal is a careful description of what your dissertation will be about and how you intend to carry out the work involved till its completion. It is a really useful document that challenges you to think very carefully about what you are going to do, how you will do it and why. It will be required in order to inform your supervisor of your intentions so that he/she can judge whether:

- The subject and suggested format conform to the requirements of the course
- It is a feasible project in respect to scope and practicality
- You have identified some questions or issues that are worth investigating
- Your suggested methods for information collection and analysis are appropriate
- The expected outcomes relate to the aims of the project.

Not only is this the main opportunity to crystallize your thoughts before you embark on the project, it is also a sober consideration of how much you will be able to actually achieve within the few weeks/months allowed. You will not be able to sit down and write your proposal without referring to your background research. A good proposal will indicate how your chosen topic emerges from issues that are being debated within your subject field and how your work will produce a useful contribution to the debate. At this level of research you do not have to make any earth-shattering discoveries, but it is necessary to produce some useful insights by the appropriate application of research theory and methods.

FIGURE 6.1   Several re-drafts will be needed.

Increasingly, the proposal is becoming an assessed part of a research methods module, so it is worth ensuring that time, care and quality are invested to (a) ensure that you pass the coursework, and (b) spend less time procrastinating at the start of your dissertation. This assignment however, is likely to be condensed into a more formal proposal at a later stage, perhaps summarized considerably for it to pass through an ethics panel and to allocate your supervisor. As this proposal must be quite short (usually not more than two sides of paper), a lot of thought needs to be put into its production in order to cover all the matter to be conveyed, in an elegantly dense manner. Several re-drafts will be needed in order to pare it down to the limited length allowed, so don't panic if you cannot get it all together first time. A really informative proposal will not only impress your supervisor, but also give you a good guide to the work, and help to get you focused back on the important issues if (probably, when) you get diverted up branching paths of investigation later on in the project.

There is a fairly standardized format for writing proposals which, if followed, ensures that you cover all the important aspects that must be included. The advice under the following headings will help you to focus on the essential matters and to make the hard choices required at this early stage in the project.

6.2   The subject title

The subject title summarizes in a few words the entire project. You will probably not be able to formulate this finally until you have completed the proposal, but you will need something to be going on with in order to focus your thinking.

A title should contain the key words of the dissertation subject, i.e. the main subjects, concepts or situations. Added to these are normally a few words that delineate the scope of the study. For example:

> Physical education in secondary schools: how much time do children spend physically active?

Start therefore by summing up the core of your chosen subject by its principal concepts. To find these, refer to the background reading you have done. What words are mentioned in the book titles, the chapter headings and the content lists? These may be quite esoteric, but should represent the very heart of your interest. This part of the title will, by its nature, be rather general and even abstract. In order to describe the nature of the project itself, more detail will be required that states limitations such as the location, time and extent. Locations can be countries or towns, types of place, or situations. Time might be historical periods, the present or during specific events.

The previous delineations help to define the extent of the project, but further factors can be added, such as under certain conditions, in particular contexts, etc. A few examples here will give you the general idea:

- In rural schools
- Within the Foundation Stage curriculum
- Contemporary trends
- Since 1989
- During unstructured play
- As part of constructive pedagogy.

6.3   The aim and objectives

The aim and objectives of the project should be summarized in three or four bullet points, certainly no more than five. This then provides a very succinct summary of the thrust of the research and an introduction to the rationale that follows. If you find this difficult to write, then you have probably not thought sufficiently about what you are actually going to do. It may well be worth revisiting the section on aims/objectives in the last chapter for further guidance on these.

6.4   The background

Anyone reading your proposal for the first time needs to be informed about the context of the project and where it fits in with current thinking. Do not assume that the reader knows anything about the subject, so introduce it in such a way that any intelligent person can understand the main issues surrounding your work. That is one function of the background section. The other function is to convince your supervisor that you have done the necessary reading into the subject, and that you have reviewed the literature sufficiently. This is why it is necessary to have plenty of references in this section.

FIGURE 6.2   It requires quite an effort to get a lot of information across in a succinct manner.

The references should refer to history, theories, relevant data, accepted practices, contentious issues and recent research publications dealing with your subject of study. It requires quite an effort to get a lot of information across in a succinct manner. Use the notes you have made from your reading. Check that the most important theories and writers have been mentioned. You will find these in the main publications about your subject. Expect to cite about ten or so references in this section.

You could spend an enormous time doing this, as the amount of previous work in the field could be extensive. Alternatively you could worry that you have missed out on essential references, especially if your searches are not very productive. Just remember that at undergraduate level you are not expected to already know everything in your chosen subject. One of the points of doing a dissertation is to widen your knowledge and understanding. So stop as soon as you can provide enough background material to give a context to your project. Your supervisor should be able to tell you if you have missed out any crucial references.

6.5   Defining the research problem

Based on the issues explained and discussed in the background section, you should be able to identify the particular part of the subject that you want to investigate. Every subject could be studied for a lifetime, so it is important that you isolate just one small facet of the subject that you can manageably deal with in the short amount of time that you are given. Once you have explained the topic of your study, and argued why it is necessary to do work in this area, it is a good idea to briefly state the research problem in one or two clear sentences. This will be a direct reflection of your title and will sum up the central question or problem that you will be investigating.

A clear definition of the research problem is an essential ingredient of a proposal; after all, the whole project hinges on this. The nature of the problem also determines the issues that you will explore, the kind of information that you will collect, and the types of analysis that you will use. The main research problem should grow naturally and inevitably out of your discussion of the background. There should be a connection between the problem and the aims and objectives of the project: everything should link up neatly.

6.6   The main concepts and variables

Every subject has its own way of looking at things, its own terminology and its own methods of measuring. Consider the differences between analysing the text of a Shakespeare play and the data transmitted back from a space probe. You will certainly be familiar with some of the concepts that are important in your subject: just look at the title you have chosen for examples of these. It will probably be necessary to define the main concepts in order to dispel any doubts as to their exact meaning. There might even be some dispute in the literature about terminology: if so, highlight the nature of the discussion.

A mention of the indicators that are used to make the concepts recognizable will be the first step to breaking down the abstract nature of most concepts. Then a description of the variables that are the measurable components of the indicators can be used to demonstrate how you will actually be able to collect and analyse the relevant data to come to conclusions about the concepts and their nature.

You do not need to write much here, just enough to convince the reader that you are not vague as to how you can investigate any abstract concepts that you might be dealing with, for example suitability, success, creativity, quality of life, etc. Even well-known terms might need to be broken down to ensure that the reader understands just how you will study them.

FIGURE 6.3 Every subject has its own way of looking at things.

6.7   Methods

What exactly will you do in order to collect and analyse the necessary information? This is the practical part of the proposal where you explain what you will do, how you will do it and why. It is important to demonstrate the way that your research activities relate to the aims or objectives of your project and thus will enable you to come to conclusions relevant to the research problem. Different methods will be required for different parts of the research. Scan through Chapters 13 to 16 in order to get an idea of the range of research methods that are available. At this stage you need not know in detail just how you will implement them, but you should quite easily be able to choose those that seem appropriate for different aspects of your enquiry. Consider the following actions that you might need to take:

- Do a literature search and critical analysis of sources
- Consult with experts
- Identify research population(s), situations, possible case studies
- Select samples – size of sample(s), location of sample(s), number of case studies
- Collect data, quantitative, qualitative and a combination of both – questionnaires, interviews, study of documents, observations, etc.
- Set up experiments or models and run them
- Analyse data – statistical tests, enumerating and classifying, data displays for data reduction and analysis
- Evaluate results of analysis – summarizing and coming to conclusions.

It is best to spell out what you intend to do in relation to each aim and objective relating these to the specific method of data collection you intend to use. Try to be precise and add reasons for what you are planning to do, i.e. add the phrase 'in order to…'. This methods section of the proposal can be in the form of a list of actions.

This whole process will need quite a lot of thought and preparation, especially as you will not be familiar with some of the research methods. But time spent now to make informed decisions is time well spent. It will make you much more confident that you can plan your project, that you have not overreached yourself, and that you have decided on activities that you will quite enjoy doing.

6.8   Expected outcomes

It is a good idea to spell out to the reader, and to yourself, just what you hope will be achieved by doing all this work. Since the proposal is a type of contract to deliver certain results, it is a mistake to 'promise mountains and deliver molehills'. Although you cannot predict exactly what the outcomes will be (if you could, there would be little point in carrying out the research), you should try to be quite precise as to the nature and scope of the outcomes and as to who might benefit from the information. Obviously, you should make sure that the outcomes relate directly to the aims of the research that you described at the beginning of the proposal. The outcomes may be a contribution at a practical and/or a theoretical level.

6.9   Programme of work

Chapter 23 deals in detail with how to plan your time, but you could even now, before reading it, make a stab at allocating your major future activities into your available timeframe. A simple bar chart showing the available time in weeks, and the list of tasks and their sequence and duration, will be sufficient. Don't forget to give yourself plenty of time to actually write up and present your dissertation. You will quickly spot if you have been too ambitious in your intentions, because the tasks just will not fit realistically into the time. If you see problems ahead, now is the time to adjust your proposal to make it more feasible. Reduce the scope of the investigations by narrowing the problem still further (you can do this by becoming more specific and by reducing the number of aims and objectives), by being less ambitious with the amount of data to collect and by simplifying the analytical stages.

6.10   What should I do now?

Write your proposal! Just follow the above recommendations and it should not be too difficult. The biggest danger is that you agonize for ages over what to do before you even write anything down. This is a mistake, for if you try to work out everything in your head you cannot realistically review it. Committing yourself to paper not only relieves your memory from having to retain all your decisions, but also forces you to construct an argument to structure your intentions. Once you have something written down, you can review it, build on it, add detail to it and alter it as required.

Using a word processor gives you the opportunity to sketch out your ideas, perhaps as a series of headings or points. You don't have to worry too much what you write down, as it can so easily be altered, moved, expanded or even deleted. You can work like a painter who first sketches out a few indicative lines, then builds on these to produce, stage by stage, a finished picture. Assuming you have a good idea of the sort of problem you wish to address, you don't even have to start at the beginning. You could work back from the desired outcomes and create a rationale on how you would get there. Or you could select the activities that you enjoy doing most and explore how you could exploit these to devise a project. Once you have a framework that looks feasible, you can add the detail – work that will require rather more reflection and reference to further information.

The final version should be set out following the structure outlined above. You will also need to add a list of references that give the details about the publications cited in your text. Check with any coursework instructions you have been given to make sure that you are fulfilling the requirements. When you have finished, even if you are not formally obliged to do so, give a copy to your supervisor and request his/her comments. Be prepared to alter your proposal in response to any comments you receive, but first think carefully about the implications of these changes. The comments should help to make life easier for you, or clarify the implications of your proposals. It is also in the interest of your supervisor that you do well and enjoy the experience of writing your dissertation.

The proposal will form a firm foundation for your research work. You should refer to it from time to time during the next weeks when you get into the detail of your work, in order to check that you are not going astray, getting too bogged down on one particular aspect, or missing out on an essential detail.

Finally, if you have written a proposal for a research methods module, ensure that you take note of the tutor's feedback on your work … don't just look at the grade but actually engage with their written feedback. If in doubt about anything, ask! It is likely that your module tutor would have supervised many dissertations in the past – use their experience.

6.11 References to more information

There are books that are solely dedicated to writing academic proposals of all kinds. The principles are the same for all of them; it is the extent and detail that vary. All are reasoned arguments to support a plan of action. If you want to read more, or find different approaches to proposal writing, you can explore some of these books. Some will be rather too detailed for your purposes, but you will undoubtedly find something useful. I have put them in order of complexity, simplest first, though you may want to look at a more subject-specific book first. Every book on how to do dissertations will also have a section on writing a proposal.

The following book is extremely useful in proposal writing:

Locke, L.F. (1999) *Proposals That Work: A Guide for Planning Dissertations and Grant Proposals*, 4th edn. London: Sage.

Other books listed here are also worth a read:

Forsyth, P. (2006) *How to Write Reports and Proposals*, 2nd edn. London: Kogan Page.

Jay, R. (1999) *How to Write Proposals and Reports That Get Results*. London: Prentice Hall.

Ogden, T.E. and Goldberg, I.A. (2002) *Proposals: A Guide to Success*, 3rd edn. London: Academic Press.

Punch, K.F. (2006) *Developing Effective Research Proposals*, 2nd edn. London: Sage.

7 How Do I Write an Introduction?

7.1 An introduction to the introduction

Although the shortest chapter in your dissertation, the introductory chapter is at the same time, perhaps the most important as it sets out the rest of your work. If you can write a solid introduction, one that engages with the reader, then they will want to read more. There is so much at stake with this first chapter: how often have you read the first chapter of a book then decided it is not for you?

If I were a cynic, I would say that as long as you have a strong introduction and a strong conclusion, then you can be forgiven for what goes on in-between: indeed this is very much like performing; people can go to sleep in the middle part of a performance however, a dramatic ending, one that awakens them from their slumber, will make them realize what quality they had missed. Alas, I am not that much of a cynic and would advise you to ensure all of your chapters are of the same quality.

The introduction is where you need to establish your focus and let the reader know why your dissertation is important; after all it must have been important to you otherwise you would have chosen a different focus. Not only do you need to explain why it is important to you but also explain why the focus is important in its own right.

The chapter will also establish the parameters of your dissertation ensuring that the reader is aware of what you intend to cover, how and where this will take place. Consequently writing the introduction is not a hard task as you would have previously considered many of the issues prior to putting pen to paper (or fingers to keyboard!)

For this reason, I would suggest that the introduction is not written immediately but saved for when you know exactly where the dissertation journey is going having read around your area extensively, established a sufficiently narrow focus and considered your methodology in detail – who you will be researching on, why, how and where. This chapter can therefore be saved for a time during your dissertation when you are tired of spending endless hours in the library or in the research setting collecting data.

There are several key elements that you should include in the introduction; each of these will be discussed in greater depth throughout this chapter.

7.2   Overview of the chapter

Defining your focus of your research

- What is your focus?
- Why have you selected this focus for your dissertation?
- Did you consider (and reject) any other ideas before settling on your selected focus? Why?
- What is the significance of the focus?
- What is the context of the research?

The environmental issues of your research

- What is your background?
- Where is the research going to take place and why?
- Who are you going to be researching and why?
- What are you hoping will be the impact of your research?

Research aim and objectives

- In one sentence, what specifically do you intend to achieve through your research?
- In supplementary sentences, how will you achieve this?

Signposting your research

- How will your dissertation unfold?

7.3   Defining your focus of your research

What is your focus?

Within the first paragraph of your introduction, the reader should be clear as to your focus for the rest of the dissertation. If there are too many initial paragraphs discussing the 'scenery', when you actually declare your focus, the reader may not have noticed unless you bring it to light with a fanfare!

Why have you selected this focus for your dissertation?

Explain to the reader why the focus is important. In terms of your profession, is the focus a topical issue which is being hotly debated? Is it an issue is becoming of increasing concern? Is it an issue that people are unaware of and you are explaining why people should be aware of this issue? Basically you will need to explain why your focus is important in relation to education (after all you do need to keep in mind that the dissertation is written in your chosen subject field … and what a vast field it is!)

There may also be personal reasons for why you have selected the focus – what makes you impassioned enough to want to dedicate a substantial amount of time and effort to exploring and perhaps resolving an issue? Why do you want to do this? How do you benefit?

Did you consider (and reject) any other ideas before settling on your selected focus? why?

There may well have been other areas you considered before deciding to settle on your selected focus. What actually led to this point in time? Did your focus evolve from a totally different issue, or is your focus related in-part to an issue? For example, you may be aware of certain constructivist approaches within science education, specifically the work of Keogh and Naylor's 'concept cartoons' (where cartoons are used to promote thinking). Could this pedagogical method be used within a different subject which is in turn the focus of your research? Perhaps you decided that using concept cartoons was not applicable, however, you utilized a different constructivist method. Consequently you would have explained the 'journey' to your specific focus.

What is the significance of the focus?

This is the 'so what?' part. So far you have kept me engaged with your introduction but my interest starts to wean. You have told me why you have selected your focus for personal and professional reasons yet am I really that interested? Take for example a focus where you explain the importance of teaching about alcohol consumption to secondary children. Would an adult without secondary-aged children really be concerned about this? (To that extent, how concerned are adults with secondary-aged children?)

If however, you explain the wider implications, that if children are not taught about drinking responsibly, potentially I am at more risk of a motor accident as a result, that my taxes are increasingly paying for health provision due to the associated risks of drinking, etc. As a consequence, your research focus is going to ensure I maintain my attention as you informed me that the problem may well be mine.

What is the context of the research?

So far you have developed a coherent argument outlining why your dissertation is of importance. Yet for all I know, you could be making up a fanciful research topic to amuse yourself or blatantly discussing an issue you have read in some obscure journal. This part of the introduction provides support for your focus by making explicit key aspects contributing to your focus. An example of this may be a survey report which states a problem exists but does not indicate how the problem could be resolved. Alternatively, there could be a parallel report which has discussed your focus in one area, yet not in another, for example, there may be plenty of research discussing outdoor play in the primary phase, yet little in the secondary phase.

You must ensure that you are not writing a miniature literature review, or just drawing out key aspects from your second chapter: instead you need to refer only to literature that demonstrates why your dissertation is worth completing.

7.4 The environmental issues of your research

Your research needs to be positioned to provide the reader with an insight into the nature of the setting, the participants, and your own expertise. All researchers have varying expertise, research settings differ as do participants: by writing a paragraph or two on the following area, you will provide a 'richness' to your dissertation.

What is your background?

Your research must be positioned not only from your research stance but also your background and your role within the research. Have you a vested interest in the area? If so, could this be politically motivated and somewhat biased?

Outlining your role as a professional and that of a researcher will provide the reader with some insight as to why you wish to conduct the research and what you may potentially gain from this. A teacher with 25 years of experience researching their own class may have different views from someone early on into their career who have only known a class for a relatively short time.

Where is the research going to take place and why?

Research needs to take place at some location: as such why have you selected the particular location you have selected? Is it because of proximity? Have you been on work experience at the setting? Is there something particular about the setting that you wish to investigate? In other words, out of all of the educational settings in your locality, why select the one you have focussed on?

It may well be worth your while finding out statistical information about the sociological diversity of where the research is taking place to provide an additional insight. For example, you could detail the proportion who may speak English as an additional language among other sociological indicators.

Who are you going to be researching and why?

Following on from the above point, are you researching a group of pupils who you have never worked with before, or are they known to you? Your role as a researcher will impact on those you study: if you are known to the participants, they are more likely to feel at ease in providing information: if you are a stranger entering their research setting, they will be somewhat guarded.

You could detail what is unique about the individual's you have selected: perhaps their level of attainment, what may be deemed to be specific educational needs, the level of support they may have, etc.

What are you hoping will be the impact of your research?

Research is a pointless activity if it is not used to inform other people, perhaps making suggestion for improvement, no matter how minor. You would have previously detailed why you had selected the area for research but what are you hoping to obtain from this? It would be worth discussing the realistic impact of your research: although you may not be able to change the world, improving some small notion may create further ripples, just as a stone being thrown into a pond.

7.5   Research aim and objectives

In one sentence, what specifically do you intend to achieve through your research? This will be the first time that you have specifically detailed to the reader what you intend to achieve: everything leading up to this point has been 'padding' however, the previous sections must logically lead up to this aim. If your focus was not particularly defined, or you have discussed an associated topic which is only part related to your aim, the reader will be taken aback if the aim springs out from nowhere! Consequently ensure that the aim relates back to the problem you have discussed.

Your aim is the crux of your dissertation and has previously been discussed in Chapter 5. It sets the focus and establishes parameters around your work. In several thousand words, your conclusion will revisit this aim, discussing to what extent your dissertation has successfully researched this in depth.

It would be worth noting that depending on advice provided by your institution or your supervisor, your objectives may actually be placed at the end of your literature review. The reasoning for this is that until you have conducted your literature review you will not be aware of what gaps actually exist in your area. Similarly if the objectives are placed in the introduction, they may seem a little out of place, with the reader thinking 'Where did they come from?' Ultimately it would be best to check such conventions with that of your supervisor.

7.6 Signposting your research

How will your dissertation unfold?

There are two ways of progressing once you have defined your aim for the reader. You could take them on a 'magical mystery tour' or discuss how you intend to set about exploring the aim. The latter is more appealing as surprises can cause discomfort in the reader: if they want to read a mystery novel in their own time, it is their choice! Alas the dissertation demonstrates that you can produce a clear, coherent and logical argument. Consequently, inform the reader briefly of how your dissertation will unfold and how aspects will link logically into a uniformed structure.

7.7 What should I do now?

Although this chapter has discussed different sections of your introduction under various headings, when writing the introduction avoid using these headings: they are for your benefit. As the chapter is one of the shortest in your dissertation, too many subheadings can spoil the flow for the reader. Consequently, ensure that the various sections logically lead from one to the other.

It would be worth however, noting the headings for the structure of this chapter, then writing key bullet points under each. You can amend these points as work on your dissertation unfolds and you may want to play about with the order to see what works best for your work.

7.8 References to more information

Although this chapter has provided a substantial overview to guide you, you may want to also refer to other sources to see what they have to say on writing an introduction. Specifically refer to the chapters on 'Writing an Introduction' or similar, noting how the authors suggest a structure. From this, identify what aspects would be most beneficial to the dissertation you are writing in order to help structure your first chapter.

Cottrell, S. (2003) *The Study Skills Handbook*, 2nd edn. Basingstoke: Palgrave Macmillan.

Mounsey, C. (2002) *Essays and Dissertations*. Oxford: Oxford University Press.

Redman, P. (2005) *Good Essay Writing*. London: Sage.

   See Chapter 6.

Rudestam, K.E. and Newton, R.R. (2001) *Surviving your Dissertation: A Comprehensive Guide to Content and Process*, 2nd edn. Thousand Oaks: Sage.

   See Chapter 4.

Soles, D. and Lawler, G. (2005) *The Academic Essay: How to Plan, Draft, Write and Edit*, 2nd edn. Abergele: Studymates.

SECTION 3

As noted in the last section, if you can establish a clear introduction to your work, explaining why your dissertation is of importance, then you have made a good start. Section 3 thus develops your work further by providing guidance on how to ensure that both you and the reader are fully informed of the important issues in the area and whether any gaps in knowledge need to be addressed.

Chapter 8 discusses how to get hold of information. In all likelihood, during your degree so far, you may have relied on the recommended readings from the module. Yet with the dissertation, you are responsible for finding your own literature. You may have had induction session on the full range of resources available at the start of your course, yet two years on, how much of this has changed … how much have you remembered? Consequently this chapter will remind you of how to access the key resources to help ensure you have the relevant information you require.

Chapter 9 outlines what to do once you have this information. Your desk may be heaving under the strain of books and journals, so to ensure you adhere to health and safety regulations on carrying heavy weights, this chapter will discuss how to make effective notes. Chapter 10 naturally follows from Chapter 9 (it would be weird if the book were to jump straight into Chapter 15 after all!), by discussing issues relating to referencing your notes.

Chapter 11 introduces the art of arguing effectively, after all your discussion is one colossal argument where you are persuading whoever reads (or marks) your dissertation as to why you should be believed. Hence this chapter outlines argumentative strategies you can employ.

The final chapter in this section discusses how you can thread your information into a structured chapter, providing the background theoretical stance to your dissertation.

8 Where Do I Get Hold of All the Necessary Background Information?

8.1 Information overload?

It is well known that this is an information age; we are drowning in the stuff! There can be no excuse that there is a lack of information on your subject. The problem is in knowing where to look for suitable information and to be able to sort it and select what is relevant and of sufficiently good quality. Any trawl through the Internet will demonstrate what a lot of rubbish there is on every subject under the sun. Even a visit to the library or a good bookshop can be a daunting experience: 'Goodness! Do I really have to read all this stuff!' is a typical reaction. No, you don't. But you will have to read some of it, and the skill is in finding what is the essential information. Luckily, there are easy-to-learn, sophisticated methods of trawling for information. No need to spend hours in dusty archives (unless that is central to your project), no need to buy lots of expensive books, but there is a need to get skilled in search and find techniques.

Where you look will depend on the subject you have chosen. Some sources cover most subjects; others are specialized in a narrow range, and will hence provide more detail.

Here are lists of places you can search.

Libraries

- Your institution's library – this should be your first choice. Here, not only will you find a huge amount of information, but you will also be able to find out about all the other information sources listed below.
- Specialist libraries – subject libraries in university departments, professional libraries in professional institutions.
- Private libraries – in stately homes, institutes, organizations.

Information services

- Government departments such as standards institutes, records offices, statistical offices.
- Pressure groups and voluntary organizations.
- Professional organizations.

The Internet and intranets

- The full gamut of the World Wide Web.
- Your own organization's intranet. Often providing lecture notes and course material as well as other specialist information, for example research papers, professorial lectures.
- Subject databases, for example the British Education Index.

People

There are experts in every field. Some will be willing to advise you. Try the members of your own university staff at first, many of whom will be involved in research. Ask a professor or key lecturer in your subject area to suggest who might have the specialist knowledge that you are seeking. Your library will contain guides to professionals and experts. In some cases, local knowledge will be needed: search out the relevant local experts (e.g. children centre managers, headteachers, education psychologists, social workers, etc.).

8.2 Library searches

The library will normally be your first access point for information. I am sure that you have used the library many times before, but have you really used all the sophisticated search facilities available? It is not sufficient at this level of study just to visit the shelves to see what is there, even if you have consulted the online catalogue first. There will be a wide range of resources and search facilities provided, together with a series of training sessions and leaflets in the use of these. Find out what is available and attend the training sessions so that you can use the full services of the library with confidence. Being adept at making searches will save you lots of time and frustration, as well as ensuring that you get hold of all the latest information you need.

Try to get the latest publications (unless you have special reasons not to) for two reasons. First, information becomes quickly outdated and new findings are constantly being made; and second, the reference lists at the end of the books which will guide you to further sources will not be too out of date. The information in fast-moving subjects, such as ICT or school management, will become rapidly obsolete, but in certain subjects like the humanities, older publications can have lasting value.

Here are some of the facilities you should investigate:

FIGURE 8.1   Library.

Library catalogues

Most libraries now have an electronic catalogue accessed through their computer terminals. You will probably be able to access this online from elsewhere too via the intranet and/or Internet. This means that you can do searches from home or from elsewhere in the institution. If the book you want is not on the shelves, reserve it so that you can receive it when it is returned. Do keep track of renewal dates: to forget can turn out to be very expensive!

To widen your search or to locate a book not available in your library, catalogues of other libraries (national and worldwide) can easily be consulted via the Web. OPAC (online public access catalogue) is the common system used and the books can be borrowed through inter-library loans. A fee is usually charged for this kind of loan.

Useful Web addresses are:

- The British Library Public Catalogue (BLPC), with details of over 10 million books, journals, reports, conferences and music scores: http://opac97.bl.uk/.
- Other academic and research libraries in the UK: http://www.nis.ac.uk/lis.
- European national libraries: http://portico.bl.uk/gabriel/en/welcome.html.
- The Library of Congress of the USA, with over 17 million books: http://www.loc.gov/catalog/.
- Looking worldwide, try: http://www.libdex.com/.
- Newspapers, including UK national, many provincial and various international papers, can be found at the British Library Newspaper's Catalogue: http://www.bl.uk/ catalogues/newspapers.htm.
- Times Educational Supplement: http://tes.co.uk/.

FIGURE 8.2   Don't forget journals and newspapers.

Don't forget the journals and newspapers. These are often catalogued and stored separately from the books in the library. As they appear regularly, they tend to be very up to date. They are based on defined subject areas, and vary in content from newspaper type articles to the most erudite research papers. To track down articles and papers in past issues, see the next two points.

If you are at home on vacation, or on placement, or if you live some distance away from your institution, you can probably arrange to use your local university or college library, certainly for reference and possibly for lending (various schemes are in operation: consult your librarian).

Databases

These are computer-based lists of publications on CD-ROM, or on the university network, or on the Web. Access to these is, depending on the licensing arrangements, from library terminals, university computers or even your own computer. Databases contain huge amounts of sources, usually searched by using key words. Some provide only citations and abstracts. Citations are the basic author and publication details; abstracts are short summaries of the contents of the article. In these cases, you will have to get hold of the book or journal article for the full information. Some databases provide the full text of the publication as plain text or even in facsimile, i.e. looking as originally printed. Citation indexes list the publications in which certain books and articles have been used as a reference.

Previous postgraduate dissertations produced in your university should be listed on a database. Copies of undergraduate dissertations might also be, though you might have to consult your own department collection. It is helpful to see what other students have done before you.

As there are many databases to choose from, and many are subject specific, it is best to consult the information provided by your library to identify the best ones for you to search. You may need to obtain a password to get access (e.g. Athens authentication); again, consult library information. Your library will also provide training sessions in using electronic databases, which will save you much time in the long run.

Several databases are of note. The following may be accessed directly through the internet or through your institution's own pages. The British Education Index (BEI) and the American equivalent, Education Resources Information Center (ERIC) provide abstracts and indexes for a vast array of education journals. Unfortunately they do not necessarily allow you to open the full text of the document, however it can provide useful references that can then be searched for on databases that offer full-text articles, for example, Academic Search Premier (ASP). Such full-text articles open in Adobe portable document format (.pdf) which can be saved to your computer (or memory storage device) and opened at a later stage. Please note that your institutional library may subscribe to a range of different databases and that it would be worth familiarising yourself with these.

Spend some time looking at the instructions on conducting searches as this will help you narrow down your results considerably (or broaden them if there appears to be little in your area).

Journals of abstracts and indexes

These are printed publications that give a summary of articles and papers in a vast range of journals, together with the details required to obtain a full copy of the publications. Although more recent publications are generally recorded on electronic databases, these printed guides cover the older sources – particularly useful for historical studies. Enough information is usually given to enable you to decide if you need to read the full paper. They are usually organized in subject areas. Older dissertations and conference proceedings can also be tracked down in this way.

A useful hint when using computer-based searches: instead of printing out your search results on paper, copy them to disk, so that you can easily view and edit them at a later time. The useful references can then be transferred to your bibliography without having to type them out again (ideally using a bibliographic database program such as Endnote).

Librarians

They are there to help you. Ask at the help desk if you get stuck. There are often subject librarians who have specialist knowledge in specific subject areas; they will be able to help you explore more elusive sources. Libraries usually run free training sessions on all aspects of searching for information, often with specialist advice in the various subject areas. Find out when these take place so that you can make the best use of the services offered.

8.3 The Internet

With thousands of pages being added every day, the World Wide Web (WWW) is the biggest single source of information in the world. However, the content is of extremely variable quality, and the biggest challenge when using it is to track down good-quality material. You can easily waste hours trawling through rubbish in search of the goodies. Careful use of search terms helps to eliminate the trash. Usually, the more precise your search parameters, the more manageable the search results will be. Not all information on the Web is free. Two useful websites for reference are:

- Intute (www.intute.ac.uk). This website has been created by a network of universities and partners. For education resources, first go to the 'social sciences' page.
- Infed (www.infed.org). This website has a range of articles and resources which can help provide information on a range of educational topics.

There are published Internet guides that can help you to make the best of this resource (try your library for lists devoted to subject areas). Some are specifically aimed at students and list useful search engines, sites and databases. Any Internet guide quickly becomes outdated, so you may have to go and buy one for the current year.

8.4 Evaluating Web sources

Anyone can add pages to the World Wide Web, so how can you judge if the information you have found is reliable? Here are seven different tests you can make to judge the quality of the contents.

- Is it accurate? Does it say what sources the data are based on? Compare the data with other sources. If they diverge greatly, is there some explanation for this?
- What authority is it based on? Find out who authored the pages and whether they are recognized experts or a reputable organization. Check if other publications are cited or if they provide a bibliography of other articles, reports or books. You may need to track down the 'home page' to get to the details. Also see if there is a postal address and phone number to indicate the 'reality' of the organization. Web addresses that end in 'ac' (meaning academic) are likely to be university or college addresses and therefore point to some intellectual credibility – no guarantee of quality but nevertheless a useful indicator.
- Is it biased? Many pressure groups and commercial organizations use the Web to promote their ideas and products, and present information in a one-sided way. Can you detect a vested interest in the subject on the part of the author? Find out more about the authors – for example does the information about animal experiments come from an anti-vivisection league, a cosmetics company, or an independent research institute?

- How detailed is the information? Is the information so general that it is of little use, or so detailed and specialized that it is difficult to understand? Investigate whether it is only fragmentary and misses out important issues in the subject, and whether the evidence is backed up by relevant data. There may be useful links to further information, other websites or printed publications.
- Is it out of date? Pages stay on the Web until they are removed. Some have obviously been forgotten about and are hopelessly out of date. Try to find a date on the page, or the date when the page was updated (perhaps on the View/Page Info option on your Web browser). Note that some updates might not update all the contents. Check any links provided to see if they work.
- Have you cross-checked? Compare the contents with other sources of information such as books, articles, official statistics and other websites. Does the information tally with or contradict these? If the latter, can you see why?
- Have you tried pre-evaluated 'subject gateways'? The information on these sites has been vetted by experts in the relevant subjects, so can be relied upon to be of high quality. Try the BUBL link at: www.bubl.ac.uk/link/.

8.5 Search techniques for online catalogues, databases and the Net

Here are a few basic hints on how to make effective searches for information. In order to find what you want, it must first be clear what you are looking for. Searches rely on single words or a combination of several words. Every subject will contain several crucial terms that distinguish it from other subjects, so the trick is to select these. If you are unfamiliar with the subject, look it up in a specialist dictionary or an encyclopaedia to see what terms are used so that you can build up your own list of key words. Remember also the use of different words and spellings in parts of the world, for example car/automobile, lift/elevator, pavement/sidewalk, organisation/organization, behaviour/behavior.

Databases usually provide the option of a free text search, or a key word, subject or index search. The former looks for your chosen word(s) in all the text contained in the database, while the latter only searches the key words, subject lists or index lists provided by the authors with their books or papers. These lists focus on the subject matter of the publication, so give a more reliable guide to the contents. Many databases include a thesaurus – a list of indexing terms that will help you to use the standard terms. Sometimes the number of articles to which the term is assigned is given.

It is usually possible to narrow your search by indicating place and time, where these are relevant. The publication date is a basic piece of bibliographic data.

Adding an asterisk (*) to words or parts of words automatically widens the search parameters in the form of wildcards. For example, 'educ*' will find all the words starting with that stem, for example 'education', 'educator', 'educational', etc. Inserting the * symbol into a word takes care of different spelling versions, for example 'behavio*r' will find 'behaviour' and 'behavior'.

Boolean logic is a fancy word for the technique of using connecting words such as 'and', 'or' and 'not'. These refine the search by defining more closely what you want to include or not. For example:

- Schools and finance: this narrows down your search by only selecting records that contain both terms.
- (Lifts or elevators): this widens your search by selecting records that contain either or both terms. Note that 'or' statements must be in brackets.
- Nurseries and playschools, not schools: this eliminates the terms that you do not want to consider. However, be careful that you do not eliminate useful records.
- It is best if you keep the search terms simple and search several times using different variations and terms.

FIGURE 8.3   In order to find out what you want, you must first be clear about what you are looking for.

8.6   What should I do now?

If you have not been to a library training session for some time, now is the time to book yourself in. There are always new sources of information being introduced, especially access to electronic databases, so make sure that you are up to date with all the facilities. You may need a password to access some, so you will not be able to sit at a terminal and work it out yourself. Also look for the latest information bulletins in the library, particularly in your subject.

It is much easier to find information if you know what you are looking for. This might sound obvious, but it does some careful thought before making searches. Make a list of

FIGURE 8.4   Keep your eyes and ears open for possible leads to information.

the all the main concepts and other terms that appear in your title, aims, background, research problem and methods sections of your proposal. This should give you a list of key words on which you can base your searches. Look up the most important ones first.

Once you have found some useful publications, use the reference list at the back to lead you on to other sources. Unfortunately, this only goes backwards in time. If you want to look the other way, consult a citation database and look up the title of the book, article, etc. you are currently reading. This will list the publications that have cited that one as a reference.

Despite what I said above about knowing exactly what you are looking for, do let chance play some part in your quest. Keep your eyes and ears open for possible leads to information. Discussions on the TV or radio, informal conversations, chance meetings are all possible sources. In the library, instead of tracking down a particular book, try exploring a section of the shelves containing books with the relevant class number, i.e. the number given according to the subject. For a start, you will imme- diately see what is actually available, and you may come across authors you are not familiar with.

Do read the next chapter before you return the publications you have borrowed. It is essential that you are systematic in taking notes and making records of the publications, and the next chapter explains how you can do this.

8.7　References to more information

I have given a short description of what you may find useful in the following books, starting with searching and reviewing the literature.

Allison, B. and Race, P. (2004) *The Student's Guide to Preparing Dissertations and Theses*. Milton Park: Routledge Falmer.

Cohen, L., Manion, L. and Morrison, K. (2007) *Research Methods in Education,* 6th edn. Abingdon: Routledge.

See pp. 242–244 for a comprehensive list of websites to help find Internet sources.

Cottrell, S. (2003) *The Study Skills Handbook*, 2nd edn. Basingstoke: Palgrave Macmillan.

Hart, C. (2001) *Doing a Literature Search: A Comprehensive Guide for the Social Sciences*. London: Sage.

The entire book is devoted to finding relevant information.

Hart, C. (1998) *Doing a Literature Review: Releasing the Social Science Research Imagination*. London: Sage.

A guide through the multidimensional sea of academic literature with techniques on how to deal with the information when you have found it.

Mounsey, C. (2002) *Essays and Dissertations*. Oxford: Oxford University Press.

Soles, D. and Lawler, G. (2005) *The Academic Essay: How to Plan, Draft, Write and Edit*, 2nd edn. Abergele: Studymates.

9 How Can I Manage All the Notes?

9.1 Introduction

A good dissertation will be based on wide reading, and contain references to all the important literature in the chosen subject. This means that you will have to spend considerable time trawling through the library and other sources of information, collecting a whole range of relevant information and views on your subject. All this collected material will have to be recorded somehow and stored for further use in such a way that you can find what you want when you need it for your writing. This requires considerable organization on your part at the outset, to get your system up and running for when you start. Trying to change your system of recording, storage and retrieval of information halfway through will be an enormous task, well worth avoiding! So you do need to have a sound system to start with, and to be very disciplined in following it through. This will ensure that you will not have to waste time searching for that oh-so-important but dimly remembered quotation, on a page you cannot remember in a book you borrowed from the library three months ago, by an author whose name you have forgotten.

The following tips will give you a range of methods to choose from, which you can adapt to your own preferred working methods and the scale of your dissertation. You will find that the skills you develop in this activity will be of invaluable use in many other fields of endeavour. Remember, this is an information age, so acquiring a sound method of avoiding information overload by good management will be well worth the effort.

FIGURE 9.1   This is an information age.

9.2   Reading techniques

Faced with a line of books on the library shelf that all seem to have some relevance to your subject, it is easy to become overwhelmed by the sheer amount of reading and recording that needs to be done. At this point you need to be aware of methods of 'filleting' a book in order to see quickly how much of it is relevant and what you need to record for later use, and different reading techniques relevant to different stages in the searching process. There is no need to read whole books in order to find the material you require. There are actually several ways of reading that can be used to good effect in the appropriate situations. Freeman and Meed (1993: 31–41) suggest the following levels of reading:

- Scanning – a focused approach, looking for one particular piece of information, as one would look in a dictionary or an encyclopaedia. Here the importance of the index is obvious. The essential thing is that you deliberately ignore everything except the one item for which you are scanning.
- Skimming – a quick review of the contents, introduction, review and abstract in order to get an idea of the content of the book to judge its relevance for your own area of study. A closer look would entail looking at the chapter headings, their introductions and conclusions, and even reading the first and last sentences of paragraphs to get a gist of the main arguments. A review of the diagrams, tables and illustrations also gives valuable clues to the content and approach.
- Reading to understand – involves detailed study of a passage, chapter or paper, in order to really absorb all the facts, ideas and arguments. It might be necessary to read it more than once, and to take notes to record and comment on the contents.
- Word-by-word reading – used when following detailed instructions when you need to understand every word. This will be needed when reading assignment and exam

questions, and instructions on the use of research methods, such as surveys or experiments.

- Reading for pleasure – used when you read for relaxation and enjoyment, for example, when reading a novel or a comic book.

Another reading technique is called 'speed reading'. This involves a technique of using the eyes to scan pages of text very quickly, getting the brain to absorb the meaning without reading along the lines as you do normally. A ruler is used to guide the eyes' progress down the lines of the pages. This is a skill that undoubtedly needs a lot of practice, and is probably suitable only for the type of reading where you need to find out the outline of a story or argument, rather than particular details. In case you are interested, and have plenty of time to practise, I have added a few references to books on this in the last section of this chapter.

9.3   Identifying useful material

First, you really do need to know what you are looking for. The easiest way to limit a search is to select a series of key words that are relevant to your subject. You may not know all of these at the outset, but you will develop a list as you become more familiar with the terminology used and the important concepts and issues involved. These will help you to track down the publications that might be relevant in the library.

Book titles generally contain the most important words used in the text, so this is the obvious place to start. Select the books that mention one or some of your key words in the title, then look at the list of contents at the beginning. Do your key words occur here? Are whole chapters dedicated to them? If so, it is worth investigating more closely. If not, look in the alphabetical index at the back. Are your key words mentioned, and if so, how many pages do they appear on? Look up some of the mentioned pages and read what is written about the word. Do this for several of your key words, and you will be able to decide whether there is enough of interest for you to use the book for further study. If your key words do not appear, or not in the sense or context that interests you, you can reject the book.

This technique can be used on any published information, though the convenient list of contents and index might not be present. Other useful places to look in a book or other publication are the introduction, the reviews on the book jacket, and perhaps the conclusions section. Academic papers normally have an abstract at the beginning that summarizes the contents very succinctly. They also often identify a list of key words. The use of key words when surfing the Internet is obviously a crucial part of the search process, as you read in the last chapter.

If you find a nugget of information in the text that seems relevant, but you need more, look to see if there is a reference cited in that passage. Then, look up the reference details at the back of the chapter or book, and there you will have another publication to track down – hopefully with more of the information you need.

Getting to the required information on websites requires similar techniques. Look at the contents list for guidance to the contents. More sophisticated sites have a search function where you can insert your key words.

9.4 Organizing your system

So now you have a pile of books or other publications in front of you, all containing what is probably valuable information. You cannot be sure if you will use all of this, because you will only discover what is really essential when you get into the writing stage, but you need to record anything that might be useful. This is why it is important to compile your own 'library' of notes that you can draw on at later stages in your dissertation.

Before considering what notes to take and how to take them, let us first look at the formats you could use for recording and storing these notes.

There are two basic formats for notes:

1   paper-based format
2   computer-based format.

Paper-based notes

The paper-based format needs no electronic equipment, though a few accessories make life easier. The principle behind this system is to write your notes on sheets of paper or card, and then order the sheets in such a way that you can find the notes when you need them later.

You can use A4 sheets of paper and store them in ring folders, or alternatively you can use index cards (the larger sizes are more useful) and store these in boxes designed for the purpose. The idea is to store your notes under certain headings so that you can find what you have collected on that subject. The headings can be various, depending on your subject and how you will be approaching it. You will have to work out the best method yourself. The kinds of headings commonly used are:

- Key words
- Author names
- Publication titles
- Dates (particularly useful in historical studies)
- Subjects – or aspects of the main subject.

Some academics advise you to make several copies of your notes so that you can file them under several headings. This way you can find the material whether, for example, you are looking for the writings of a particular author, or information about a particular subject or about a particular date. It is best to keep the notes short, that is, concentrated on one topic or aspect of the subject. Start another page or card when the topic or your

FIGURE 9.2   You can make and take your notes anywhere.

notes change. This is because you may want to search out all your notes on one topic, so you can pull out all the pages or cards under that topic heading. Several ring binders will be needed for storing your A4 sheets, or filing boxes for storing cards.

The greatest advantage of this format is that you can make and take your notes any-where without needing any equipment apart from paper or card and a pen. The main disadvantage is that you will need to rewrite the material from your handwritten notes on the word processor when you use them.

Computer-based notes

The computer-based formats rely on various database programs. These are set up to deal with lots of bits of information so that you can easily store and retrieve them. The most common non-specialist database programs come with standard program packages, such as Microsoft Access. More specialized programs are aimed at exactly this job of notes and referencing. The current main ones are Endnote, Procite and Citation. Check if they are available on your institution's network. You can even devise a simple system using your normal word processing package.

The basic requirements of the system using a computer format are similar to those of a paper-based one. Notes should be short and on a single topic, they should be thoroughly referenced, and they should be stored under allotted headings. The major advantages of a computer-based system are that you have much more powerful search facilities; your notes are easily retrieved, copied, revised and edited; and you do not need to rewrite your reference information (lots of complicated formatting and punctuation), you can just copy it for lists, etc. You can also store all your notes on a compact floppy disk. The main disadvantage is that, in order to avoid copying out, you need to have your own computer with you wherever you need to make the notes – not such a problem if you own a laptop. You will also have to spend time learning how to use the program.

Obviously, you can devise a system that uses the best features of each format. Whichever format you want to use, you need to decide exactly how you will do it, and test it out before putting it into general use.

Notes content

There are several bits of information that you must record for each and every one of the notes that you take. These are:

- The author(s) of the text – surname and first names. Perhaps the name on the book is the editor of the book, who has compiled a series of chapters or papers by various authors. In this case you will also need all the name(s) of the author(s) of the relevant text.
- The title of the book – including any subtitle. If it is a journal or a newspaper, you will have to record the full name of the journal or newspaper.
- If it is an article or a paper in an edited book, journal or newspaper with different authors for different chapters or papers, then the title of the relevant chapter or paper is also required.
- If it is a website, the URL (Web address).
- The date of the publication (in a book, look on the reverse of the title page for this).
- The place it was published (ditto).
- The name of the publisher (ditto).
- The number(s) of the page(s) containing the information you have made notes from.
- Also useful is a reference to where you found the information, for example the library and the book code number, so that you can easily track it down again.
- You might also use material from lectures or conferences. In this case, give full details including speaker, title of talk, conference title, venue and date.

This information, attached to every note, will enable you to fully reference it, and to find the original information again if you need to.

So how will you set about recording the information that you want to collect?

9.5 Taking notes

The purposes of note taking are to make:

- A record – when you develop your ideas and start writing you will need to have your collected information and ideas to hand. Your notes will be your own 'library' of relevant material. This will include direct quotations as well as transcripts.

- A précis – to make the information manageable, it is usually necessary to distil out the valuable essences relevant to your subject of study.
- An interpretation – your own view of the value and quality of the information and opinions found in the literature is an important component of the dissertation. Recording these in your notes helps to invoke an analytical approach to reading.
- A commentary – notes need not always be directly related to the pieces of text that you are reading. Often it is worth recording your thoughts in relation to your study as they occur. Often, flashes of inspiration or insight occur at unexpected moments, and are quickly forgotten if not written down immediately.

Making notes also helps you to concentrate on what you are reading, and to listen carefully at lectures and conferences.

Notes are really useful when you come to writing the first drafts of your dissertation. You can use them as a prompt to start; after all, you have already begun writing as soon as you have started taking notes. They can be used to help you structure your writing, perhaps by physically laying out the notes in sequence on a table. Reviewing and reordering the sequence is simple and fast. The requirement that notes are single subject, short and well defined is obviously of great value in this context.

FIGURE 9.3   Flashes of inspiration.

There are many recommendations made by lecturers about how to actually do note taking. Here are some dos and don'ts:

- Do ensure that you have a supply of your chosen medium for recording notes always to hand, or at least a notebook of some kind. Notes made on the back of an envelope always get lost!
- Don't make notes on the book or publication that you are reading: it spoils your and anyone else's later reading of the text, and loses the point of extracting information for your own 'library' of notes.
- Do use your own words. This demands not only that you have understood the text, but that you will understand what it means when you come to read it again. It is best to read the passage in question carefully, then put it aside as you make the notes from memory. This will also avoid any danger of plagiarism.
- Don't mix up direct quotations, your own notes summarizing the text, and your own commentary on the text (opinions, prompted ideas, comparisons, etc.) Make a separate

note 'card' for each. Quotations should be short and make a significant point, or explain an important concept.

- Do keep notes to one subject or key word. This will help you greatly when you want to find everything you have noted on one subject or key word.
- Don't forget to insert all the reference information on each note, including page number where it can be found.
- Do sort your notes into your system as soon as possible, especially if you have made them in a non-standard format that needs transferring to your system (e.g. card system or computer database).

Make a list of all the publications you have referred to, using a standard format. You can generate this list automatically when using a bibliographic database program.

9.6 What should I do now?

You should, before you start reviewing the literature and taking notes, devise your personal system for recording, storing and retrieving them. The average dissertation might use 100–150 notes based on 40–50 references, so it is definitely worth getting a well-organized system in place. On the basis of what you have read above, explore the options for what format and medium to write your notes, how you will sort them into categories, and how you will store them and retrieve them as you need them.

Here are some questions that you should answer. It will provide a checklist to develop and test your system.

- Will you use a paper/card-based system or a computer database system? This is a pretty fundamental decision. It really depends on your familiarity with computers and learning new computer programs whether you have the confidence (and time) to go electronic. Although you do not necessarily need your own laptop, it does simplify the process and eliminate copying out notes. However, many generations of researchers have managed perfectly well with paper-based systems.
- If you decide to use a paper-based system, will you print out standard forms on paper or cards? If you do so, you will be prompted to fill in the important reference details every time you start a new note.
- If you decide to use a computer system, which database program will you use? You will have to find out which ones are readily available to you (check on your university or college intranet), and ideally choose one that you can install on your laptop if you have one. The easiest to use will be programs designed for bibliographic purposes, unless you are very familiar with setting up databases from scratch.
- How will you store your notes? This is not a problem with computer-based systems, apart from the issue of keeping backups in various formats (e.g. hard disk, floppy disk, server file). Paper-based formats need more thought. Keep in mind that you may want to search in different ways, for example by subject or by author. Consider colour coding and separate folders for paper, or card boxes with dividers for cards (old card boxes are

usually easy to acquire cheaply). You might even want to go to the extent of duplicating notes and filing under different headings.

- How will you retrieve your notes? This is where the use of key words or subject categories becomes essential. In any system, if you can easily find all the notes you made on the particular aspect of your subject that you want to write about, you are halfway to producing your first draft.

FIGURE 9.4   How will you retrieve your notes?

Try out your system with a set of about 10–15 notes. Make real notes that will be useful to you anyway, and make them as diverse as possible, so as to test your storage and retrieval system thoroughly. You could even explain your system to a colleague and ask him/her to try to extract some specific piece of information: unfamiliarity with the notes will create a sterner test.

9.7   References to more information

First, some books about note taking and organizing your information. Most books about how to do research will have a section on this, but you may want to compare advice and approaches with those given in this chapter. The first two are examples of these; there are plenty more mentioned at the end of earlier chapters in this book.

Blaxter, L., Hughes, C. and Tight, M. (1996) *How to Research*. Buckingham: Open University Press.

Chapter 4 deals with reading and note taking quite comprehensively, although there is nothing on computer-based bibliographic databases.

Cottrell, S. (2003) *The Study Skills Handbook*, 2nd edn. Basingstoke: Palgrave Macmillan.

See Chapter 6.

Rudestam, K.E. and Newton, R.R. (2001) *Surviving your Dissertation: A Comprehensive Guide to Content and Process*, 2nd edn. Thousand Oaks: Sage.

Chapter 10 looks at using the computer to keep track of notes and references.

Below is information about bibliographic database programs. Check what is available on your college/university network before you make an expensive decision to buy a program yourself.

Endnote. Institute for Scientific Information at: http://www.endnote.com.

Procite. ISI Research Software at: http://www.procite.com/pchome.html.

Citation. Oberon Development Ltd at: http://www.citationline.net.

Nice website with free download demo version.

If you are interested in speed reading, here are some books. But beware, these skills take time and practice to perfect. Have you really got the time now?

Berg, H.S. (1992) *Super Reading Secrets*. London: Little, Brown and Company.

Buzan, T. (2006) *The Buzan Study Skills Handbooks: The Shortcut to Success in Your Studies with Mind Mapping, Speed Reading and Winning Memory Techniques*. London: BBC Active.

Konstant, T. (2002) *Speed Reading in a Week*, 2nd edn. London: Hodder Arnold.

10 What About Referencing?

10.1   Why should I bother about references?

Writing a dissertation is not an exercise in creative writing. You will not be relying on your imagination as a source of your text. Almost everything you write will need to be based on the work of others and on your own research work. At this level you will not be required to produce an original contribution to knowledge. You might generate some new data if you do some fieldwork, for example surveys, experiments, etc. and you will certainly have to express opinions and judgements that are genuinely your own. Your input will primarily be the building up of an argument or discussion from existing material, collected and organized by yourself. To do this you will need to read quite widely in order to study the background to your subject and to investigate what work has already been done in your chosen field. You will also need to consult textbooks about research methodology, and possibly track down relevant statistics and other data.

In order to record the sources of this information, and also to substantiate facts and claims that you make in your text, you must include citations within the text of your dissertation and make a list of references. The use of a sound referencing system is essential. It is also good academic practice, and if properly applied is bound to impress your examiner. Not only does it demonstrate your high ethical standards, but it also gives a very good record of the number and type of books and other publications to which you have referred during your study. Expect the examiner to know who the important writers are in the subject you have chosen, so you need to ensure that you have consulted the appropriate books.

From the ethical point of view, correct referencing ensures that you do not pass off as your own any ideas, writings, diagrams or information created by someone else.

FIGURE 10.1   Penalties for plagiarism are stiff.

In academic writing there is absolutely no shame associated with referring to, using or manipulating other people's work. In fact, much time is spent by academics doing just this. As long as you are 'up-front' and acknowledge your sources, you cannot be criticized. If you are reviewing existing ideas and knowledge on a subject, your text could legitimately be riddled with acknowledged excerpts and quotations. If, however, you are sloppy and forgetful, even unintentional borrowings are regarded as theft of intellectual property, commonly referred to as plagiarism. As you will see from your university or college regulations, penalties for plagiarism are stiff, and rightly so. It is not at all difficult to conform to the accepted standards of referencing, it just needs a bit of care and forethought.

Not only is referencing used to acknowledge the contribution of others to your text, it is also very useful as a guide to the reader to check on the quality of the sources and perhaps to acquire more detailed information. The best test of a referencing system is to try to find the original information, opinion, or idea referred to from the reference information given. For example, if you quote that 23 per cent of school leavers cannot read and write sufficiently to fill in a job application form, can the actual published statistics be tracked down from your reference?

10.2   Keeping track

There are several established systems for achieving this task. What you need for all of them is a full record of the source of your information. This is why I stressed very strongly in Chapter 9 that you should always attach details of the author, publication, page number, date of publication, and publisher to each note that you have taken from your reading sessions. Without this information you will be at a loss to provide a full reference; many wasted hours can be spent trying to track down the source of a really useful quotation or a relevant theory or opinion, perhaps months after you have read them.

It is the best idea to incorporate all the referencing details while preparing your drafts. This will prevent the references from becoming 'detached' from the relevant text and will save much time later on in the production of the finished script. The citation is the acknowledgement within the text to indicate the source of the opinion or information. This is expanded to the full details in the reference found in the list of references at the end of the chapter or dissertation. Don't confuse this with a bibliography, which is a list of books you have referred to or which expand on the subject, but which may not have been actually cited in your text. Correct referencing can quite easily be done if you use one of the systems I suggest below.

10.3 Right ways of doing it

Here are two alternative systems that you can use: the British Standard (numeric) system and the Harvard (author/date) system. Generally within education, most institutions have adopted the Harvard referencing system. Even within this system, there are numerous variations in terms of detail. An alternate system is the British Standard (numeric) system. Depending on your predominant subject discipline (e.g. if you are taking a major in history), the British System may be more familiar. No doubt your institution would have provided you with the exact referencing format, probably detailed in a course handbook. Ensure, however, that this is the system used for the dissertation by asking your supervisor if in doubt. Ultimately the basics of referencing are standard and generally, as long as you are consistent in your dissertation, you shouldn't have too many problems.

British standard (numeric) system

This is ideally used for shorter pieces of text, or for separate chapters, articles or papers. It is suitable for use in your proposal. The citation is simply a number in brackets at the appropriate spot in the text (i.e. after the statement or piece of information to which it refers). You can include several numbers or a range of numbers to refer to several publications. Note, the punctuation is always after the brackets. Use the same style of brackets throughout – square or round. For example:

> The order came from the king who was at Gloucester at the time (1). Although, according to traditional views, 20,000 troops were in readiness (2), Jones and Eldred (3) estimated only 5000 on the basis of the latest evidence discovered in a contemporary journal (4). Morton et al. described the state of the troops as 'full of confidence and ready for battle' (5). There are varying assessments of the readiness of the opposing forces (6–9).

The reference gives the full details of the publication and is placed in number order in the list of references. The sequence of information for books is: author, title, edition (if not the first), place, publisher, date, relevant pages. Books containing the work of several authors put together by an editor need details of the author cited as well as the editor, so lists: author, title of his/her chapter, editor, title of the book, place, publisher, date, relevant pages. Journal references are slightly different: author, title of article, title of journal, volume/issue or part number, date, relevant pages. See also examples below of newspapers, Internet sites, etc.

Here are some examples that show the details in different cases. Take particular care to be consistent with the punctuation, spaces, use of capitals and italics.

1   Jacob, J.R. *The king's commands in battle*. Cambridge: Jason, 2001, p. 78.
2   Hendred, R.S. *Common 19th century myths*. In: Bracknell, L.S. ed. History in turbulent times. London: Stolls, 1998, pp. 45–47.
3   Jones, A.H., Eldred, K.Y. *Readings in cathedral archives*. 2nd edn. Oxford: Boles, 2000, p. 138.
4   Ponsford, S.J. *Diaries of a journeyman*. British Museum Manuscript, 1345, p. 13.
5   Morton, R.M., Smith, J. and Rogers, D. The battle of Coombe Hill. *Journal of Studies in Medieval History*, 51(3), 1998, p. 57.
6   Daly, G.S. Controversy reigns about historic battle. *Daily Express*, 24 June 2001, p. 3.
7   *Gloucestershire Past Website*. No date. Retrieved 25 May 2003 from: http://glospast.gobenet/views.htm.
8   BBC History. *Medieval battles*. Produced and directed by James Notts, 1999, videocassette, 30 min.
9   Open University. *Texts in medieval history*. 2002. Retrieved 24 June 2003 from: http://www.open. ac.uk/history/resources.htm.

Harvard (author/date) system

This is used internationally. It has the advantage that brief details of the publication are given in the citation in the text and the list of references is arranged alphabetically. This eliminates the need to synchronize the order of citations and references, so easily disturbed if you rearrange the text. Another advantage is that the basic information supplied by the citation remains with the relevant text wherever you might move it. It is therefore ideal for using in extended texts, such as dissertations, theses and books, subject to several drafts and revisions.

Below is the same text as in the example above, but using the Harvard system:

The order came from the king who was at Gloucester at the time (Jacob, 2001, p. 78). Although, according to traditional views, 20,000 troops were in readiness (Hendred, 1998, pp. 45–47), Jones and Eldred (2000, p. 138) estimated only 5000 on the basis of the latest evidence discovered in a contemporary journal (Ponsford, 1345, p. 13). Morton et al. described the state of the troops as 'full of confidence and ready for battle' (1998, p. 57). There are varying assessments of the readiness of the opposing forces (Daly, 2001, p. 3; Gloucestershire Past Website, no date; BBC History, 1999; Open University, 2002).

Note that the names of the authors mentioned in the immediately preceding text do not have to be repeated in the citation.

FIGURE 10.2   So easily disturbed if you rearrange the text.

The references are given in alphabetical order in the list of references. Note the different order of the items and use of punctuation. The date is given in brackets after the name of the author, rather than near the end. This is quite useful, as there might be several works by one author but of different dates. List these in date order. If there is more than one reference of the same date, then letter them, for example (1999a), (1999b), (1999c). Use the same lettered date in the citation.

BBC History (1999) *Medieval battles.* Produced and directed by James Notts. Videocassette, 30 min.

Daly, G.S. (2001) Controversy reigns about historic battle. *Daily Express,* 24 June, p. 3.

Gloucestershire Past Website (no date or n.d.) Retrieved 25 May 2003 from: http://glospast.gobenet/views.htm.

Jacob, J.R. (2001) *The king's commands in battle.* Cambridge: Jason, p. 78.

Jones, A.H. and Eldred, K.Y. (2000) *Readings in cathedral archives.* 2nd edn. Oxford: Boles, p. 138.

Hendred, R.S. (1998) Common 19th century myths. In: Bracknell, L.S., ed. *History in turbulent times.* London: Stolls, pp. 45–47.

Morton, R.M., Smith, J. and Rogers, D. (1998) The battle of Coombe Hill. *Journal of Studies in Medieval History* 51(3): 57.

Open University (2002) *Texts in medieval history.* Retrieved 24 June 2003 from: http://www.open.ac.uk/ history/resources.htm.

Ponsford, S.J. (1345) *Diaries of a journeyman.* British Museum Manuscript, p. 13.

Other reference systems differ in detail. If you use a reference database program such as Procite, Endnote or Citation, the program will automatically draw up reference lists correctly in a choice of many referencing systems on the basis of the details you entered on the database.

10.4   How many references do I need?

There is no simple answer to this question. It all depends on the type of dissertation you are writing. Also, some sections of the dissertation will have many more references than others. So where and when should these references appear? Here is a list of these instances, some more obvious than others:

- In a general description of the background to your chosen subject. This will appear in your proposal and in the introduction to your dissertation. What are the main factors, ideas, approaches in the subject?
- In a literature review of the particular issues raised by your research question or problem. Just about every dissertation will have one of these reviews. Who wrote what – state-of-the-art information and comparisons?
- In the descriptions of the methodology you have used to do your research. Again, every dissertation should contain some of these. What are the sources of your information on research methods?
- Appealing to higher authorities as a way of justifying your arguments. The opinion of an expert usually carries more weight than that of an undergraduate student. Who said it, where?
- Using secondary data sources. You might use government or other statistics. Where do they come from?
- Inserting quotations, diagrams and illustrations. Always a useful and attractive feature. You must acknowledge the sources. Where did they come from?

You will see from the above that the type of dissertation that will be full of references is one that reviews the work of others, for example in a critical analysis of historical interpretations, an evaluation of economic theories, or a review of different practices. Where most of the writing describes your actions and your own collected information, for example in carrying out an experiment or survey, then references will rarely be required. But every dissertation will need to refer to ideas, information, methods and material produced by others: nothing is new, everything comes from somewhere.

Given that some dissertation subjects will automatically require more references than others, how can you judge for yourself, apart from the material you have collected anyway, how many references will be enough, or even too many? The latter is easier to answer. Don't bolster your list for the sake of trying to impress. Adding spurious or irrelevant references will actually count against you.

As to the question of how many is enough, this is a matter of both knowledge and judgement. If you are a particularly keen and effective sleuth you will unearth more relevant secondary material than if you are a reluctant searcher. What you must ensure is that you have included the essential references to the most important work in your subject. You will not know what these are unless you find out! After having done your searches, if you can, check with your supervisor or a specialist in your subject whether you have missed anything important. Swapping information with your fellow students can also help at this stage.

Assuming you have included the basic minimum of references, your method of enquiry and style of writing will influence how you use references. Be alert to making unsubstantiated statements: add a reference or give some supporting information. In the end, you will have to judge what you are comfortable with.

10.5   What should I do now?

If you haven't been systematic in recording your references in your notes, now is the best time to go back and do it. The later you leave it, the more likely you will have forgotten the sources of your information and quotations.

If you have been meticulous in keeping the references with the notes, then whatever note taking and storing system you have used, you will manage the referencing without problem. When you prepare a draft of a chapter or section, include the citations and references straight away. I know that it is tedious and tends to break up your flow of thought, but if you don't do it immediately it will take much longer to go back and do it later.

Do check through your drafts to spot any assertions, quotations, descriptions or other material that are not purely based on your own individual work.

FIGURE 10.3   A particularly keen and effective sleuth.

10.6   References to more information

Referencing conventions tend to vary from University to University with different interpretations of the Harvard Referencing System predominantly being used for education.

First, consult your own library or supervisor to find any guidance handouts they might produce. These should be ideally suited to your needs. If you really need more information, then here are some books (you might have noticed that the reference style I have used differs slightly from the given models):

Bosworth, D. (2004) *Citing Your References: A Guide for Authors of Journal Articles and Students Writing Theses or Dissertations.* Thirsk: Underhill.

Redman, P. (2005) *Good Essay Writing: A Social Sciences Guide.* London: Sage.

See Chapter 9.

11 How Do I Argue My Point Effectively?

11.1 Introduction

Your dissertation is probably your first lengthy piece of independent writing. The big question when faced with such a task is how to structure the work so that it forms an integral whole. The structure will provide a guide to the reader, as well as a framework for you to fill as you write. In academic writing, the aim is not to tell a story as one might in a novel, but to set up an argument to support a particular view, analysis or conclusion. In fact, argument will pervade all that you write: you will be trying to persuade the reader that what you have done is worthwhile and based on some kind of intellectual process.

Whatever the subject of the inquiry, there has to be a focus, a central issue that is being considered. You should be able to define this quite clearly when you prepare your proposal, by explanation and persuasion. The body of the dissertation will then revolve around this focal point, perhaps considering it from different perspectives, or examining causes or finding explanations for the situation. At the end you will have to come to some conclusions, and this is where argument is required. You will need

FIGURE 11.1   Argument will feature as a basic ingredient.

to base these conclusions on evidence, and you should produce some reasoned argument about how this evidence leads to your conclusions. This is where argument is required.

You will also have to argue why you have gone about your investigations in the way you have. Lots of choices will be open to you as to how to carry out your investigations, for example which issues to treat as important, which data to collect and which to ignore or reject, who to consult and how to analyse the data, etc. It is up to you to convince the reader that you have good reasons for doing what you have done, and to demonstrate that it needed to be done in order to produce suitable evidence on which to base your conclusions.

No wonder that argument is an important topic to understand. So as argument will feature as a basic ingredient of your dissertation, what exactly does it consist of, and are there different types of argument?

11.2   The use of language

Let's just start with a quick review of some of the most important aspects of language. Why? Because language is the medium for argument. An argument without language becomes a fight!

We often fail to appreciate the complexity and subtlety of the many uses of language. Here, as in many other situations, there is a danger in our tendency to oversimplify.

FIGURE 11.2   To communicate.

But here we go with such a simplification. Copi (1982: 69–72) divided the use of language into three very general categories, which have been found useful by many writers on logic and language.

FIGURE 11.3   To express.

- To communicate information, to inform: Normally this is done by devising propositions and then maintaining or refuting them, or presenting an argument about them. This is not to say that the information is true or that the arguments are valid; misinformation is also included in this category. The function of informative discourse is to describe the world and to reason about it.
- To express: Poetry, evocative prose, even sales talk and political haranguing, exploit expressive possibilities to the full. Alliteration, analogies, rhythms, rhymes and other devices are often used.
- To direct: For the purposes of causing (or preventing) overt action. The most obvious examples of directive discourse are commands and requests. When a soldier is told to fire his gun, there is no informative or emotional content in the command. The form of language is directed at getting results.

FIGURE 11.4   To direct.

In your dissertation you will primarily use the informative function of language, even though you might be studying the use of other forms, for example when analysing poetry. In order to inform, it is necessary to assert a statement in such a manner as to get the reader to believe in it. So what are statements and how are they used?

11.3   Statements

According to Reynolds (1977: 67–76), statements can be classified into two groups: those that state that a concept exists, and those that describe a relationship between two concepts.

Existence statements

These state that a concept exists, and provide a typology or a description. Here are some statements that make existence claims:

- That object is a cat.
- That house is black and white.
- That (event) is a rainstorm.

Each of these statements follows the same basic pattern: it provides a concept, identifies it by a term, and applies it to a thing or an event. The above are examples of existence statements in their simplest form. They can, however, be more complicated without losing their basic form. For example:

- If…
  ○ there are four individuals in a group
  ○ each individual plays a stringed instrument and
  ○ each individual cooperates in the group to perform pieces from the string quartet repertoire
- then … the group is a string quartet.

Existence statements can be 'right' or 'wrong' depending on the circumstances. Take for example the rather abstract statement 'It is 5 o'clock in the afternoon here'. This can be seen to be correct anywhere once a day. If, however, we state in a more concrete fashion that 'It is 5 o'clock in the afternoon on 15 November in London', this can only be correct once and in one place. It can thus be seen that the level of abstraction of a statement has a powerful influence on its potential for correctness, i e the more abstract a statement, the more capacity it has for being right, and conversely the more concrete a statement, the more capacity it has for being wrong.

Relational statements

These impart information about a relationship between two concepts. By referring to the instance of one concept, they state that another concept exists and is linked to the first. We rely on relational statements to explain, predict and provide us with a sense of understanding of our surroundings.

There are two broad classifications of relational statements. The first describes an association between two concepts, and the second describes a causal relationship between two concepts.

Here is an associational statement:

- If a person is an athlete, then he will be physically fit.

By slightly changing the wording of this sentence you can transform it into a causal statement:

- Becoming an athlete will make a person be more physically fit.

That is, becoming an athlete will cause that person to be more physically fit.

There are three possible types of correlation between two concepts:

1 Positive: e.g. fast cars have large engines (and vice versa), i.e. high value in one concept associated with high value in second concept, or low value associated with low value.
2 Negative: e.g. grass at low altitudes grows longer, i.e. low value in one concept associated with high value in second concept.

3   None: e.g. men and women have equal rights in a democracy, i.e. no information about associated high or low values in either concept.

The degree of association is often measurable and is usually expressed as 1.0 for maximum positive correlation, 0.0 for no correlation, and 1.0 for maximum negative correlation. Needless to say, this is useful for drawing conclusions from statistical tests and, however, more problematic for qualitative research.

Causal statements describe what is sometimes called a 'cause and effect' relationship. The concept or variable that is the cause is referred to as the 'independent variable' (because it varies independently), and the variable that is affected is referred to as the 'dependent variable' (because it is dependent on the independent variable). For example, in 'running fast makes you out of breath', 'running fast' is the independent variable and 'out of breath' is the dependent variable.

Causal statements can be deterministic, meaning that under certain conditions an event will inevitably follow, for example 'if you drop an apple, it will fall'. However, it is not always possible to be so certain of an outcome, so a probabilistic statement might be more suitable, for example 'if parents are intelligent, their children are likely to be intelligent too'. A quantification of the order of probability may be possible, for example with a probability of 0.7.

Abstraction

Statements of any kind can be made on three levels of abstraction:

1   Theoretical statements: abstract statements based on theoretical concepts, e.g. 'bodily comfort depends on environmental conditions'.
2   Operational statements: less abstract in that they are based on the definitions of theoretical concepts, which are capable of measurement, e.g. 'the rate of heartbeat relates to the surrounding still air temperature and the level of activity'.
3   Concrete statements: based on specific findings, i.e. the measurements themselves, e.g. 'the heart beats at 102 beats per minute at a surrounding air temperature of 32 degrees centigrade at an energy consumption level of 42 kilocalories per hour'.

11.4   Argument

Statements on their own provide information on discrete units. When they are strung together to form a larger structure, they are often referred to as a discourse. Just as with language generally, discourse can be used for information, expression or direction. Again, for your dissertation you will primarily be using the informative type of discourse, sometimes called assertive discourse. This type of discourse consists of, or contains, assertive statements. These are the discourses that invite us to approach them from a logical point of view.

In some assertive discourses, statements are not merely presented for our information (or misinformation, as the case may be); they are connected in a specific logical way. Some of the statements are offered as reasons for others. This kind of discourse is termed an argument. It is a discourse that not only makes assertions but also asserts that some of those assertions are reasons for others.

In the case of ordinary speech the term 'argument' is often used when referring to a dispute, or a situation in which people who hold different views on some controversial subject try to bring the other person around to their way of thinking. But as a technical term in logic, argument is a special kind of discourse, in which a claim is made that one or more particular statements should be accepted as true, or probably true, on the grounds that certain other statements are true. Put another way: by the process of reasoning, using the operation of logic, a conclusion is inferred from the statements given. An argument can be seen as the verbal record of this reasoning.

The minimal ingredients of an argument are:

- At least one statement that is reasoned for (this is the conclusion of the argument). This can be detected by words such as: therefore, hence, thus, so, implies that.
- At least one statement that is alleged to support the conclusion (this is the premise of the argument). This can be detected by words like this: for, since, because, for the reason that, in view of the fact that. Ensure that the premise is reliable as a weak premise would result in a weak argument and weak conclusion.
- Some signal or suggestion that an argument is under way.

It is sometimes difficult to determine whether a discourse is an argument: there are cases, especially in a complex piece of text, when it is impossible to be sure whether the minimal ingredients of an argument are indeed present.

11.5   Different types of argument

In essence, your whole dissertation should be in the form of an argument. Why is this? Because whatever you are writing about, it must be your concern to persuade the reader that you are writing sense, that your conclusions follow from your evidence, and that you are making some valid points about your chosen subject. A dissertation that comes to no conclusions is not worthy of the name; it would be better called a summary or an account.

In the light of what has been discussed above, the nature of your argument will be very much influenced by your philosophical standpoint. It may be based on a purely scientific approach, dealing with facts and looking for verifiable causes and effects, or alternatively it may be based on gaining some kind of understanding of complex social issues where nothing can be stated for certain. You may combine the two approaches where it is relevant. Whatever you do, though, your dissertation should convince the reader that there are good reasons why you come to your conclusions.

So, what are the characteristics of an argument? The most important requirement is the use of logic. This allows us to move from making statements to reaching conclusions. Here are two examples of very basic arguments:

Example 1:

- All cows are animals.
- Daisy is a cow.
- Therefore, Daisy is an animal.

Example 2:

- Fred is rich and drives a large car.
- John is rich and drives a large car.
- Mike is rich and drives a large car.
- Therefore, rich people probably drive large cars.

Compare these two short arguments, and you will doubtless notice that the conclusions differ. The first conclusion is a categorical statement, while the second only asserts a probability. In fact these arguments start from exactly opposite directions.

The first is an example of deductive thinking. It starts by making a general statement and then deducing a particular instance from this. The second is an example of an inductive argument. It makes statements about particular cases and then draws a general conclusion from these.

If the statements (premises) of a deductive argument are true, and if the argument correctly follows the rules of logic (i.e. is valid), then the conclusion must be true. In this way it is like a mathematical calculation, either true or false depending on the correctness

FIGURE 11.5   Probably drive large cars.

of the input and the method. There is nothing you can add to the premises to make the conclusion more true (e.g. that all cows have four legs, they all drink water, etc.).

Inductive arguments are more flexible in the sense that, even with correct logic, the conclusion cannot be said to be definitely true or false, only more or less probable. The more the supporting evidence you can bring to bear, the greater the probability of the conclusion being correct. For example, if you could name thousands of rich people, all of whom drove large cars, your conclusion would be strengthened. Even if one or two of them only had small cars, the conclusion would not be incorrect.

Just to make things a bit more complicated, inductive arguments do not necessarily only use individual cases to make a general conclusion. They can also be turned round to make a conclusion about a particular case from a general statement, for example:

- Most clever students get good exam grades.
- Julie is a clever student.
- Therefore Julie will probably get a good grade in her finals.

What really marks this out from a deductive argument is that additional statements (premises) can have serious effects on the probability of the conclusion. If Julie also got good grades in her last exams, she attends all the lectures, works hard, etc. then the conclusion will be reinforced. If however, she is bone idle, never reads a book or goes to lectures, and gets paralysed by nerves during examinations, then you might reach just the opposite conclusion.

To make things slightly more complicated, from the two categories of argument (inductive and deductive), there are a number of different argument types that can be developed. According to Weston (2000) arguments may take the following forms:

- Inductive arguments
  - Arguments by example
  - Arguments by analogy
  - Arguments from authority
  - Arguments about causes
- Deductive arguments
  - *Modus ponens* (the mode of putting)
  - *Modus tollens* (the mode of taking)
  - Hypothetical syllogism
  - Disjunctive syllogism
  - Dilemma

Please don't be put off by the names of the deductive arguments … all will be explained as we go on! To demonstrate how these arguments are structured, one key theme will be considered across all of the arguments: whether A levels are really getting easier, or whether students are improving. I will allow you to make up your mind from reading the following arguments.

Arguments by example

In this form of arguing, specific examples are provided to support a generalization. The key to this argument is to ensure that the examples are accurate and representative of a sample of instances. Furthermore you will need to ensure that your examples are supported with relevant literature opposed to just writing these straight from your mind in order to provide credibility. The following example demonstrates such an argument:

- Over the past couple of decades, there has been an increase of students taking A levels.
- Over the past couple of decades, the average points a student obtains with their A level results has steadily increased.
- More students are entering higher education than in previous years.
- Graduating students are tending to be awarded higher degree classifications than in previous years.
- Therefore it would appear that students are improving in their academic skills.

Arguments by analogy

This form of argument is an exception to providing a number of examples as for the previous argument. Parallels are highlighted between two different examples which may share a number of similarities, thus reasoning that because they share so many similarities, they may well be alike in one further specific way. An example of this argument is:

- A level attainment has increased steadily over the past couple of decades. Therefore why shouldn't students be achieving higher degree classifications?

Arguments from authority

In this argument, an 'expert' in the field states something, therefore because they are deemed to be an 'expert', the argument must be true. A word of warning though, ensure that you utilize your critiquing skills to ensure that the source of the argument is unbiased! Such an example is:

- Professor X, who has conducted several prominent studies on student achievement, concludes that students are working harder than ever before.

Arguments about causes

This is where a correlation between two different events are explained through the evidence. It is important to keep in mind the direction of the cause: does A cause B or does B cause A? A good argument should therefore identify the direction of the cause and why this has occurred. Could it be just down to coincidence or does one actually impact on the other. Weston (2000: 36) illustrates this with an example, noting that 'the rise and fall of women's hemlines correlated for years with the rise and fall of the Dow Jones Industrial Average'. An example of an argument about causes is:

- As students are increasingly funding their own education, they are working harder with their studies to ensure they achieve a good graduate career.

There, that wasn't too difficult I hope! In the main, the above arguments are the types predominantly used in education dissertations. If you really want to show off, demonstrating that you have grasped the fundamentals of philosophic arguments, please read on …

In the following types of argument, letters are used to represent various sentences, similar to linguistic algebra. This may appear a little confusing at first but it would be worth reading these through a couple of times, perhaps even noting down a different example to the ones provided to ensure you can formulate your own deductive arguments.

Modus ponens (the mode of putting)

This argument is developed by explaining and defending both of the premises before discussing how one relates to the other. Consequently one effects the other positively.

- If P then Q.
- P.
- Therefore, Q.

If 'A' level results are improving (P), then teaching standards are improving (Q).
A level results are improving (P).
Therefore, it seems likely that teaching standards are improving (Q).

In the above example, it would then be necessary to provide evidence illustrating that results are improving and that teaching standards are improving. This could be achieved through collecting data from league tables, etc.

Modus tollens (the mode of taking)

This argument is developed by taking Q, then as a result taking P. The relationship between these two then prove the non-existence of each other. Consequently one effects the other negatively.

- If P then Q.
- Not-Q (denial of Q).
- Therefore, not-P.

If standards are falling in school (P), then A level results will fall (Q).
A level results are not falling – they are improving (Not-Q).
Therefore, standards in school must be improving (Not-P).

In the above example, it would be necessary to provide evidence to demonstrate that results are not falling (again through analysing league tables) which would then suggest that standards cannot be falling in school.

Hypothetical syllogism

This argument is formed through establishing a major premise (P), a minor premise (Q) and a conclusion (R). In a manner, this argument logically links a number of premises through cause and effect, while explaining why these link.

- If P then Q.
- If Q then R.
- Therefore, if P then R.

  If teaching standards are improving (P), then students will achieve more (Q).
  If students are achieving more (Q), then A level results will be better (R).
  Therefore, if teaching standards are improving (P), A level results will be better (R).

In the above argument, improved teaching standards impact on exam results as students improve through better teaching. Therefore the evidence that would need to be collected is on whether teaching standards are improving and if results are improving. If results are not improving but teaching standards are, the argument would not hold.

Disjunctive syllogism

This form of argument is based on which one of two statements is correct, through the use of the word 'or'.

- P or Q.
- Not-P.
- Therefore, Q.

  Either A level results are improving because of easier examinations (P) or better teaching methods (Q).
  Politicians tell us that examinations are not getting easier (P).
  Therefore, A level results are improving because of better teaching (Q).

Within this argument, it would be necessary to obtain information on either P – what the politicians say, or Q – proof that teaching methods are improving. The problem exists that it could be both! Therefore the word 'or' is used inclusively, whereby either one or both statements are correct. The word 'or' can however, be used exclusively whereby only one statement can be correct. For example:

  Either I will walk to work or I will cycle.
  My bike has a puncture and I cannot cycle.
  Therefore, I will walk to work.

Dilemma

A dilemma is a choice between two possible options with the associated outcomes.

- P or Q.
- If P then R.
- If Q then S.
- Therefore, R or S.

A levels are getting easier (P), or students are getting better (Q).
If A levels are getting easier (P), students will obtain higher grades (R).
If students are getting better (Q), students will obtain higher grades (S).
Therefore, students are obtaining higher grades (R or S).

From this argument, R and S are the same and although technically the final sentence could be written, 'Therefore, students are obtaining higher grades or students are obtaining higher grades', however, saying it once is enough!

So, are students actually improving … well you have got this far in your studies so I would hope so! (Hhm – I wonder what sort of argument that was!)

11.6   Do I need to use logic in my argument?

The simple answer is Yes! Whatever argument you follow, even if it is based on qualitative data of the most subjective kind, you need to make a case to support your conclusions. In order to do this, your argument needs to be based on a logical sequence of evidence and conclusions. What does this involve? Well, there are basic rules of logic that can be simply learned, though applying them in a complex argument is a bit more difficult. The aim is to be able to detect a correct logical structure in an argument to determine whether the argument is valid or invalid. So what are the characteristics of logic that govern the structure of argument?

You must remember that logic is concerned not with the truth or falsity of premises (statements) or conclusions, but rather with the correctness of arguments. Therefore we do not say that arguments are true, incorrect or untrue, but we say that they contain valid deductions, correct inductions, or at the other extreme, assorted fallacies. The strict rules below really apply only to deductive arguments as these are limited to reaching firm conclusions solely based on the stated premises: no 'probably', 'might', 'likely to' as is seen in the conclusions of inductive arguments.

11.7   Fallacies in argument

Logic is the protection against trickery and sloppy thinking. Logic deals with arguments that are based on reason. Mistakes are possible and even frequent in applying forms of logical argument. These mistakes are termed fallacies. However, not all mistakes in argument are genuine mistakes; there are innumerable examples of the calculated use of quasi-reasoning used in order to convince or convert the unwary.

The recognition of fallacies is not new, many of them having been noted as early as Aristotle. You can probably devise an argument yourself which is entirely logical, whose validity is clearly demonstrated by the conclusion being derived from the premises, and which carefully follows all the rules of syllogism, but which is based on premises that are phoney, tricks and delusions. There are brilliant deceptions for getting people to accept all sorts of false premises as true, and these tricks of argument are so common that even when people realize that they are being hoodwinked they tend to let it pass.

The daily use of argument in normal and academic life is a highly complicated human activity and you cannot successfully study it in a sort of vacuum. There is no simple connection between the presentation of an argument on one side, and the acceptance of it on the other. Emotional and referential signals often add a significant subtext. For example, even the most abstract and exotic

FIGURE 11.6   Valid logical structures.

television commercial usually contain some kind of argument, some assertion of reasons and drawing of conclusions, for example, 'must buy this because it's so romantic'. Even when you read books on logic you find that the arguments are seldom spelled out fully, except in the examples.

The word 'fallacy' is often used in two ways. Sometimes it is used to describe any kind of attitude that is fraudulent or deceitful, and at other times it is used, in a more narrow sense, to indicate a defective manner of reasoning or a wily or cunning form of persuasion. In the following analysis of fallacies, it is the second meaning that is taken, i.e. when an argument purports to abide by the rules of sound argument but in fact fails to do so. There are two main categories of fallacy, formal and informal.

Formal fallacies have some error in the structure of the logic. Although they often resemble valid forms of argument, the logical route only takes us from A to B by way of disjointed or missing paths. In brief, the fallacy occurs because the chain of reasoning itself is defective.

Informal fallacies, on the other hand, often use valid reasoning in terms that are not of sufficient quality to merit such treatment. They can be linguistic, and allow ambiguities of language to admit error, and leave out something needed to sustain the argument, or permit irrelevant factors to weigh on the conclusion, or allow unwarranted presumptions to alter the conclusions that are reached.

There is not room here to discuss all the different types of fallacy in detail, but I have selected some of those with the greatest relevance to academic research work. Most types of fallacy have been given titles or technical names and are well known to logicians. It is not necessary that you remember the names, though it will impress people if you point out the shortcomings in their arguments by quoting the type of fallacy by its name! The following examples demonstrate a few of these:

- 'If I run too much I will be tired. Since I have not run at all, I am not tired'.
    - Formal fallacy – denying the antecedent. The writer does not recognize that the same result can be produced by different causes.
- 'The duchess has a fine ship, but she has barnacles on her bottom'.
    - Informal fallacy – linguistic. This is a case of careless grammatical construction that causes an ambiguity of meaning.
- 'The ship of government, like any other ship, works best when there is a strong captain in charge of it. That is why government by dictatorship is more effective'.
    - Informal fallacy – relevance presumption. Analogies are often a useful way of describing unfamiliar concepts: in the above, equating government to a ship. The mistake is to assume further similarities that may not exist.
- 'Talk of the Loch Ness monster is nonsense. We know that it does not exist because every single attempt to find it has failed utterly'.
    - Informal fallacy – relevance intrusion. Just because we lack knowledge about something, it is a fallacy to infer that the opposite is the case.
- 'All musicians are really sensitive people. It happens that some really sensitive people are not properly appreciated. So some musicians are not properly appreciated'.
    - Formal fallacy – undistributed middle. The middle term 'really sensitive people' in this example does not refer to all sensitive people – so musicians might not be included.
- 'If the Americans wanted good trade relations, they would encourage the production of specialist goods in other countries. Since they do support this type of production, we know that they want good trade relations'.
    - Formal fallacy – affirming the consequent. In an 'if … then' construction, the 'if' part is the antecedent, and the 'then' part is the consequent. It is all right to affirm the antecedent, but not vice versa. Affirming the consequent is fallacious because an event can be produced by different causes.
- 'I don't think we should employ Mr Smith. I am told that he is a poor golf player. Careless people are bad at golf, so I don't think it is a good omen'.
    - Informal fallacy – omission. When statements are made about a class, they may be about all or some (or none) of the members. This fallacy occurs when ambiguity of expression permits a misunderstanding of the quantity that is spoken of (i.e. in this example, is it all or some careless people who are bad at golf?).

The above examples will give you an idea of some logical pitfalls. In more sophisticated arguments the logic can become very complex, with parts of an argument depending on others, for example if not this, then that. Obviously, it is important to recognize fallacies when you read or listen to people's arguments. It is just as important to avoid fallacies in your own writing (or to use them to best effect if you intend to deceive!). At this level, you will have to rely on careful reading and analytical thinking and quite a lot of common sense. The above examples are only a small selection of types of fallacy.

11.8 Building up your argument: the essential thread

So, what has all this theoretical stuff got to do with your dissertation work? As has been mentioned several times before, the whole point of doing a dissertation is to identify a particular question or problem, to collect information and to present some answers or solutions. It is up to you to convince the reader that you have collected information relevant to the question or problem and that you have based your answers and conclusions on the correct analysis of this information. You will need to use some logical argument in order to do this convincing.

Taylor (1989: 67) offers a useful list of the sorts of argument you might make in your dissertation. You might:

- Agree with, accede to, defend or confirm a particular point of view
- Propose a new point of view
- Concede that an existing point of view has certain merits, but that it needs to be qualified in certain important respects
- Reformulate an existing point of view such that the new version makes a better explanation
- Dismiss a point of view or other person's work on account of its inadequacy, irrelevance, incoherence, etc.
- Reject, rebut or refute another's argument on various reasoned grounds
- Reconcile two positions that may seem at variance by appeal to some 'higher' or 'deeper' principle
- Retract or recant one's own position in the face of arguments or evidence.

Imagine yourself to be a lawyer making a case in court. You set out to solve the problem (who committed the crime and how) by analysing the situation, collecting the evidence, then making a case for your conclusions about 'whodunnit' and how. The jury will have to decide whether the argument is convincing and the evidence is sufficiently strong. In the case of a dissertation, you will be setting the problem and laying out your case, and the examiner will be your jury.

Just as a lawyer will be careful to make it clear just how he/she has reached his/her conclusions, so must you make it obvious how you came to yours. Always refer to the evidence when you make statements, whether it be by citing some kind of authority or by referring to your data and analysis. Careful cross-referencing is essential here. Always give page numbers of where the evidence is to be found (whether in a reference or in your dissertation), and refer to diagrams and graphs by number when relevant.

It is a good idea initially to set up a skeleton of your argument by making a diagram that starts with the question or problem at the top, then follows logical steps to the conclusions. There may be branches along the way that take in particular aspects of the subject, i.e. subquestions that need to be covered. But all the threads should come together at the end to provide the main answer or solution to the main question or problem. In this way, you will be able to track the route of your argument and spot gaps,

FIGURE 11.7   A lawyer making a case in court.

fallacies, meanderings or dead-ends. The examiner should be able to draw a similar diagram from reading your completed dissertation.

Weston (2000) provides some useful guidance for structuring an argument:

- Explore the arguments on all sides of the issue
- Question and defend each argument's premises
- Revise and rethink arguments as they emerge
- Explain the question
  - Why have you set this question? Why is there a problem? Make the reader aware of the issue
- Make a definite claim or proposal
  - Be specific in what you are proposing. What are you actually claiming? What decision have you arrived at
- Develop your arguments fully
  - How have you arrived at your decision? What argument or arguments are you going to use to make your case?
- Consider objections
  - What would be the impact of your claim? Are there any disadvantages to what you have posited? How could these potentially be addressed?
- Consider alternatives
  - Why is your argument better than other possible alternatives to addressing your question?

Obviously before you have completed the work, you will not be able to finalize the argument. But it is important to have a clear 'route map' so that you can check your progress and fill in gaps. Expect to change some components of your argument as you get further advanced in your work. When you have completed the first draft, consciously check, by scanning through your main sections, that you have clearly stated the question or problem, that you have explained how you will tackle it, that the data collected are relevant, the analysis produces good reasons for your conclusions, and your conclusions actually address the question or problem stated at the outset. It is surprising how often students get somehow lost in the process and come to conclusions that do little to address the initial problem. If you do this preparation and checking, you won't be one of them.

11.9   Gathering your results

Ideally you will have the research questions at the forefront of your mind throughout the time working on your dissertation. However, this is not always possible as you grapple with the learning of new techniques and methods and the problems of organizing your data collection and analysis. But you must come back to them regularly in order to ensure that you are keeping to the intentions of the project, and will end up with relevant material in order to be able to suggest answers to the questions.

Coming to conclusions is a cumulative process. It is unlikely that the problem you have chosen is simple, with questions raised that can be answered with a simple yes or no. Even if they can, you will be required to describe why it is one or the other and make an argument to support your case. Normally, you will find that the questions have several sub-questions, and even these can be broken down into components requiring separate investigation. Throughout the analysis part of your work you will be able to make conclusions about these fragments of the main issues. The skill is to gather these up at the end in the concluding chapter to fit them together into a 'mosaic' that will present the complete picture of the conclusion to the entire dissertation.

Just as you should be able to summarize the main problem that your dissertation addresses in one or two sentences, so you should be able to state the conclusion equally briefly. This belies the complexities that lie in between. You can picture your dissertation as having a continuous thread of argument running through it. The beginning and

FIGURE 11.8   Coming to conclusions.

end of the argument are fat and tightly woven. But in between, the separate strands fan out, become twisted and frayed as different aspects are investigated, but manage to web together before reaching the end.

The secret to success lies in the sound construction of your argument.

11.10   What should I do now?

Try and experiment with different ways of constructing an argument. One way to do it is to write all the elements of the argument on bits of paper, and then arrange them on a tabletop until you are satisfied that they follow through logically. You will see where there are missing links, where additional evidence is needed, and what is the shortest route to the conclusions. You can easily reject or add bits of paper. You will also be able to track any parallel arguments that you may need to make when you take several aspects of the problem into account. Do they all add up at the end to form a plausible main conclusion?

When you are satisfied with the framework, you can produce a diagram to record your 'route map'. You could probably also do this exercise on the computer, using a program that is designed to create diagrams of this kind. The next thing to do is to translate how this map will guide the structure of the written work. Does it fall neatly into chapters? Ensure that the steps in the argument remain clear. It is also a good idea to explain the structure of your argument in the introductory chapter. This not only forms a useful guide to the reader, but will impress the examiner with your lucid thinking and organization.

11.11   References to more information

You can quickly get into deep water on the subject of thinking and argument. I would recommend Brink-Budgen to start with, and perhaps follow-up the references in there if you want to find out more on specific issues. The others I have listed require either that you have a special interest or that you have chosen a dissertation topic that focuses on aspects of these subjects.

Brink-Budgen, R. (2000) *Critical Thinking for Students: Learn the Skills of Critical Assessment and Effective Argument*, 3rd edn. Oxford: How To Books.

Cottrell, S. (2003) *The Study Skills Handbook*, 2nd edn. Basingstoke: Palgrave Macmillan.

   See Chapter 10 for an introduction to critical analytical thinking.

Cottrell, S. (2005) *Critical Thinking Skills: Developing Effective Analysis and Argument*. Basingstoke: Palgrave Macmillan.

Fisher, A. (2004) *The Logic of Real Arguments*, 2nd edn. Cambridge: Cambridge University Press.

Hodges, W. (2001) *Logic: An Introduction to Elementary Logic*, 2nd edn. London: Penguin Books.

Weston, A. (2000) *A Rulebook for Arguments*, 3rd edn. Indianapolis: Hackett.

12 How Do I Write a Literature Review?

CHAPTER CONTENTS

12.1 Why is a literature review needed?

A literature review outlines the theoretical perspective which in turn serves as a foundation for your dissertation. The literature review outlines the scope of your subject area, themes and trends and previous research, demonstrating your awareness of work within the area.

12.2 Who am I writing the literature review for?

Predominantly your work on the literature review should inform you of the issues in the area you have selected, developing and deepening your understanding of the area. It would be pointless if you spent your time researching an area which has already been researched several times before: your work should identify potential gaps in knowledge which in turn provides you with a rationale from which to develop your work. Consequently the literature review discusses the work previously completed in the area as a foundation for your work to develop.

At the same time, it is worth remembering the reader's perspective and that the reader may not necessarily be an expert in your field consequently you will need to strike a balance of providing sufficient background to the issue before progressing to discuss the finer issues. Of course the principal reader of your dissertation will be an examiner.

They will be assessing your work in terms of balancing depth and scope of your literature review with the relevance to your chosen subject area.

12.3   What areas should the literature review cover?

Your literature review should be more than just listing the relevant work associated to your focus – you need to actually discuss the themes and trends within the literature. The previous chapters in this section discuss identifying relevant literature and what to do once you have obtained it, in the form of critiquing. Indeed previous assignments on your course would have got you to engage with literature to some extent. Now is the time to write a relatively lengthy, yet focused assignment on an area of your choice.

The literature review should comment on specific arguments raised by others, assessing parallels or differences between such arguments, leading towards a conclusion where you highlight the key aspects in your subject area while discussing potential future directions for research. This in turn allows you to develop your research objectives associates to what you have discussed in your literature review. All of the aspects of defining the topic, identifying sources of information, keeping accurate references and making relevant notes discussed in the previous chapters will now be of immense benefit!

As with any assignment or presentation, there needs to be a definitive introduction, development and conclusion. Each of these will be analysed in turn:

Introduction

This defines the framework for the rest of the literature review and why you have selected this framework. Although the reader will have already ascertained from your introductory chapter the focus of your dissertation, this part of the literature review defines how you will explore the background of the topic. You will also need to provide your reasoning for conducting a literature review: for example, informing the reader of certain trends and analysing potential gaps in existing knowledge.

There are different ways in how you can go about reviewing the literature. You may decide to chronologically discuss trends if your dissertation is based on a historical element of education. Alternatively you could focus from the macro, or wide-scale, to the micro or narrow-scale. An example of this is where you take a national policy (macro), before focussing on particular elements of it that may have been informed by previous research in a specific area (micro).

Development

This is where your literature review explores the selected sources in detail. You may have selected a themed approach in which case you discuss in turn the different themes you have identified. The different themes should interrelate and not require subheadings, however, if you decide subheadings will help in signposting your work, it may be worth discussing this with your supervisor or with a critical friend.

Conclusion

Finally your literature review should summarize the major elements you have discussed, although try to avoid just listing these but actually engage the reader with the key issues and how they have related in order to develop your line of reasoning. From this, demonstrate where there are gaps in the knowledge or areas where further research could be informative. This should relate smoothly into your research objectives.

Research objectives

Again, you may want to refer back to Chapter 5 which discusses the research aim and research objectives. As a summary, the objectives should explain how you intend to explore your aim by subdividing the aim into discrete areas of investigation.

12.4   How do I structure the literature review?

If we refer back to the hourglass approach to research, the first half of the hourglass narrows the focus of your work towards the objectives. A considerable part of this first half is the literature review. Indeed, if the hourglass is dismantled, we are left with an inverted triangle (Illustrations 12.1 and 12.2).

The introduction, conclusion and research objectives are in their natural place yet the area of concern is the enormous chunk of detail and associated wording in the central, development area. How can this element be structured appropriately?

One way of looking at this is to concept map a number of areas related to your focus. Remember we covered concept mapping in Chapter 4. From this, a number of key areas will have been identified and possible links explored. This should lead you to develop a structure for your literature review based on the way your concept map has developed.

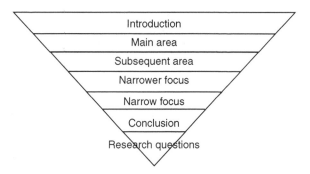

ILLUSTRATION 12.1   Literature review structure.

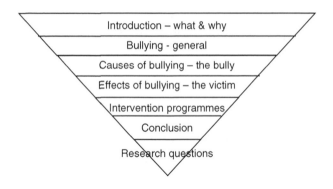

ILLUSTRATION 12.2   Example of a literature review structure related to bullying.

From the concept map, list the key areas of strips of paper, then physically arrange and rearrange these into what would appear a logical order. Try sounding this out as if you were telling a story to someone by discussing how and why the areas lead from one to another. If something doesn't quite fit, rearrange it. Once you are happy with the overall structure, perhaps jot this down on the inverted triangle. Keep in mind that the different sections of the triangle need to logically flow from one to the other.

It is worth noting that within each of these areas on your triangle, you could micro-manage the structure: each segment could be composed of another triangle which has an introduction, development and conclusion, thus narrowing to a focus. This level of planning may not suit everyone but it does however, break the task on this lengthy chapter into manageable chunks.

An alternative to this model is suggested by Rudestam and Newton (2001). They highlight a colleague's analogy (Joseph Handlon) between the literature review and making a movie, whereby there are 'long shots', 'medium shots' and close-ups'. Rudestam and Newton (2001: 62) summarize these as:

- A long shot suggests that the material is background for a particular topic. Background material needs to be acknowledged but not treated with the same detail as foreground material; it is not figural.
- The medium shot … requires a bit more descriptive material.
- The close up requires careful examination of the research and is reserved for those studies that have the most direct relevance to the proposed research question.

Rudestam and Newton (2001: 63) also suggest using a Venn diagram (Illustration 12.3) to help develop the literature review, whereby they note:

The long shots … are represented by the portions of the three primary variables that are independent of the other two variables. The medium shot is illustrated by the intersections of any two variables. The close-up … refers to the joint intersection of all three variables.

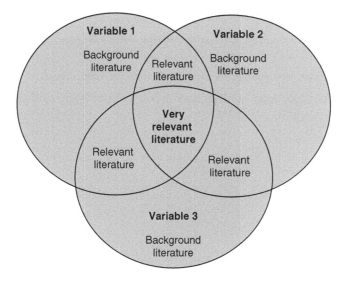

ILLUSTRATION 12.3 Venn Diagram guide to the literature review (adapted from Rudestam and Newton, 2001:64, Fig. 4.1).

Play about with the relevant models cited in this section to see what is best for you and the way you would prefer to work.

12.5   What should I do now?

Read! Make sure you get as much information as necessary to fully inform the discussion on the background to your focus. How much is enough though? This is really up to you to identify from the available sources. Avoid using literature just because it is there, use literature that illustrates your argument. This will mean that you are selective from all of the sources you collated.

Try planning out the literature review. Keep a copy of the concept map to hand also the structure of the chapter. You could use separate file dividers to collate the various readings under each of your themes.

12.6   References to more information

This section of the book would have provided you with a strong foundation from which to work. You may also want to read through the following.

Cottrell, S. (2003) *The Study Skills Handbook*, 2nd edn. Basingstoke: Palgrave Macmillan.

Hart, C. (2001) *Doing a Literature Search*. London: Sage.

Hart, C. (1998) *Doing a Literature Review*. London: Sage.

Levin, P. (2004) *Write Great Essays! Reading and Essay Writing for Undergraduates and Taught Postgraduates*. Maidenhead: Open University Press.

Mounsey, C. (2002) *Essays and Dissertations*. Oxford: Oxford University Press.

Northledge, A. (2005) *The Good Study Guide*, 2nd revised edn. Buckingham: Open University Worldwide.

Redman, P. (2005) *Good Essay Writing: A Social Sciences Guide*. London: Sage.

Roberts-Holmes, G. (2005) *Doing Your Early Years Research Project: A Step by Step Guide*. London: Paul Chapman.

See Chapter 5.

Soles, D. and Lawler, G. (2005) *The Academic Essay: How to Plan, Draft, Write and Edit*, 2nd edn. Abergele: Studymates.

This section introduces you to the various research activities that you may conduct for your research. As noted in the Introduction, this book is not specifically a research methods book: there are several weightier volumes you will be directed to: what this section does however, covers the basic data collection techniques predominantly used in educational dissertations.

Chapter 13 discusses a range of issues relating to data, exploring different types of data and how much data is required.

Chapter 14 analyses different philosophical stances you could adopt as a researcher. This is where the way in which you view the world impacts on your research, thus identifying your philosophical stance and informing the reader of this establishes where your research is coming from.

There are different data collection methods available for your research purposes and you may use one or more for your work. The choice of research method depends on one basic factor; fundamentally will it enable you to answer your research question(s)?

Chapters 15, 16 and 17 discuss the three predominant data collection techniques used within educational research at this level, namely interviews, questionnaires and observation. Each of these chapters introduce the key elements for each technique along with a number of considerations to ensure that data collection is efficient and effective. It must be noted that these chapters provide an overview of the methods and that greater reading of research methodology texts would be beneficial to your dissertation.

Chapter 17 demonstrates how the methodology chapter of your dissertation can be constructed and the main elements that need to be considered.

13 What Sorts of Data Will I Find and How Much Do I Need?

13.1 The nature of data

'Data' means information, or according to the *Oxford English Dictionary*, 'known facts or things used as basis for inference or reckoning'. Strictly speaking, 'data' is the plural of 'datum', and so is always treated as plural. When you do any sort of enquiry or research, you will collect data of different kinds. In fact, data can be seen as the essential raw material of any kind of research. They are the means by which we can understand events and conditions in the world around us. This chapter discusses the nature of data and their different characteristics.

Data, when seen as facts, acquire an air of solidity and permanence, representing the truth. This is, unfortunately, misleading. Data are not only elusive, but also ephemeral. They may be a true representation of a situation in one place, at a particular time, under specific circumstances, as seen by a particular observer. The next day, all might be different. For example, a daily survey of people's voting intentions in a forthcoming general election will produce different results daily, even if exactly the same people are asked – because some change their minds according to what they have heard or seen in the interim period. If the same number of people is asked in a similar sample, a different result can also be expected. Anyway, how can you tell whether they are even telling the truth about their intentions? Data can therefore only provide a fleeting and partial glimpse of events, opinions, beliefs or conditions.

Not only are data ephemeral, but they are also corruptible. Inappropriate claims are often made on the basis of data that are not sufficient or close enough to the event. Hearsay is stated to be fact, second-hand reports are regarded as being totally reliable and biased views are seized on as evidence. The further away you get from the event, the more likely it is that inconsistencies and inaccuracies creep in. Memory fades, details are lost, recording methods do not allow a full picture to be given, and distortions of interpretations occur. Harold Pinter, the English playwright, described the situation like this:

> Apart from any other consideration, we are faced with the immense difficulty, if not impossibility, of verifying the past. I don't mean merely years ago, but yesterday, this morning. What took place, what was the nature of what took place, what happened? If

FIGURE 13.1 How can you tell whether they are telling the truth about their intentions?

> one can speak of the difficulty of knowing what in fact took place yesterday, one can I think treat the present in the same way. What's happening now? We won't know until tomorrow or in six months' time, and we won't know then, we'll have forgotten, or our imagination will have attributed quite false characteristics to today. A moment is sucked away and distorted, often even at the time of its birth. We will all interpret a common experience quiet differently, though we prefer to subscribe to the view that there's a shared common ground all right, but that it's more like a quicksand. Because 'reality' is quite a strong firm word we tend to think, or to hope, that the state to which it refers is equally firm, settled and unequivocal. It doesn't seem to be, and in my opinion, it's not worse or better for that. (1998: 21)

It is therefore a rash researcher who insists on the infallibility of his or her data, and of the findings derived from them. A measure of humility in one's belief in the accuracy of knowledge, and also practical considerations which surround the research process, dictate that the outcomes of research tend to be couched in 'soft' statements, such as 'it seems that', 'it is likely that', 'one is led to believe that', etc. This does not mean, however, that progress towards useful 'truths' cannot be achieved.

It is important to be able to distinguish between different kinds of data, because their nature has important implications for their reliability and for the sort of analysis to which they can be subjected. Data that have been observed, experienced or recorded close to the event are the nearest one can get to the truth, and are called primary data. Written sources that interpret or record primary data are called secondary sources. For example,

FIGURE 13.2   Population densities.

you have a more approximate and less complete knowledge of a political demonstration if you read the newspaper report the following day than if you were at the demonstration and had seen it yourself. Not only is the information less abundant, but it is coloured by the commentator's interpretation of the facts.

A pair of other distinctions can be made between types of data. Much information about science and society is recorded in the form of numbers, for example temperatures, bending forces, population densities, cost indices, etc. The nature of numbers allows them to be manipulated by the techniques of statistical analysis. This type of data is called quantitative data. In contrast, there is a lot of useful information that cannot be reduced to numbers. People's opinions, feelings, ideas and traditions need to be described in words. Words cannot be reduced to averages, maximum and minimum values or percentages. They record not quantities, but qualities. Hence they are called qualitative data. Given their distinct characteristics, it is evident that when it comes to analysing these two forms of data, quite different techniques are required.

Let us examine the nature of these two pairs of characteristics of data.

13.2   Primary and secondary data

Primary data

Primary data are present all around us. Our senses deal with them all our waking lives – sounds, visual stimuli, tastes, tactile stimuli, etc. Instruments also help us to keep track of factors that we cannot so accurately judge through our senses: thermometers record the exact temperature, clocks tell us the exact time, and our bank statements tell us how much money we have. Primary data are as near to the truth as we can get about things and events. Seeing a football match with your own eyes will certainly get you nearer to what happened than reading a newspaper report about it later. Even so, the truth is still somewhat elusive – 'Was the referee really right to award that penalty? It didn't look like a handball to me!'

FIGURE 13.3   First and most immediate recording.

There are many ways of collecting and recording primary data. Some are more reliable than others. It can be argued that as soon as data are recorded, they become secondary data owing to the fact that someone or something had to observe and interpret the situation or event and set it down in the form of a record; i.e. the data have become second-hand. But this is not the case. The primary data are not the actual situation or event, but a record of it, from as close to it as possible – that is, the first and most immediate recording. 'A researcher assumes a personal responsibility for the reliability and authenticity of his or her information and must be prepared to answer for it' (Preece, 1994: 80). Without this kind of recorded data it would be difficult to make sense of anything but the simplest phenomenon and be able to communicate the facts to others.

So what sorts of primary data are there? I can think of four basic types:

- Observation – records, usually of events, situations or things, of what you have experienced with your own senses, your eyes, ears, etc. perhaps with the help of an instrument, for example camera, tape recorder, microscope, etc.
- Participation – data gained by experiences can perhaps be seen as an intensified form of observations, for example the experience of learning to drive a car tells you different things about cars and traffic than just watching.

- Measurement – records of amounts or numbers, for example population statistics, instrumental measurements of distance, temperature, mass, etc.
- Interrogation – data gained by asking and probing. For example, information about people's beliefs, motivations, etc.

These can be collected, singly or together, to provide information about virtually any facet of our life and surroundings. So, why do we not rely on primary data for all our research? After all, they get as close as possible to the truth. There are several reasons, the main being time, cost and access. Collecting primary data is a time consuming business. As more data usually means more reliability, the efforts of just one person will be of limited value. Organizing a huge survey undertaken by large teams would overcome this limitation, but at what cost? Also, it is not always possible to get direct access to the subject of research: for example, many historical events have left no direct evidence.

Secondary data

Secondary data are data that have been interpreted and recorded. We could drown under the flood of secondary data that assails us every day. News broad-casts, magazines, news-papers, documentaries, advertising, the Internet, etc. all bombard us with information wrapped, packed and spun into digestible soundbites or pithy articles. We are so used to this that we have learned to swim, to float above it all and only really pay attention to the bits that interest us. This technique, learned through sheer necessity and quite automatically put into practice every day, is a useful skill that can be applied to speed up your data collection for your dissertation.

Chapter 8 discusses the sources of secondary information; here we will look at the different types of secondary data that you might want to uncover. Depending on the subject of your choice, particular types of data will probably be more important to you than others. The descriptions given below will help you to decide where to focus your search efforts.

Books, journal papers, magazine articles, newspapers present information in published written form. The quality of the data depends on the source and the methods of presen-tation. For detailed and authoritative information on almost any subject, go to refereed journals: all the papers will have been vetted by leading experts in the subject. Other serious journals, such as some professional and trade journals, will also have authoritative articles by leading figures, despite the tendency of some to put emphasis on one side of the issues, for example a teaching union's journal will support arguments for improving pay and conditions at work rather than considering counter-arguments (as if there are any!). There are magazines for every taste, some entirely flippant, others with useful and reliable information. The same goes for books – millions of them! They range from the most erudite and deeply researched volumes, for example specialist encyclopaedia and academic tomes, to ranting polemics and commercial pap.

It is therefore always important to make an assessment of the quality of the information or opinions provided. You actually do this all the time even without noticing it. We have all learned not to be so gullible as to believe everything that we read. A more conscious approach entails reviewing the evidence that has been presented in the arguments. When no evidence is provided, on what authority does the writer base his/her statements? It is best to find out who are the leading exponents of the subject you are concentrating on. Apart from getting marks for recognizing these and referring to them, you will be able to rely on the quality of their writings. At this stage of your studies, you are not expected to challenge the experts – leave this for when you do a PhD!

Television broadcasts, films, radio programmes, recordings of all sorts provide information in an audiovisual non-written form. The assertion that the camera cannot lie is now totally discredited, so the same precautions need to be taken in assessing the quality of the data presented. There is a tendency, especially in programmes aimed at a wide public, to oversimplify issues. Also, the powerful nature of these media can easily seduce one into a less critical mood. Emotions can be aroused that cloud one's better judgement. Repeated viewings help to counter this.

The Internet and CD-ROMs combine written and audiovisual techniques to impart information. Remember the issues raised in Chapter 8 about assessing the accuracy of any data presented on the World Wide Web.

You cannot always be present at an event, but other people might have experienced it. Their accounts may be the nearest you can get to an event. Getting information from several witnesses will help to pin down the actual facts of the event.

FIGURE 13.4 So gullible as to believe everything we read.

It is good practice, and especially necessary with secondary data, to compare the data from different sources. This will help to identify bias, inaccuracies and pure imagination. It will also show up different interpretations that have been made of the event or phenomenon. Far from being an annoyance, this could provide a rich subject of debate in your dissertation. Academic writing thrives on controversy. You will thus have the opportunity to weigh up the evidence, to set up your argument, and to come to your own conclusions on the matter.

13.3   Quantitative and qualitative data and levels of measurement

The other main dual categories applied to data refer, not to their source, but to their nature. Can the data be reduced to numbers or can they be presented only in words?

It is important to make a distinction between these two types of data because it affects the way that they are collected, recorded and analysed. Numbers can provide a very useful way of compressing large amounts of data, but if used inappropriately they lead to spurious results. So how can these two categories be distinguished?

Quantitative data

Quantitative data have features that can be measured, more or less exactly. Measurement implies some form of magnitude, usually expressed in numbers. As soon as you can deal with numbers, then you can apply mathematical procedures to analyse the data. These might be extremely simple, such as counts or percentages, or more sophisticated, such as statistical tests or mathematical models.

Some forms of quantitative data are obviously based on numbers: population counts, economic data, scientific measurements, to mention just a few. There are, however, other types of data that initially seem remote from quantitative measures but can be converted to numbers. For example, people's opinions about league tables might be difficult to quantify. But if, in a questionnaire, you give a set choice of answers to the questions on this subject, then you can count the various responses. The data can then be treated as quantitative.

Typical examples of quantitative data are census figures (population, income, living density, etc.), economic data (share prices, gross national product, tax regimes, etc.), performance data (sport statistics, medical measurements, engineering calculations, etc.) and all measurements in scientific endeavour.

There are different ways of measuring data, depending on the nature of the data. These are commonly referred to as levels of measurement – nominal, ordinal, interval and ratio.

Nominal

If you have a diverse collection of different animals, you could sort them into groups of the same type, for example lion, tiger, elephant, giraffe, etc. This most basic level of measurement is called nominal (i.e. referring to names). You might think that there is not much mathematical analysis you can apply to a list of names – counting the number of names and the number of cases in each category is about it! However, you can represent this information on a bar graph to compare the different sizes of the groups. You can also compare percentages of each group to the total, or one to another, and find the mode (the value that occurs most frequently in the groups). If you have two types of nominal measurement of a group, for example types of front teeth (sharp and pointy or flat and blunt) and eating habits (carnivore, herbivore, mixed), you can use the chi-squared statistical test to show up the differences between the expected and the observed values (although more straightforward statistical tests are discussed in Chapter 19).

Common uses of the nominal level of measurement in research are male/female, religious affiliations, racial types, occupations, naming of chemicals, plant species, building types, etc.

FIGURE 13.5   Nominal.

Ordinal

If the animals were well behaved, you could perhaps stand them in a row in order of height. Now you have measured them in an ordinal fashion, i.e. put them into an order – big to small – by comparing bigger and smaller rather than actually measuring their size. They probably will not be in equal steps of size; there may be a few very big or very small animals, and a lot somewhere near the middle. Now you can analyse data measured at this level by finding the mode and the median (in this case the middle size). You can also determine the percentage or per centile rank, and again, if you have two types of measurement (e.g. size and fierceness), you can use the chi-squared test. You can also show relationships by means of rank correlation.

Examples of the ordinal level of measurement are levels of education (none, primary, secondary, college or university), skills (unskilled, semi-skilled, skilled), clothes sizes (S, M, L, XL, XXL), and many devised especially for multiple-choice answers to questionnaires (like very much, like, neutral, dislike, dislike very much).

Interval

If you ask some people how much they like the different animals in your collection, scoring them in a range from 1–10 (the higher the more liked), then you will be getting them to measure on an interval scale. Unlike the uneven steps in animal sizes, the equal steps in this measurement scale give an accurate gauge of the distance between levels of liking, for example you can work out an average score for each animal and get an accurate comparison of their popularity. However, as there is no meaningful nought, you cannot say that a score of 4 indicates half the popularity of a score of 8. This would be like saying that a room with a temperature of 45°F is half as hot as one measured at 90°F.

Actually, temperature is a good example of an interval scale: in neither Fahrenheit nor Celsius measures does 0° mean a total absence of warmth. You can however, truthfully say that the difference between scores of 4 and 8 and between 2 and 6 is the same, just as you can say that the difference between 45°F and 90°F and between 65°F and 110°F is the same. You can use additional quite sophisticated statistical tests on this level of measurement (e.g. standard deviation, t-test, F-test and the product moment correlation).

Ratio

If you counted how many lions, tigers, elephants, giraffes, etc. you had in your collection, then you would be using the ratio level of measurement. Here the nought will mean no animals. Any kind of measurement that has a meaningful nought falls into this category, for example distances in miles, light measurement in lux, age in years – you will be able to think of many more yourself. The distinctive quality of the ratio level of measurement is that you can express values in terms of multiple and fractional parts, for example half as big, three times as expensive, etc. This is the most versatile level of measurement, open to a wide range of statistical tests, but I will not bore you with the names of them all!

Qualitative data

Qualitative data cannot be accurately measured and counted, and are generally expressed in words rather than numbers. The study of human beings and their societies and cultures requires many observations to be made that are to do with identifying, understanding and interpreting ideas, customs, mores, beliefs and other essentially human activities and attributes. These cannot be pinned down and measured in any exact way. These kinds of data are therefore descriptive in character, and rarely go beyond the nominal and ordinal levels of measurement. This does not mean that they are any less valuable than quantitative data; in fact their richness and subtlety lead to great insights into human society.

Words, and the relationships between them, are far less precise than numbers. This makes qualitative research more dependent on careful definition of the meaning of words, the development of concepts and the plotting of interrelationships between variables. Concepts such as poverty, comfort, friendship, etc., while elusive to measure, are nonetheless real and detectable.

Typical examples of qualitative data are literary texts, minutes of meetings, observation notes, interview transcripts, documentary films, historical records, memos and recollections, etc. Some of these are records taken very close to the events or phenomena, while others may be remote and highly edited interpretations. As with any data, judgements must be made about their reliability. Qualitative data, because they cannot be dispassionately measured in a standard way, are more susceptible to varied interpretations and

FIGURE 13.6   Concepts such as comfort, while elusive, are nonetheless detectable.

valuation. In some cases even, it is more interesting to see what has been omitted from a report than what has been included. You can best check the reliability and completeness of qualitative data about an event by obtaining a variety of sources of data relating to the same event; this is called triangulation.

The distinction between qualitative and quantitative data is one of a continuum between extremes. You do not have to choose to collect only one or the other. In fact, there are many types of data that can be seen from both perspectives. For example, a questionnaire exploring people's political attitudes may provide a rich source of qualitative data about their aspirations and beliefs, but might also provide useful quantitative data about levels of support for different political parties. What is important is that you are aware of the types of data that you are dealing with, during collection or analysis, and that you use the appropriate levels of measurement.

13.4   Where are the necessary data found?

Data (the plural form of 'datum') are the raw materials of research. You need to mine the subject of your focus in order to dig out the ore in the form of data, which you can then interpret and refine into the gold of conclusions. So, how can you, as a prospector for data, find the relevant sources in your subject?

Although we are surrounded by data, in fact bombarded with them every day from TV, posters, radio, newspapers, magazines and books, it is not so straightforward to collect the correct data for our purposes. It needs a plan of action that identifies and uses the most effective and appropriate methods of data collection. This chapter briefly explains the most common methods. You should read this with your research problem in mind, so that you can select the most promising approaches for further investigation.

You are probably wasting your time if you amass data that you are unable to analyse, either because you have too much, or because you have insufficient or inappropriate analytical skills or methods to make the analysis. I say probably, because research is not a linear process, so it is not easy to predict exactly how many data will be 'enough'.

What will help you to judge the type of and amount of data required is to decide on the methods that you will use to analyse them (see Chapters 19 and 20 for this). In turn, the decision on the appropriateness of analytical methods must be made in relation to the nature of the research problem and the specific aims of the research project. This should be evident in your overall argument that links the research question/problem with the necessary data to be collected and the type of analysis that needs to be carried out in order to reach valid conclusions.

Whatever the focus of your research, collecting secondary data will be a must. You will inevitably need to ascertain the background to your research question/problem, and also get an idea of the current theories and ideas. As such, you would have completed this with your literature review however, you may well need supplementary secondary data such as histories, commentaries, diaries, letters, etc. and records, which are contemporary, impersonal recordings of events, situations and states, and may be descriptive or statistical. Any of them can be qualitative or quantitative in analysis.

One of the main problems faced by the researcher seeking such recorded data is that of locating and accessing them. Another is often that of authenticating these sources, and another is the question of interpretation.

Collecting primary information is much more subject specific, so you will have to judge what is appropriate here. Consider whether you need to get information from people, in single or large numbers, or whether you will need to observe and/or measure things or phenomena. You may need to do several of these: for example, you may be looking at both the education system and the building and its effects on the pupils.

This entails going out and collecting information by observing, recording and measuring the activities and ideas of real people, or perhaps watching animals, or inspecting objects and experiencing events. This process of collecting primary data is often called survey research.

You should only be interested in collecting data that are required in order to investigate your research problem. Even so, the amount of relevant information you could collect is likely to be enormous, so you must find a way to limit the amount of data you collect to achieve your aims. The main technique for reducing the scope of your data collection is to study a sample, i.e. a small section of the subjects of your study. There are several things you must consider in selecting a sample, so before discussing the different methods of data collection, let us first deal with the issue of sampling.

13.5   Sampling

When you organize any kind of limited survey to collect information, or when you choose some particular cases to study in detail, the question that inevitably arises is: how representative will the collected information be of the whole population? In other words, will the relatively few people you ask, or situations you study, be typical of all the others?

When we talk about 'population' in research, it does not necessarily mean a number of people. Population is a collective term used to describe the total quantity of cases of the type that are the subject of your study. So a population can consist of cases that are objects, people, organizations or even events, for example school buildings, miners, police forces, revolutions.

Where the objects of study are big and complex, for example towns or businesses, it might only be possible to study one or very few cases. Here, a case study approach is applicable, which enables a detailed investigation into the selected case or cases. You will have to judge which cases you choose on the basis of how typical they are of their type (population).

If you wish to survey the opinions of the members of a small club, there might be no difficulty in getting information from each member, so the results of the survey will represent the opinions of the whole club membership. However, if you wish to assess the opinions of the members of a large trade union, apart from organizing a national ballot, you will have to devise some way of selecting a sample of the members who you are able to question, and who are a fair representation of all the members of the union. Sampling must be done whenever you can gather information from only a fraction of the population of a group or a phenomenon that you want to study. Ideally, you should try to select a sample that is free from bias. You will see that the type of sample you select will greatly affect the reliability of your subsequent generalizations.

There are basically two types of sampling procedure – random and non-random. Random sampling techniques give the most reliable representation of the whole population, while non-random techniques, relying on the judgement of the researcher or on accident, cannot generally be used to make accurate generalizations about the whole population.

Random sampling

Random sampling at its simplest is like a competition draw. Represent all the cases in your population on slips of paper, put them into a hat, and draw out the slips in a random fashion. As with all samples, the larger the sample, the better. However, the issues are not always as simple as this. Here are a few basic guidelines.

First, a question should be asked about the nature of the population: is it homogeneous or are there distinctly different classes of cases within it? Different sampling techniques are appropriate for each. The next question to ask is which process of randomization will be used? The following gives a guide to which technique is suited to the different population characteristics.

- Simple random sampling: This is used when the population is uniform or has similar characteristics in all cases, for example a production of chocolate bars from which random samples are selected to test their quality.
- Simple stratified sampling: This should be used when cases in the population fall into distinctly different categories (strata), for example a business whose employees are of three different categories – sales, production and administration. An equally sized randomized sample is obtained from each stratum separately to ensure that each is

equally represented. The samples are then combined to form the complete sample from the whole population.

- Proportional stratified sampling: Used when the cases in a population fall into distinctly different categories (strata) of a known proportion of that population, for example a university in which 40 per cent of students study arts and 60 per cent study sciences. A randomized sample is obtained from each stratum separately, sized according to the proportion of each stratum to the whole population, and then combined as previously to form the complete sample from the population.
- Cluster sampling or area sampling: Here, cases in the population form clusters by sharing one or some characteristics but are otherwise as heterogeneous as possible, for example shoppers at supermarkets. They are all shoppers, each cluster experiencing a distinct supermarket, but individuals vary as to age, sex, nationality, wealth, social status, etc.
- Systematic sampling: This is used when the population is very large and of no known characteristics, for example the population of a town. Systematic sampling procedures involve the selection of units in a series (e.g. on a list) according to a system. Perhaps the simplest is to choose every nth case on a list, for example, every fiftieth person in a telephone directory or list of ratepayers. It is important to pick the first case randomly, i.e. don't necessarily start counting from the first name on the list. The type of list is also significant – not everyone in the town owns a telephone or is a ratepayer.

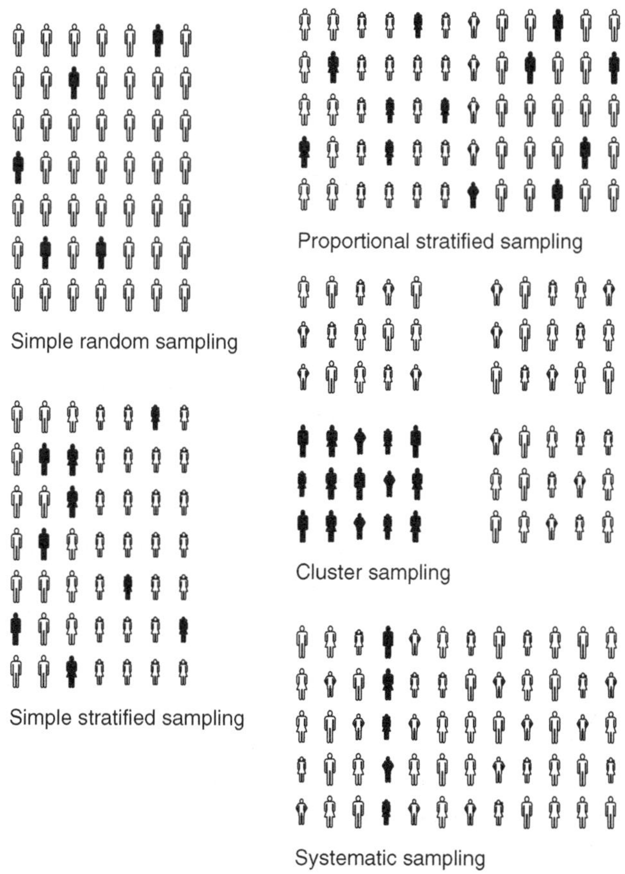

Simple random sampling

Proportional stratified sampling

Simple stratified sampling

Cluster sampling

Systematic sampling

FIGURE 13.7   Random sampling diagrams.

Non-random sampling

Non-random sampling can be useful for certain studies, but it provides only a weak basis for generalization.

- Accidental sampling or convenience sampling: This involves using what is immediately available, for example studying the building you happen to be in, examining the work practices in your firm, etc. There are no ways of checking to see if this kind of sample is in any way representative of others of its kind, so the results of the study can be applied only to that sample.
- Quota sampling: Used regularly by reporters interviewing on the streets, quota sampling is an attempt to balance the sample interviewed by selecting responses from equal numbers of different respondents, for example equal numbers from different political parties. This is an unregulated form of sampling, as there is no knowledge whether the respondents are typical of their parties. For example, Labour respondents might just have come from an extreme left-wing rally.
- Theoretical sampling: A useful method of getting information from a sample of the population that you think knows most about a subject. A study on homelessness could concentrate on questioning people living in the street. This approach is common in qualitative research where statistical inference is not required.

Another three methods can be briefly mentioned. Purposive sampling is where the researcher selects what he/she thinks is a 'typical' sample. Systematic matching sampling is when two groups of very different size are compared by selecting a number from the larger group to match the number and characteristics of the smaller one. Finally, the snowball technique is when you contact a small number of members of the target population and get them to introduce you to others, for example of a secret society.

Sample size

Once you have selected a suitable sampling method, the remaining problem is to determine the sample size. There is no easy answer to this problem. If the population is very homogeneous, and the study is not very detailed, than a small sample will give a fairly representative view of the whole. In other cases, you should consider the following.

If you want great accuracy in the true representation of the population, then the sample must be large. It should also be in direct relationship to the number of questions asked and the amount of detail required in the analysis of the data. Normally, conclusions reached from the study of a large sample are more convincing than those from a small one. However, you have to take into account the practicalities of your resources in time, cost and effort.

The amount of variability within the population (technically known as the standard deviation) is another important factor in deciding on a suitable sample size. Obviously, in order that every sector of a diverse population is adequately represented, a larger sample will be required than if the population were more homogeneous.

If statistical tests are to be used to analyse the data, there are usually minimum sample sizes specified from which any significant results can be obtained. Chapter 19 deals briefly with statistical methods.

If you are going to do some kind of a survey or case study research, you might think that all this about sampling is a bit elaborate for the scale of your dissertation. But in fact, you will gain extra marks if you can show that you have considered the issue of sampling, even if your survey is small or your case study is an obvious choice. Demonstrate your knowledge by briefly discussing the relevant options and argue the case for your conclusions. Describe how you have carried out the sampling. One of the main points of doing a dissertation is to gain some experience of applying research methods – valuable marks are allotted for this.

Case studies

Sometimes you may want to study a system, an organization, an event, or even a person or type of personality. It can be convenient to pick one or a small number of examples of these to study them in detail, and make assessments and comparisons. These are called case studies. This is usually based on the argument that the case studies investigated are a sample of some or many such systems, organizations, etc. and so what you can find out in the particular cases could be applicable to all of them. You need to make the same kind of sampling choice as described above in order to reassure yourself, and the reader, that this in fact holds good.

Alternatively, if there is a large variation between such systems, organizations, etc. it may not be possible to find 'average' or representative cases. What you can do here is to take several very different ones, for example those showing extreme characteristics, those at each end of the spectrum and perhaps one that is somewhere in the middle. Take for example discipline in schools. You could compare one school that tends to rely on sanctions, one school that tends to rely on rewards, and one school that combines both rewards and sanctions. Other examples could include how schools teach spelling or reading strategies, whether physical education is more competitive or cooperative, schools which specialize in one curriculum area subject compared to a school with a different specialist subject. You can probably think of some more relevant to your subject.

13.6   What should I do now?

You will soon have to begin collecting information about your topic of research. When doing your background reading, you have probably already seen what information has been collected and analysed by other people. This could give a good indication of what kind of data you will be searching for. Consider the types of data that you might, or are planning to, collect and first ask yourself these questions:

- Has the information you want already been recorded somewhere by someone else?
- Or do you have to go out to collect the information yourself directly from people or by observing phenomena?

- Are the data you will collect easily quantifiable and measurable?
- Or are they difficult to describe and pin down exactly?

These might be surprisingly difficult questions to answer, as it is not always obvious what data will be required and from where they can be obtained. You might well have to spend some time thinking about this. It is a good idea to make some lists of data you will need to collect, and then try to sort them into categories: primary and secondary; quantitative and qualitative. These pairs are not connected, so do the same exercise with each pair.

If for example you are interested in the types and quality after-school provision, the data might be already available in statistics collected by the government or other organizations (secondary data). On the other hand, you may want to pinpoint particular schools to see how these compare (primary data). How you measure the type and quality of after-school provision is not easy to do in a general way. What does 'after-school provision' mean? Can you break it down into several categories (nominal measurement) or into degrees of provision (ordinal measurement)? Both of these will be quantitative data in the sense that you are putting some kind of measurement to them, though you will have to make a qualitative assessment in order to fit them into these orders. How do you measure quality? Can you do it by counting the number of staff and the hours they are in attendance (quantitative data) or will you assess the attitudes of the staff to the children by observing their behaviour (qualitative data)?

Very often, unmeasurable, abstract concepts such as effectiveness, efficiency, etc. have to be broken down into components in order to apply them in a meaningful way to your investigation. Some of these components will be measurable and dealt with quantitatively; others will be qualitative and rely on descriptions and comparisons. So if you are using general abstract terms like this in your dissertation title, and in the questions you are posing, ask what they mean in the context you are using them. Try to see how they can be broken down into less abstract components that can be studied and measured more easily. (It would be worth referring back to the section on 'Statements' in Chapter 11 for additional explanation of this.)

You are likely to end up with a variety of data types you need to collect. This is altogether normal, and actually an advantage, as you can then demonstrate to the examiner of your dissertation how well you can deal with the collection and analysis of a range of different kinds of data.

13.7   References to more information

What counts as data, and what to do with them, are a big subject in research and get dealt with exhaustively in most books about academic writing, which can be overwhelming at this stage of your studies. Below are some useful other ways of looking at this aspect, without getting too deeply into technicalities. If you have other books about research to hand, look up the index to see what they have to say about data.

Bell, J. (2005) *Doing Your Research Project: A Guide for First-Time Researchers in Education, Health and Social Science*, 4th edn. Maidenhead: Open University Press.

Briggs, A.R.J. and Coleman, M., eds (2007) *Research Methods in Educational Leadership and Management*, 2nd edn. London: Sage.

See Part B of the book.

Cohen, L., Manion, L. and Morrison, K. (2007) *Research Methods in Education*, 6th edn. Abingdon: Routledge.

Denscombe, M. (2003) *The Good Research Guide for Small-Scale Social Research Projects.* Buckingham: Open University Press.

de Vaus, D. (2001) *Research Design in Social Research.* London: Sage.

MacNaughton, G., Rolfe, S.A. and Siraj-Blatchford, I. (2006) *Doing Early Childhood Research: International Perspectives on Theory and Practice.* Maidenhead: Open University Press.

Opie, C., ed (2004) *Doing Educational Research: A Guide to First Time Researchers.* London: Sage.

Roberts-Holmes, G. (2005) *Doing Your Early Years Research Project: A Step by Step Guide.* London: Paul Chapman.

See Chapter 3.

Robson, C. (2002) *Real World Research: A Resource for Social Scientists and Practitioner-Researchers*, 2nd edn. Oxford: Blackwell.

Rudestam, K.E. and Newton, R.R. (2001) *Surviving your Dissertation: A Comprehensive Guide to Content and Process*, 2nd edn. Thousand Oaks: Sage.

See Chapter 3.

14 What's All This About Philosophy?

14.1 Can I believe what I see? Do I see what I believe?

You might well ask, 'Why a chapter about philosophy? After all, I'm doing a degree in education?' The simple answer is, that your whole life is determined by your philosophical approach, whether you realize it or not. Everyone is a philosopher – everyone has his/her own concept of the world.

> The alternative to philosophy is not *no* philosophy but *bad* philosophy. The 'unphilosophical' person has an unconscious philosophy, which they apply to their practice – whether of science, politics or daily life. (Collier, 1994: 16)

The research work involved in doing your dissertation requires you to take a conscious stance with regard to the nature of knowledge, its acquisition and analysis, and the quality and certainty of the conclusions that can be reached from it. You cannot assume that your position will necessarily be shared by your reader, so you will have to make clear to the reader what your philosophical approach is.

So what is it that makes up this philosophical approach, and how can one recognize its nature? The best way is to look at some of the debate about different approaches to knowledge and enquiry – the sorts of issues that are inherent in the process of producing a dissertation. There is a wide spectrum of attitudes in the debate about research, with

FIGURE 14.1   Your position will not necessarily be shared by your reader.

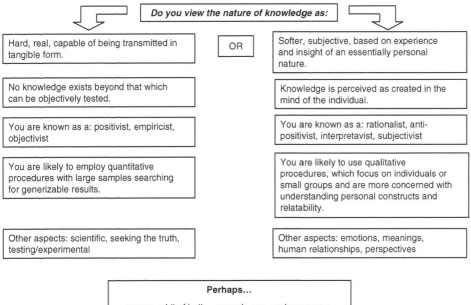

Do you view the nature of knowledge as:

| Hard, real, capable of being transmitted in tangible form. | OR | Softer, subjective, based on experience and insight of an essentially personal nature. |

No knowledge exists beyond that which can be objectively tested.

Knowledge is perceived as created in the mind of the individual.

You are known as a: positivist, empiricist, objectivist

You are known as a: rationalist, anti-positivist, interpretavist, subjectivist

You are likely to employ quantitative procedures with large samples searching for generizable results.

You are likely to use qualitative procedures, which focus on individuals or small groups and are more concerned with understanding personal constructs and relatability.

Other aspects: scientific, seeking the truth, testing/experimental

Other aspects: emotions, meanings, human relationships, perspectives

Perhaps...
you are a bit of both...as such, you are known as a
reconciliationistor eclecticist.

ILLUSTRATION 14.1   Different philosophical stances (adapted from Opie, 2004:13, Fig. 1.3 An overview of research paradigms).

two opposing camps, the positivists and the relativists (sometimes referred to as inter-pretivists), at the extremes, and a range of intermediate stances. I will briefly compare these divergent attitudes, and describe the position near the centre, often called the rec-onciliationists although also known as eclecticism. The main distinctions between these approached is summarized in Illustration 14.1.

14.2 Positivism (also known as empiricist, objectivist)

On the one hand, the positivists maintain that in order to know something it should be observable and measurable. The observer must stand apart and take a detached and neutral view of the phenomenon. For example, an engineer testing the strength of a beam will make careful measurements of loading and deflection, and careful observations of cracks and signs of failure. It should not make any difference if the engineer's dog had died that morning and he/she was feeling really low. Any other engineer doing the same test elsewhere would come up with identical results and knowledge about that beam.

This is simple enough to understand when dealing with controllable inanimate material and forces. But extreme positivists would go further. They would say that any observable phenomenon can be understood and explained in a logical way, if only enough was known about all the complexities of the situation. Hence, for example, the development of life on earth will be fully explained when enough information is gained and enough experiments are carried out to successfully test the theories about the process.

Inherent to this way of thinking is a set of assumptions. It is these that underpin the positivist approach and form the basis of scientific method that has brought us so many advances in science and technology. The main assumptions are as follows:

- Order: There is a conviction that the universe has some kind of order, and because of this, it is possible that we should be able to achieve some kind of understanding of it. Consequently, we can find out the links between events and their causes and thus understand 'the rules of the game'. This then allows us to make predictions, for example the engineer can predict that other beams of the same type as that tested above will fail if subjected to the same destructive force. Admittedly, some phenomena are so complicated that it is very difficult to possess enough information and understanding to make reliable predictions (e.g. long-range weather forecasting).
- External reality: This maintains that everyone shares the same reality and that we do not all live in different worlds that follow different rules. Although there is much philosophical debate about the nature of reality, the positivists rely on the assumption that knowledge is shareable and verifiable: that is, you see the same as I do when, say, looking down a microscope. A theory built upon observations can therefore be tested by any observer to see if it is reliable, in order that the theory can achieve general acceptance.
- Reliability: Human intellect and perceptions are reliable. You can depend on your senses and methods of thinking. Despite the dangers of deception and muddled thinking, careful observation and logical thought can be depended on. The accuracy of memory is also an important feature of this assumption.
- Parsimony: This maintains that the simplest possible explanation is the best. Needless complexity should be avoided. Einstein's formula $E = mc^2$ that sums up his momentous theory of relativity, is a good example of this.
- Generality: It is no good if the results of one experiment are only relevant to that one case, at that particular time, in that particular place. It must be possible to generalize from particular instances to others, for example from the performance of one tested

FIGURE 14.2   Find out the links between events and their causes.

beam to the predicted performance of other similar beams. It is impossible to see every instance of a phenomenon, for example water boiling when it is heated, but it is possible to maintain that any water will boil if heated sufficiently.

The underlying thrust of this understanding of reality, based on the human capacity to think logically and mathematically, is that:

Once a fully natural science was available, including especially a natural science of human beings and human behavior, then it could be applied, in the form of technology, to make human life perfectly happy, with all human needs supplied by the most efficient method which science could devise. (Matthews, 1996: 181)

When society is organized in a 'scientific' way, logical methods can be applied to all aspects of life, so as to share all the increasing benefits equally and to ensure that people themselves act rationally. This approach is often labeled modernism, and promotes the fundamental interrelated ideas of reason, science, objectivity and happiness. Wouldn't you be happy if you won the lottery and could afford all the latest equipment and facilities? If you think not, perhaps you tend to the relativist point of view.

14.3   Relativism (also known as interpretivism, anti-positivist, subjectivist)

On the other hand, the relativists maintain that we humans are inextricably bound up with the events of the world, and that it is impossible for anyone to stand aside and observe it impartially, as it were, 'from on high'. We are all encumbered by our own experiences and viewpoints, and are enmeshed in our society. However, well established they are, facts are human interpretations of reality, and may well change with time or be understood quite differently by different cultures.

This approach is particularly relevant when studying anything to do with human society. Scientific method is poorly equipped to track the inconsistencies, conflicts and subtleties of beliefs, ideals and feelings that form such an important part of human life.

> The world is not an object such that I have in my possession the law of its making; it is the natural setting of, and field for, all my thought and all my explicit perceptions. (Husserl, 1964: 11)

FIGURE 14.3 We are all encumbered by our own experiences and viewpoints.

But even in what is regarded as pure scientific research, for example astronomy, physics and biology, the mindset of society, referred to as the current paradigm, is an enormously powerful force that distorts thinking away from idealistic detachment and channels it into socially (and sometimes religiously) 'acceptable' routes. A striking example of this in the past was the complicated solutions devised to explain the movement of the heavenly bodies to conform to the belief that the earth was the centre of the universe. A more modern situation is the enormous momentum that political and economic favour gives to a particular direction in scientific enquiry to the virtual exclusion of exploration of alternative theories, for example in research into global warming. Commercial pressure can also distort scientific efforts, for example, in the development of particular drug treatments where heavy investment almost 'requires' that it be shown that the treatment works.

In order to understand this basically different approach to understanding reality it is revealing to compare the relativists' attitudes to the previously listed assumptions that underlie the positivist position.

- Order: The creation of some kind of order in our understanding of the world is based on our own human perceptions of the world. As time passes, our ordering of the world changes, not because the world has changed but because our attitudes to life, society and beliefs have changed. However, much knowledge is gained, we will never reach a definitive understanding of the world order. The 'rules of the game' are constructed by our intellect which is irrevocably bound up in our society and individuality.
- External reality: Our perceptions of the world are uniquely individual. The world we actually perceive does not exist of a series of stimuli that we interpret through our senses

and make sense of logically in a void. Rather, we already have a picture of the world, and what we perceive is interpreted in relation to our feelings and understanding – our reality. Admittedly, we might share reality by using the same meanings of words in language (even that is debatable), but this sharing is only a tiny part of our individual experience. We look on the world from within it, and from within ourselves.

- Reliability: Can we believe our senses? Does our memory always fool us? We will answer 'not always' to the first and 'quite often' to the second, if we believe that human nature is inevitably bound up in its culture and past experiences. These lead us to a personal interpretation of our perception and memorizing of events in our surroundings. Our senses can be tricked in many ways, and our memory is far from perfect, so researchers cannot rely on these to give a definitive record and measurement of the work. However, our skills of reasoning must be taken as a reliable method of organizing data and ideas, even though there may be several ways of interpreting data.
- Parsimony: Life and society are not so simple and uniform that a simple explanation is possible. Hence, simplification usually implies oversimplification. Although needless complexity should be avoided, it is rarely possible to sum any situation up in the form of a neat formula.
- Generality: Relativists tend to reject the importance, or even possibility, of categorizing individuals and events into classes. Owing to the uniqueness of each person and the uniqueness of each event it is very difficult to predict what may happen in the future under similar conditions; it is dangerous to generalize from studied cases.

The function of language becomes an important issue in this debate. Actually, this issue is widened into the subject of communication, which goes beyond just the spoken and

FIGURE 14.4   Our senses can be tricked in many ways.

written message. We communicate by all sorts of gestures; we assume roles and follow conventions. Consider how difficult it is to gauge people's meanings and feelings when you are in a strange country where different social rules apply, even if you understand the language. This subject of communication is called discourse. How things are communicated is often as important as what is communicated: discourse analysis recognizes these important factors and stresses that there is no 'neutral' way of communication.

14.4   Reconciliationism (also known as eclecticism)

The reconciliationists try to find a 'middle way'. They maintain that we can know certain things with a degree of certainty that makes prediction possible, for example technological and scientific subjects, but that we are still undeniably human with all our inherent complications and failings, so many subjects are open to debate and different interpretations. A particularly elegant solution to bridge the opposing views was formulated by Roy Bhaskar (Collier, 1994: 107–9). He saw the whole gamut of scientific enquiry as a formation of strata, each layer using the previous one as a foundation for more complexity.

At the base is physics – the fundamental and abstract play of forces. Standing on this, but extending beyond, is chemistry – the study of types of matter. This conforms to the laws of physics but also adds its own laws. Biology encompasses both physics and chemistry, but in its turn adds its own unique features, such as life. Subject to all the laws of these are the human sciences, the highest stratum, which adds even greater complexity and has its own social 'laws'. Thus, although all humans are subject to physical forces, are composed of chemicals, and conform to laws of biology, the study of humanity cannot be reduced to the study of physical, chemical and biological properties alone.

The complexities of the upper strata of this stratified world obviously present problems when one wants to study them scientifically. While the stratified system is an open system, it is easier to isolate phenomena in the lower strata, for example to isolate a chemical process that occurs within an organic process. However, it is not possible to isolate an organic process from the effects of chemical processes, since it has its origin in them. Thus, the higher up the hierarchy we go, the more complicated things get and the more difficult it is to isolate phenomena in order to study them individually. Complex interrelationships result in large systems that contain so many factors that it is impossible to predict the outcome of any action or event.

14.5   How do these attitudes affect your dissertation?

You will need to think about this. Your own personal philosophy about how we can see and understand the world around us will be a fundamental factor in your attitude to your investigations. There are many ways in which any situation can be analysed. Each approach will have a tendency to be based on a particular philosophical line that influences what you look at, the data you collect and the types of conclusions that you aim at. This is best explained using an example.

Suppose that you have decided to carry out some research into children's playgrounds in cities. You could base your research on official statistics about how many playgrounds there are in relationship to population figures, their sizes, facilities and locations, and records of vandalism and child crime. Or you could arrange interviews with children and parents to find out what they felt about different playgrounds. You could also observe the playgrounds from above and plot children's playing patterns in the form of geometrical shapes; or you could observe from nearby and record how the children used each piece of equipment. You could also make measurements of how much force is exerted by children playing on the equipment, test its strength and measure rates of corrosion, in order to ensure that it is safely built. Each of these approaches involves basic theoretical as well as methodological decisions.

So, for example, if you wanted to establish correlations between 'social facts', you would favour collecting official statistics. However, if you were concerned with finding 'social meanings', then interview studies would be more appropriate. If you were more interested in theories of interactionism or ethno-methodology, you would make a close observation of what people did, either as a whole or in detail. Finally, if you were interested in the technical performance of play equipment, then tests and experiments according to scientific method would produce the relevant answers.

FIGURE 14.5   You will need to think about this.

Accordingly, you will have to decide which philosophical standpoint(s) to adopt when carrying out your research. This is not to say that any approach is better or more true than any other. Your research approach will depend on the characteristics of your research problem and your own convictions about the nature of research. The decision will help you to determine the nature of your enquiry, the choice of appropriate research methods, and the characteristics of the outcomes that you can expect.

14.6 Two opposite approaches to enquiry: induction and deduction

While we are discussing the issue of philosophy in research, it is appropriate to consider the two different approaches to enquiry: induction and deduction. These are the methods of structured thinking expressed as opposite approaches. Explained simply, they describe opposing extremes, which are actually equally impossible to carry out in a pure form. However, it is always easier to explain things when they are compared as being as different as black and white. There is nothing weird about these ways of thinking: you do it like this all the time, sometimes more one way, sometimes more the other. So what are we talking about?

Induction

In one phrase, induction is 'going from the particular to the general'; or, if you prefer the *Oxford English Dictionary* definition, 'the inference of a general law from particular instances'. If, like the Moravian monk Gregor Mendel (1822–84), you observed over many years the occurrence of red and white blossoms on the peas that you carefully cultivated from generations of seeds derived from these plants, you might have come to the same conclusions about the exact ratios of inherited characteristics with regard to blossom colour. You might even have been able to formulate some basic general rules about dominant and recessive genes. This would have been the result of inductive thinking – observing many particular instances (of pea blossoms in this case) to derive a general rule applicable to many other situations. You start with observations and then work out a theory that fits the phenomena you have recorded.

This approach can be traced back to Aristotle, whose empirical scientific observations particularly in the field of biology (for example the development of the chick embryo) were unparalleled in the ancient world and laid the foundations for both Islamic and later western scientific thought. Galileo (1564–1642), Newton (1642–1727) and other scientists of that time heralded the scientific revolution with this method of enquiry. As the philosopher Francis Bacon (1561–1626) summed up: in order to understand nature, one should consult nature, rather than the writings of ancient philosophers and the *Bible*.

There are three conditions that must be satisfied in order to make generalizations from observations legitimate:

1 There must be a large number of observations.
2 The observations must be repeated under a large range of circumstances and conditions.
3 No observations must contradict the derived generalization.

Despite the undisputed success of this approach, there are several inherent problems. The 18th-century philosopher Hume pointed out that the logic on which the justification for this form of argument is based is circular, that is, it uses its own argument to justify itself. Notice the same method of deriving a general rule from numerous observations:

- Induction worked successfully on one occasion.
- Induction worked successfully on a second occasion.
- And so on.
- Therefore the principle of induction always works.

The other problems are about the number of observations and conditions required in order to come to reliable conclusions. How many times do you have to put your hand in the fire to conclude that fire burns? How many cigarette smokers do you have to observe to conclude that smoking can cause cancer? How can you avoid missing the possible exceptions to the rule? You cannot review every possible case in the universe.

These problems have led to the attitude that, although there may be overwhelming evidence for a certain theory, it can never be claimed to be irrevocably true. The greater the number of observations under the greater number of conditions, the greater is the probability of the truth of the generalization.

Deduction

Deduction starts from the other end. In one phrase again, deduction is 'going from the general to the particular'; or again, if you prefer the *Oxford English Dictionary* definition, 'the inferring of particular instances from a general law'. For example, medieval astronomers were convinced that the earth was the centre of the universe. All their calculations about the movement of the heavenly bodies were based on this theory. Despite this erroneous 'law' they managed to predict the positions of the planets and stars at different times in the future with considerable accuracy. The calculations for their predictions were based on deductive thinking founded on the general idea of the earth-centred solar system.

This approach is often associated with the ancient Greek philosopher Plato, who relied on our powers of reason to make sense of the world. He developed the doctrine that the material things that we handle and see around us, and abstract concepts such as 'justice', are ephemeral and imperfect copies of ideal and perfect entities that exist outside the physical world. He called these 'ideas' or 'forms'. This kind of knowledge puts theory before observation. Reality was interpreted in terms of these theories, and any observations that appeared to contradict them must automatically be wrong.

This may seem to be a silly way to do research. You could invent any kind of theory, for example that cars have personalities and feelings, and argue that evidence to the contrary must be mistaken (though you might even be able to make a good case for this!). But this approach has its uses. After all, you cannot really begin to do research with a completely unstructured idea of what you are looking for. There are so many things to observe around us: where will you begin? It is essential to have some theoretical basis for your investigations. What if you had strong feelings (i.e. had a theory) that trying to teach very young children to read and write is counter-productive?

After all, Einstein's theory of relativity could not be tested until long after it was formulated. Since Einstein's theory was formulated, scientists have struggled to find ways in which the theory could be tested. Despite this, relativity theory has been useful in developing scientific thought. It is only recently that technology has provided the means to produce equipment that could investigate the forces that are the subject of the theory. This issue of testing theories brings us to the main approach to modern scientific investigation.

Hypothetico-deductive method

This approach combines the focusing power of deductive thinking with the observative power of inductive thinking. It was formulated by Karl Popper in the 1930s, and consists of a basically simple process of four steps. These are:

- Identification of a problem
- Formulation of a hypothesis or tentative solution (synonymous with a theory in deductive thinking)
- Practical or theoretical testing of the hypothesis or solution (synonymous with observations in inductive thinking)
- Elimination or adjustment of an unsuccessful hypothesis or solution (this is the significant step in this process).

How does this work in practice? Let's take a simple example:

- Problem – to what temperature do you have to heat water in a kettle in order for it to boil?
- Hypothesis – water boils in an open vessel at 100°C.
- Testing – heat up water and measure the temperature at which it boils in as many situations as possible.
- Results – it is found that water boils at 100°C at sea level, but at lower temperatures at altitude.
- Adjustment of hypothesis – water at 1 atm pressure boils in an open vessel at 100°C.

You can even develop a new hypothesis on the basis of this work, i.e. that the temperature at which water boils is affected by the surrounding pressure.

This method is often referred to as 'scientific method'. In practice, problems are rarely as simply defined as this; nor can one straightforward practical hypothesis sufficient to set up a testing regime be formulated. Generally, the hypothesis to a research problem is more abstract in nature, and from it subhypotheses can be derived. These are at a more concrete level, enabling them to be subjected to practical testing. You read about this in the previous chapter.

14.7   What should I do now?

In the light of what you have read in this chapter, how does your thinking about your dissertation topic fit in with the different philosophical approaches? Are the assumptions of positivist thought acceptable in your research approach, or is a more relativist basis appropriate?

In order to examine what might be an appropriate philosophical stance to the issues of your research, first look carefully at the subject of your dissertation. Now ask yourself the following rather general questions, and consider the comments I have made in response to the different options you may be offered.

- Is your study concerned with things or people, or does it include a study of both, perhaps of their interrelationships?

The study of things can usually be carried out using scientific method. Are you going to look at the things themselves and their properties and performance, for example the performance of certain materials in certain situations, or will you look at processes or procedures in their manufacture or use? A positivist approach is quite suitable for either option, as the uncertainties of human interaction, feelings and habits are not an issue.

If it is people that you are going to study, will you look at trends in society, i.e. taking an overview of large groups or classes of people, or will you investigate personal relationships within small groups or between individuals?

The large amounts of quantitative data involved in the former also imply that taking a positivist approach is possible if you think that there are 'natural' or inevitable forces and laws that determine social events on a large scale. If you believe that the uncertainties of human reactions and beliefs operate even at this large scale, then a more relativist stance is appropriate. Scientific method could be used to examine the data.

The latter, examining individuals and small groups, is more likely to be approached in a relativist manner as your own background and attitudes make it difficult to see the situation from a purely neutral stance. Even so, if you were a psychologist or neurologist, you might disagree: there might be a purely scientific biological basis for all our actions.

If you are examining the relationships between people and things, at what scale will you be working? You could be using a large scale via general principles, for example the design of school buildings; on operational scale in systems studies, for example the workforce organization in a particular educational setting; or a small scale in practical studies, for example the design of personalized learning strategies for a specific child.

In every case, the technical and organizational aspects will be influenced by the human aspects. Hard science will need to be adapted to cater for the abilities, feelings and habits of people. You will need to adapt your approaches to these different aspects.

- Can your problem be analysed and explained in terms of forces or inner physical processes, or rather in terms of meanings and subjective forces?

Clearly a positivist approach is appropriate here, with the use of scientific method being a strong contender as a way ahead.

- Are notions of causation an important aspect, or are you seeking to find explanations in order to reach an understanding of a situation?

FIGURE 14.6   Causation has a sort of inevitability about it.

Causation has a sort of inevitability about it, as if it followed certain rules: 'If these certain events take place, then they will cause this other event to happen.' In the natural sciences the role of human relative values plays little part, for example the rules of aerodynamics can be harnessed to make a plane fly even without a pilot. A positivist approach is appropriate here. When the issues have a more human perspective, then certainties are more elusive, for example what are the causes of good behavior? Understanding and explanations will be more subjective and relativistic. Perhaps a reconciliationist view would be appropriate: in this case you could argue that our animal urges drive us to aggression and our cultural mores moderate these instincts.

- Will knowledge be gained through impartial observation and/or experimentation, or will you have to immerse yourself in the situation and make subjective interpretations or value-laden observations?

Here is a clear distinction between a positivist approach and a relativist approach. The very assumption that you can observe impartially implies a belief in the possibility of detachment and neutrality, while experimentation rests on assumptions that you can really control certain selected variables. Subjective interpretations and value-laden observations can only make sense when you recognize the partiality of the researcher.

- Are you trying to find solutions to a perceived problem, explain reasons for events, investigate to discover new knowledge, or compare and criticize the work of others?

How you approach these tasks depends on what the problem, events, type of knowledge or work of others consist of.

Do remember though, when thinking about the philosophical attitude you have developed to the subject of your project, that the positivist, relativist and reconciliationist stances are crude formulations of the range of approaches one could take. What may be appropriate for one aspect of your study might be inappropriate for another. The main thing is to be aware of your attitudes, and to question your assumptions when you formulate the design of your research activities. It is a good exercise to explain your motivations for choosing your particular topic: this might quite clearly reveal your attitudes towards the subject.

14.8 References to more information

You could spend an awful lot of time reading about philosophy and its impact on enquiry and research. If you get interested in this subject, beware of getting bogged down and spending too much time exploring. You could carry on for a lifetime! Still, you can follow-up all the interesting aspects after you have finished your dissertation.

Hughes, J. (1997) *The Philosophy of Social Research*, 3rd revised edn. Harlow: Longman.

MacNaughton, G., Rolfe, S.A. and Siraj-Blatchford, I. (2006) *Doing Early Childhood Research: International Perspectives on Theory and Practice*. Maidenhead: Open University Press.

See Chapter 3.

Pring, R. (2001) *Philosophy of Educational Research*. London: Continuum.

Seale, C., ed. (2004) *Researching Society and Culture*, 2nd edn. Thousand Oaks: Sage.

For a simple general introduction to philosophy, seek this one out. This approachable book explains the main terminology and outlines the principal streams of thought:

Thompson, M. (2006) *Teach Yourself Philosophy*. London: Hodder.

And here are books that deal in more detail with some aspects of philosophy – really for the enthusiast!

Collier, A. (1994) *Critical Realism: An Introduction to Roy Bhaskar's Philosophy*. London: Verso.

Husserl, E. (1964) *The Idea of Phenomenology*. W. Alston and G. Nakhnikian (trans.) The Hague: Martinus Nijhoff.

Matthews, E. (1996) *Twentieth-Century French Philosophy*. Oxford: Oxford University Press.

And these I have selected which are more focused on the research process – mostly in great detail. They could provide inspiration and a few enlightening revelations, but you will have to work at it. If you do delve into these, seek out the bits on the philosophical approach(es) – not always clearly stated!

Booth, W., Colomb, G. and William, J.M. (2003) *The Craft of Research*. Chicago: University of Chicago Press.

Mouly, G. (1978) *Educational Research: The Art and Science of Investigation*. Boston: Allyn and Bacon.

May, T. (2001) *Social Research: Issues, Methods and Process*, 3rd revised edn. Buckingham: Open University Press.

Neale, J. and Liebert, R. (1986) *Science and Behaviour: An Introduction to Methods of Research*, 3rd edn. New York: Prentice Hall.

15 How Do I Conduct Effective Interviews?

15.1 Introduction

An interview is a way of finding out information by speaking to and importantly, listening to another. Before we progress any further with this chapter, it is worth remembering that you are probably an expert in interviewing already! What do I mean by this? If we take the course of a week, how many interviews do you conduct, how many are you subjected to yourself as an interviewee and how many do you act as an observer? For example, catching up with a friend, watching the news or a chat show on the television, or listening to the radio are all examples of interviews: they are so common that we hardly take any notice of how well the interview is conducted, or how many we see/hear in the course of a day. As an exercise over the next day or so, take note of the different types of interview and how effectively they take place.

So if an interview is finding out information, how can this be achieved effectively so that you can get the data required to answer your research questions? The most important aspect with any form of data collection is to spend sufficient time in the planning and preparation of your research to ensure that you will capture exactly what you require.

15.2   Different types of interview structure

There are three main ways an interview can be structured: structured, semi-structured or unstructured. Each have relative advantages and associated disadvantages as discussed below.

Structured

In a structured interview, the interviewer has a set of specific questions that they ask in order to each respondent. The advantage of this format is that everyone is asked the same, thus responses can be compared on specific questions, although this structure can also be problematic should the interviewer want to follow up on a response. This type of interview is generally used for more quantitative studies, where the researcher is interested in establishing the number of views on a given topic, how many are similar, etc.

Semi-structured

With semi-structured interviews, the interviewer may have a specific set of questions, although only a few are key questions that they must ask. This allows the interviewer to ask supplementary questions, or leave out questions that have been answered or are not relevant. This type of interview can either be used for quantitative or qualitative purposes and you may want to ask additional questions for clarification.

Unstructured

An unstructured interview is a conversation with a purpose. It allows a free-flowing exchange between the interviewer and respondent, whereby either the interviewer or respondent can lead the interview. Although this will allow a depth for discussion, the problem arises that the interviewer may have little which is appropriate for their research. It is also problematic if the researcher was to seek comparable views on a specific issue. In the main, an unstructured interview is used for qualitative purposes, where real depth behind an issue can be explored.

Focus groups

A focus group is where a group of people are interviewed together in order to assess the views of a group. This is an ideal way of saving time interviewing a number of separate people. Respondents in the focus group should be from the same homogenous groups, for example, age, gender, ethnicity, etc. as too diverse a group may not provide representative responses.

It must be noted that the responses from the focus group are shared opinions and that people may respond in a different way than if interviewed individually. However, in contrast to this, the individual may feel more comfortable responding in a group setting and may actually say more than they would in an individual interview.

Focus groups can be problematic in trying to get a number of people together at a certain time, although this may be less problematic if using pupils. A further problem is in trying to capture the information. Although an audio-recording device can be used, when it comes to transcribing the recording, identifying who said what, especially if several people are talking at the same time, can make the researcher want to give up! In order to negate this, a microphone could be passed to the current speaker in order to directly capture their response.

It is worth noting that when working with children, sometimes if they sit with a friend, they may feel more relaxed. Although you may only be interested in a certain child's answers, allowing another child or a couple of children to also be interviewed in a focus group may be beneficial to your purposes. As such there is no need to transcribe everything!

A focus group can either be structured, semi-structured or unstructured. You may want to provide a questionnaire to each individual prior to the focus group, where they can note down ideas and responses for feedback at the focus group, ensuring that they have something to say.

Ultimately having decided on the interview structure, this will have a direct relation to the type of data you collect in terms of qualitative and quantitative data. Generally the less-structured interview format allows for greater qualitative data, whereas the structured interview promotes quantitative data. This will be discussed in greater detail in the next section.

15.3   Preparation

You should have already ensured that your research aim and objectives are refined, opposed to just considering that you would like to conduct interviews. As noted previously, the aim/objectives are central to your dissertation. It may even be worth pinning these to your desk to keep yourself focussed on them.

What objective/s?

The next aspect to consider is the research objective that may be achieved through interviewing. For example, one of your objectives may be to analyse different attitudes on a specific policy. Although a questionnaire could similarly enable you to collect attitudes, the interview may provide additional depth as people tend to say more than they are prepared to write. It would be worth assessing each of your objectives in order to ascertain the relative strengths and weaknesses that interviewing or questionnaires may provide for your research.

Quantitative or qualitative?

Interviews can be used for qualitative and quantitative data collection or indeed both, depending on the sample you are researching and time factors involved. For example, if you were collecting as many respondent's views as possible on a topic, you may have a few quantitative questions you will ask. If however, you were after detailed comments, more qualitative questions would be set.

After considering whether you wish to obtain quantitative or qualitative data, a further consideration is the type of question you use. Such questions are usually referred to as open or closed questions. An open question is one that invites the respondent to provide a full answer, stopping when they have decided that they have said enough. Open questions tend to invite extended answers to a question especially if the question engages their opinions and feelings. Generally these questions start with 'what' or 'how', for example:

- What do you think about the new Government policy on x?
- What would make an ideal outdoor play area?
- How do you know that a child is learning?

A closed question tends to demand a specific answer with specific detail, or a fixed choice of answers are provided for a selection to be made. Generally these questions start with 'who', 'when', 'where' and 'did', for example:

- Who do you consider to be the most influential children's author?
- When did you think of entering the education profession?
- Where do you think the 'Iron Man' (from the Ted Hughes book) came from?
- Do you like music being played when you are concentrating on your work? Please respond with either 'Yes' or 'No' or 'Sometimes'.

One key word which so far has been omitted is 'why?', a wonderful question that can turn a closed question into an open question. If you revisit the closed questions above, adding the word 'why?' to the respondent's answer will extract far greater depth to an answer. Try however, to avoid overuse of the 'why' word: ensure that your questions are suitably open-ended to allow for a full-response when considering the questions you are likely to use for your interview.

One problem with open-ended questions is that they can encourage silence while the respondent considers their answer. This is something that at first feels awkward, where you may want to ask a supplementary question or rephrase your original question. Allow sufficient time for the respondent to formulate their answer. Generally, it can take 6–8 seconds for a person to consider their answer depending on the complexity of the question, and as such, you need to be prepared to wait this long.

Once you have considered the questions you will ask and the objective(s) they may help you to meet, decide on the natural order of how the interview should proceed, for example, trying to ensure that questions are organized into blocks on specific issues. You may also want to consider asking some introductory 'warm up' questions in order to put the respondent at ease.

Respondents

Who are you going to interview for your research? This is a further consideration that impacts on your research and once you have decided on who you want to interview, can you ensure that they actually want to take part? As interviews can be quite lengthy, do they have the time to commit to yours? What is the benefit to them for helping you out with your research? Furthermore you will also need to consider who potentially, would be suitable to interview for your research and if necessary, identify others as a back up. As such, it is important to keep in mind that people are more likely to commit to a ten minute interview rather than half-an-hour. Therefore, keep your interview questions to a minimum while ensuring that you ask sufficient questions to address your objectives.

Capturing the information

No doubt you will want to record the interview in some format so that you can go over the responses at a later stage. Unfortunately this can lead to a quagmire of problems! There are different ways of recording an interview, each with their relative advantages and disadvantages as summarized in Table 15.1.

One aspect that the above method of capturing information does not consider is non-verbal body language. A person may provide a wonderful answer to a question on how much they like a specific policy, yet their body language may be completely closed, for example by crossing their arms/legs during their answer, thus indicating that although they are telling you what they think you want to hear, they do not actually agree with what they are saying.

A book could be written on such use of body language (and indeed many have!) yet for the purpose of this chapter, it may be worth trying to consider a way in which you can record body language while conducting your interview. An example of such a form may be found in Table 15.2.

Interview setting

Where and when will you actually conduct the interview? Again, careful thought needs to be given to this. If conducting the interview in a classroom or staffroom, background noise may cause a hindrance. Furthermore, will your respondent provide full, honest responses where other people may hear what they say? Alternatively, the respondents may feel more comfortable answering your questions in the familiar surroundings of a classroom or staffroom. This needs to be balanced with the issues of working ethically and perhaps working alone with children.

If to avoid background noise, you choose to work in a quiet area, try to ensure that the area is familiar to the respondent (not a broom cupboard!) and that there are other people about so the respondent does not feel isolated or you are put at risk. Furthermore, try to ensure that you select a place where you and the respondent can feel comfortable: is the setting too hot or cold, is there a breeze blowing through, are there distractions

TABLE 15.1 Associated implications of various recording methods.

Recording Method	Advantage	Disadvantage	Overcoming limitations
Audio-recording device: Tape-recorder/ dictaphone	Captures exactly what is said and the context in which it is said, taking tone of voice, pauses, etc. into consideration.	Recording can make the person feel uncomfortable. Ethical issues of recording. Time it takes to transcribe the recording.	Position the microphone out of sight of the other person, either to the side of the interview, or cover it with a sheet of paper. Ensure however, that the recording can be heard on playback by trialling different positions and recording levels. Only transcribe what is required for your objective – the full interview will not need to be transcribed.
Written notes by interviewer (detailed)	Captures exactly what is said. Notes recorded at the time save transcribing at a later stage.	Does not capture the context, tone, etc. Notes may not make much sense. Lack of body language between interviewer and respondent due to the interviewer constantly writing. This may disengage the respondent.	Ensure that the response relates to the question by preparing a form to complete.
Written notes by interviewer (brief)	Interviewer can note the important aspects of the interview.	May not capture important aspects. Notes may not make much sense.	As above
Written notes by another person		Finding a suitable person to record the interview. Respondent may feel awkward or distracted by another person in the room.	Ensure the person is familiar to the respondent. Sit the person out of sight or the respondent, perhaps pretending that they are working on something else. This can help negate ethical issues of being left alone with the respondent however, it also raises ethical issues concerning the research process.
Written notes after the interview	Allows the interviewer to engage more directly with the respondent. Less formal and more natural approach.	Unable to capture exactly what was said, and how it was said. Limits the 'purity' of responses.	As soon as it is possible post-interview, write down as much as you can recall. Highlight aspects that you remember clearly in one colour while also highlighting more dubious aspects in a different colour.
Use of video recorder	Captures the purity of the interview. Allows interviewer to engage directly with respondent.	As with other forms of recording, it can make the person feel uncomfortable. Ethical issues are also a concern.	Make the video recorder unobtrusive, filming from a tripod set in the distance (using the zoom facility as appropriate).

TABLE 15.2   Example of an interview record.

Interviewee:		Interviewer:	
Date:		Time:	
Setting:			

Question	Response (Continue on blank sheet if necessary)	Tone of voice (Please tick)	Body language (Please tick)
1. Please can you tell me about your educational background.		Thoughtful Engaged Animated Aggressive Defensive Other…	*Open* Relaxed and engaged Gesturing Plenty of eye contact Other … *Closed* Defensive positioning Arms crossed Legs crossed Lack of eye contact Other …
2. How long have you been working at this place?		Thoughtful Engaged Animated Aggressive Defensive Other …	*Open* Relaxed and engaged Gesturing Plenty of eye contact Other … *Closed* Defensive positioning Arms crossed Legs crossed Lack of eye contact Other …
3. What do you think is the most important curriculum subject and why?		Thoughtful Engaged Animated Aggressive Defensive Other …	*Open* Relaxed and engaged Gesturing Plenty of eye contact Other … *Closed* Defensive positioning Arms crossed Legs crossed Lack of eye contact Other …

happening outside, are the chairs comfortable to sit on? Such physical issues can impede an interview, as can the way you structure the room.

The interview setting also depends on the age of the person you are interviewing. Younger children would feel more comfortable in the relative normality of their classroom to feel at ease, whereas older children may prefer to be away from their peers by being outside of the classroom. If you are a relative stranger to the setting (for example if you have not worked in the setting for long) you may want to get another person to conduct the interview on your behalf, someone the child knows again letting them feel comfortable during the interview process. This however, raises issues about the skilfulness of the interviewer and how you can ensure that they conduct an interview to the same quality you want. You could provide guidance to this person and allow them time to practice their skills on a new respondent who is not part of your research sample.

You may well have been interviewed in the past for a job, or indeed are familiar with the intimidating aspects of an interview panel where a person or group of people sit behind a table asking numerous questions to the individual sitting on the isolated chair. Such settings are structured to put people under pressure, yet do you really need to conduct your interview in this way? If you similarly consider the typical, more comfortable chat-show set-up, where the interviewer is sitting at 90° from the interviewee, where there are seldom items of additional furniture (like desks). Such a setting helps to make the respondent more comfortable and thus more open to the questions.

As such, try to ensure that when conducting your interview:

- You are not sitting directly opposite the respondent
- You are sitting at the same height, thus not dominating the interview
- There are no physical barriers that may act as mental barriers to the free-flow response of the respondent
- There is water available for the respondent. This serves two purposes, if they are thirsty through talking, the lubrication will allow them to continue to talk. Furthermore, they can take a sip while thinking about a response to a question, ensuring that they feel less pressured to provide an immediate answer.

Putting the respondent at ease

If the respondent can feel at ease about the interview process, they are more likely to provide full answers. In order to achieve this, a few measures can be taken:

- Ensure that the interview starts with a general, easy topic. This could be to do with the weather, what they have been up to, how their day is going, etc.
- Make clear to the respondent the purpose of the interview, what you are trying to find out and why.
- Outline the ethical considerations you will be adopting for the interview, for example asking if they are willing to take place with your research, if they would be happy for you to record the interview (either by an audio-recording device) and how you will store and use their information, that they have a right to leave the interview whenever they want, etc.
- Ask a mixture of open and closed questions to vary the pace of the interview.
- Ensure that the key questions you want to ask are placed midway through the interview. This will ensure that, even if you run out of time, you would have captured the main responses required.
- Thank the respondent for their time.

Although you have a set of questions you want to ask the respondent, it is important to also make them feel engaged with you in the process. Paying attention to your body language while also trying to listen to what they are saying, writing notes or planning to ask the next question can cause you to appear detached. Therefore, try to actively listen to what the respondent is saying which will encourage them to open up providing more complete answers. A few strategies you may want to try are:

- Listen to the respondent!
- Do not interrupt the respondent. If you appear rude, they will close down the interview by not answering as fully as possible. However, there is a fine line between interrupting them and letting the respondent know that you have enough information for your purposes.
- Make eye contact when you are asking the question.
- Make regular eye contact when they are answering. (Too much eye contact can also make the person feel uncomfortable!)
- Ensure that your body language is not 'closed' (crossed arms/legs can appear defensive, very much like having a desk in the way).
- Be animated, for example by occasionally nodding your head, use of hand gestures, etc. Ensure however, that you do not become so animated as to be a distraction!
- If you feel the need, you can make comments such as 'that's interesting', 'hmm', 'can you tell me more about...', etc. to encourage the respondent to talk further.
- Copy their body language. This demonstrates a level of subconscious familiarity with the respondent, thus making them feel more comfortable in the setting.

Before engaging with your interviews, it would be worth practicing your interview technique with your friends, so that you can get their feedback on how well you acted as an interviewer. Did you nod your head too much or demonstrate another behaviour that distracted them? Did they feel that you were actually listening to them? Did they feel comfortable with the interview process?

15.4   Advantages

Interviews offer several advantages as a method of data collection. Predominantly they offer the researcher flexibility whereby an answer can be followed up with a supplementary question in order to gain greater depth of information. Furthermore an interview actually engages with the respondent, whereby the respondent is the centre of attention opposed to being a solitude participant as with a questionnaire.

15.5   Disadvantages

The fundamental disadvantage to conducting an interview is the time it can take to structure, conduct and interpret. A lot also depends on the quality of the interviewer in order to extract information from a respondent: two interviewers could have the same set of questions, yet one could be more successful in obtaining detailed responses than the other.

Interpretation of the response to a question can be problematic, whereby a respondent may *say* one thing yet their body language reveals that they actually *mean* something else.

15.6 What should I do now?

This chapter has highlighted a number of aspects to consider in preparing an interview. If you have identified that interviews could potentially be used for your dissertation, it would be worth becoming attentive of the interviews taking place around you on a day-to-day basis, critiquing what was useful and what could have been improved.

Identify what you are actually trying to find out for your dissertation in order to meet your research objectives and from this, make a list of the associated subject areas. Once you have identified these, evaluate and re-evaluate which are the most important, which of these appear linked to another area and which of these are not really that necessary. A list of four or five key areas would be ideal for an interview.

Consider the logical order to place these areas: does one area naturally lead into another, or do they appear disjointed. If it is the latter, your respondent may become confused and confusion can limit their responses. Once you have an appropriate structure for these areas, list a number of questions associated with each. Play about with the various question types: would an open or closed question be more appropriate. Could the question be ambiguous: could it be interpreted in more than one way?

When you have an appropriate list of questions for each area, leave them for a while and come back to them at a later stage to see if they make sense to you. Keep the useful questions and gradually hone these so that you have one or two key questions for each specific area. Try these questions out on your friends or a small pilot study and take feedback to assess whether they need to be changed.

Ensure that you have suitable time and resources to conduct the interview or interviews. It may be worth working back in time: when is the ideal time to interview? Is there sufficient time to rearrange the interview if the respondent is unavailable at the last minute, or will your dissertation come to a grinding halt? Consequently ensure that you leave additional time as a back-up.

Remember that interviews take longer than envisaged in conducting them and analysing them! Allow for this time. Finally, you may want to explore the use of interviews in greater depth through obtaining some of the references listed below.

15.7 References to more information

Research methodology books that have previously been cited deal with interviews effectively, for example:

Aubrey, C., David, T., Godfrey, R. and Thompson, L. (2000) *Early Childhood Educational Research.* London: Routledge.

Briggs, A.R.J. and Coleman, M., eds (2007) *Research Methods in Educational Leadership and Management*, 2nd edn. London: Sage.

See Chapter 13.

Cohen, L., Manion, L. and Morrison, K. (2007) *Research Methods in Education*, 6th edn. Abingdon: Routledge.

See Chapter 16.

Denscombe, M. (2003) *The Good Research Guide for Small-Scale Social Research Projects*. Buckingham: Open University Press.

See Chapter 7.

MacNaughton, G., Rolfe, S.A. and Siraj-Blatchford, I. (2006) *Doing Early Childhood Research: International Perspectives on Theory and Practice*. Maidenhead: Open University Press.

See Chapters 11 and 12.

McNiff, J., Lomax, P. and Whitehead, J. (1996) *You and Your Action Research Project*. London: Routledge.

See Chapter 5.

Opie, C., ed (2004) *Doing Educational Research: A Guide to First Time Researchers*. London: Sage.

See Chapter 6.

Roberts-Holmes, G. (2005) *Doing Your Early Years Research Project: A Step by Step Guide*. London: Paul Chapman.

See Chapter 7.

Robson, C. (2002) *Real World Research: A Resource for Social Scientists and Practitioner-Researchers*, 2nd edn. Oxford: Blackwell.

See Chapter 9.

Verma, G.K. and Mallick, K. (1999) *Researching Education: Perspectives and Techniques*. London: Falmer Press.

The following books also provide an excellent source of information:

Aldridge, A. (2001) *Surveying the Social World: Principles and Practice in Survey Research*. Buckingham: Open University Press.

Another comprehensive book: find what you need by using the contents list and index.

Fink, A. (2003) *The Survey Kit: How to Design Surveys*. London: Sage.

Nine volumes covering all aspects of survey research!

Fowler, F.J. (2001) *Survey Research Methods*, 3rd edn. London: Sage.

This book goes into great detail about all aspects of the subject of doing surveys. Good on sampling, response rates, methods of data collection – particularly questionnaires and interviews. Use it selectively to find out more about the particular methods you want to use. This book will also be useful later for analysis and has a section on ethics too.

Jaber, F., ed (2002) *Handbook of Interview Research: Context and Method*. London: Sage.

Keats, D.M. (2000) *Interviewing: A Practical Guide for Students and Professionals*. Buckingham: Open University Press.

Wengraf, T. (2001) *Qualitative Research Interviewing: Biographic, Narrative and Semi-Structured*. London: Sage.

16 How Do I Structure Effective Questionnaires?

16.1 Introduction

Perhaps one of the most widely-used data collection methods for undergraduate educational research is that of the questionnaire. As with interviews, the questionnaire is widely known to people as we appear to be surrounded with such sheets of paper, whether module evaluation forms, medical questionnaires, insurance forms, etc. Basically a questionnaire asks for information in a written format.

Many of the issues previously discussed for interviews are applicable for questionnaires, for example, the phrasing of questions and whether these are open or closed, etc. Unfortunately, the questionnaire does not offer the same flexibility that an interview offers: a supplementary question can be asked in an interview, yet once the questionnaire has been circulated, this is almost impossible!

The questionnaire appears simple to prepare and administer, easy to use with a target sample, analysis is relatively straightforward, there appear less ethical constraints (for example in recording verbally or visually respondents) and there is a sense of accomplishment when they have been returned and processed. Yet despite the many advantages of the questionnaire, there are a range of issues to be considered.

The key to using questionnaires effectively for your research is to ensure that you consider exactly what you want to find out and whether the questionnaire is the most suitable data collection method for this purpose. Needless to say, this applies for all data collection methods, yet the questionnaire can be used as the first choice due to the relative ease although may not necessarily yield usable data when it comes to analysis. Ultimately, the golden rule when preparing a questionnaire is to 'KISS' it …

Keep
It
Short and
Simple

16.2   Preparation

Many of the issues relating to the preparation of questionnaires can be derived from the previous chapter on interviews, for example, the type of question, structure, etc. There are however, some important differences applicable for questionnaires.

What objective/s

As noted in the last chapter, the research aim and objectives are fundamental in ensuring that questionnaires are an appropriate method for data collection for your research. There are similarities between the questionnaire and interviews in terms of questioning: however, a questionnaire may have distinct advantages if you are trying to capture a lot of respondents' views initially, then identifying themes that you want to explore in greater depth with a few selected interviews. Consequently, objectives which specify assessing a broad range of views on simplistic aspects may well lend themselves to questionnaire. An example of this would be in collecting demographic data on staff in a large school (gender, age, years in teaching, etc.) or a parental survey assessing views on school uniform, how they transport their children to school, etc.

From assessing whether your objectives lend themselves to use of questionnaire, it is then necessary to identify the important aspects about which you require information. Take for example assessing how children get travel to school. What information would be important for such a questionnaire? A 'typical' simplistic questionnaire could consist of the following categories:

- Number of children:
- Age of child/children:
- Distance from home to school:
- Mode of transport taken to school: Walk, cycle, bus, train, car

This questionnaire may appear to assess the key aspects on school transport; however, there are a number of issues that may also need to be considered that have not been listed on this questionnaire:

- The modes of transport available
  - If the parent does not own a car, then by default they would walk, opposed to the parent who chooses to walk their child to school yet could equally drive them or put them on a bus! Can attitudes be measured just by asking the parent what mode of transport they use?
- Whether there are any health problems for either the child or parent?
  - A child may travel to school by car due to a health issue, even though they live relatively close. Similarly, a parent may need to use a car due to their own health issues.
- If the mode of transport changes depending on the weather, where the child/parent are heading afterwards, etc?
  - A parent may only drive their child to school when it rains, or if the child is taken some distance after school for swimming lessons, or if the school is on the way to their place of work, or if the parent intends to go shopping afterwards.

Consequently, the questionnaire could be structured to account for a range of other issues that may not at first appear important.

Quantitative or qualitative

The same issues apply as for interviews, whereby questionnaires can be used for both quantitative and qualitative purposes depending on the sample you are researching and time factors involved. Open and closed questions can be used; however, it must be noted that the more complex issues explored through a questionnaire may impact on issues such as the number of responses obtained: basically the longer the questionnaire, the less likely a person will be to complete it! With this in mind, questionnaires are less likely to provide information on the 'why' of events and issues but used more for more quantitative questions, for example, the who, when, where, etc.

It may be worth considering placing the closed questions at the start of the questionnaire in order to allow the respondent to gain a sense of completion, before the more open-ended questions are included. Furthermore, limiting the number of open-ended questions, perhaps to just a couple will ensure that there is a higher response rate with greater detail. Therefore it is vital that you consider the specific data you wish to collect and how this will inform your objectives.

As previously discussed, you may however, wish to use the questionnaire to gain an insight into the sample population before using more focussed, alternative data collection techniques in order to assess the depth of values and opinions.

Below are examples of question types that could be employed for your questionnaire. Try and ensure, however, that your questionnaire does not become too complex by having too many question types. Remember the questionnaire needs to be KISSed!

16.3   What types of question can be used in a questionnaire?

Generally there are several ways a question could be asked depending on whether the data you require. The main ways are listed below:

- Open ended – One line
- Open ended – Comment box
- Choice – Single answer
- Choice – Multiple answer
- Rating scale – One answer
- Rating scale – Matrix
- Ranking question

Each of these will be demonstrated in turn with examples related to reasons for studying at University.

Open ended – one line

A question is set with a short space to answer.

Example:

Name:	
Age:	
What is the name of your university?	

Open ended – comment box

A question is set with a longer space to answer.

Example:

Why did you take the course you are studying? (Please write your answer in this box)

Choice – single answer

A question is set with several answers that could be selected. Only one answer can be selected.

Example:

What is your main reason for selecting the course you are studying? (Please tick one box)	
It will lead to a worthwhile career	
I have always been interested in the subject	
The course has a good reputation	
I was not accepted onto any other course	
My friend is also taking the same course	

Choice – multiple answer

A question is set with several answers that could be selected. One or more answers can be selected.

Example:

Why did you choose to study at your higher education institution? (Please tick all boxes that are relevant)	
It is close to home	
It is far away from home	
It has a good academic reputation	
The student facilities are impressive	
The geographical location (e.g. next to the sea, in a warmer or cooler location)	
I know people who have previously studied there	
A friend of mine is studying there	
There are a good range of social activities	
There are a good range of sporting activities	
It was the only institute that offered me a place	

Rating scale – one answer

A question is set with a continuum of answers. Only one answer can be selected.

Example:

How do you rate your academic attributes? (Please tick one response for each category)	Poor	OK	Good	Excellent
Your attendance at lectures				
Your contribution to seminar sessions				
The effort you put into completing assessments				
The amount of time you study each week				

Ranking question

A question is set with a continuum of answers. Each answer needs to be placed in an order.

Example:

Why did you choose to study at your higher education institution? (Please use the numbers 1 to 5, using each number only once. 1 indicates the most important feature, 5 indicates the least important)	
It has a good academic reputation	
The student facilities are impressive	
The geographical location (e.g. next to the sea, in a warmer or cooler location)	
There are a good range of social activities	
There are a good range of sporting activities	

Respondents

The anonymity of questionnaires can make the respondent feel unwanted ... why should they bother with something, when it is likely that somebody else may complete the questionnaire? To this extent, trying to personalize questionnaires can be useful. This can be achieved through the following:

- Address the questionnaire to a named person. You can still offer anonymity in return by not asking the respondent to complete their name on the questionnaire.
- Provide a covering letter with the questionnaire, or write a couple of paragraphs at the top of the questionnaire. This will provide the respondent with information about why their views are of importance by outlining the scope of your study.
- Inform the respondent as to how long it may take to complete the questionnaire so that they are aware of their commitment.
- Writing a sentence at the end of the questionnaire thanking the respondent. For example, 'Thank you for your time in completing your responses', or words to that effect.
- Enclose a pre-paid envelope for postal questionnaires. Sometimes envelopes and stamps are not easy to come by, therefore, questionnaires remain uncompleted. Making the process as easy as possible for the respondent to reply will bring greater responses.

Common sense and respondents cannot always be taken for granted. As such, it is worth providing information on how to complete the questionnaire. You may have used an elaborate system to record responses, yet will the respondent be aware of this? If you want answers circled, then state: Please circle your answer. If you want respondents to place a series of statements in order, then state: Please number your responses in order of preference, with 1 being the most important and 5 being the least.

It would be useful, as with interviews, to trial your questionnaire with a small sample to ensure that the questionnaire makes sense and that you obtain the information you require. Assessing the time it took to complete the questionnaire and whether the ordering and language of the questions were appropriate can also be achieved through such a pilot study. This will again ensure a higher response rate of valuable data when it comes to conducting your research over a larger sample.

Capturing the information

There are a number of simple rules for devising a questionnaire:

- You must establish exactly which variables you wish to gather data about, and how these variables can be assessed. This will enable you to list the questions you need to ask (and those that you don't) and to formulate the questions precisely in order to get the required responses.
- The language must be unmistakably clear and unambiguous and make no inappropriate assumptions. This requires some clear analytical effort.
- In order to get a good response rate, keep questions simple, and the questionnaire as short as possible.
- Clear and professional presentation is another essential factor in encouraging a good response. Try to ensure that the questionnaire is easy on the eye with plenty of white space to avoid your questionnaire looking cluttered.
- A generally cited rule is to try and ensure that your questionnaire only takes two sides of a sheet of paper: if a respondent sees many pages stapled together, they are less likely to invest in time to complete it.

Analysing the information

An important aspect to consider is how you will process the information from the questionnaire. This in turn may influence the questions selected and layout. The key aspect to this is reducing the data to a useable format. Being confronted with a hundred questionnaires can be daunting! For quantitative questions, it is useful to devise a scoring sheet to tally responses to a specific question (e.g. male/female, age, etc). You may want to use more elaborate systems, for example using a spreadsheet in order to record responses which will help in statistical analysis at a later stage. Please refer to Chapter 19 for further information on quantitative analysis.

For qualitative data, responses can again be reduced to the key elements, perhaps noting the key words within a response, and noting this on a table along with other people's responses. You may also want to devise a system to score responses by writing supplementary notes against a response on the questionnaire. This is known as coding and will be discussed in Chapter 20 on qualitative analysis.

16.4 How do I get my questionnaire to respondents?

There are three basic methods of delivering questionnaires: personally, by post and becoming more frequent, are Internet questionnaires; each has its own merits and problems.

Personal

The advantages of personal delivery are that you can help respondents to overcome difficulties with the questions, and that you can use personal persuasion and reminders to ensure a high response rate. You can also find out the reasons why some people refuse to answer the questionnaire, and you can check on responses if they seem odd or incomplete. This personal involvement enables you to devise more complicated questionnaires. Obviously, there are problems both in time and in geographical location that limit the scope and extent to which you can use this method of delivery.

Postal

Postal questionnaires do not suffer from the limitations of time and location. However, the most serious problem is that the rate of response is difficult to predict or control, particularly if there is no system of follow-up. The pattern of non-response can have a serious effect on the validity of your sample by introducing bias into the data collected. Consider the cost in choosing postal distribution. It might be your only method of questioning people spread over a large area or situated in relatively inaccessible regions.

Internet

A relatively cost-effective method of distributing and analysing questionnaires is through the Internet, either by setting up a website and encouraging respondents to visit, Alternatively e-mailing an internet link to various respondents.

There are a number of internet survey tools available online, ranging from the free to the costly. Running a quick website search on 'survey tools' will yield a range of results although you may want to look at the following as an example of online software you could use. Some of these sites offer free, although limited surveys, others may have an evaluation period in which to try their product. It may also be worth asking your tutors whether your institution subscribes to such a survey website.

- www.coolsurveys.com
- www.infopoll.com
- www.instantsurvey.com
- www.surveymonkey.com
- www.statpac.com
- www.zoomerang.com

Although online surveys can be used to reach a large number of respondents with ease, there are setbacks to consider.

It takes time to learn to use such software, therefore you need to balance the time and effort you invest into learning and setting up your questionnaire against the time and effort you would need to invest in a paper version and the associated data input and analysis. It may also take an inordinate amount of time to e-mail a group of people or create a website to post your survey and advertise the link, opposed to actually taking your questionnaire to a group of people.

People tend not to like reading off a screen for extended periods, therefore your questionnaire needs to be short and specific. Response rates can be poor whereby a person may start to complete a questionnaire, then decide to answer their e-mails instead. With a paper questionnaire, the respondent can actually see and assess how long it may take to respond opposed to the unknown factor with online versions.

It is also problematic in identifying your sample size. Many online questionnaires are posted on websites, yet it is difficult to assess how many visitors have actually completed the questionnaire. You may have 100 completed surveys however, this may only account for less than 1 per cent of the visitors to the website, therefore can the responses truly be used as a representative sample?

16.5   Advantages

One of the main features of a questionnaire is its impersonality. The questions are fixed, i.e. do not change according to how the replies develop, and they are the same for each respondent, and the person posing the questions is remote. The responses can be completely anonymous, allowing potentially embarrassing questions to be asked with a fair chance of getting a true reply. Another feature is that there are no geographical limitations: the respondents can be anywhere in the world as long as they can be reached by post. Questionnaires can be a relatively economic method, in cost and time, of soliciting data from a large number of people. Time for checking facts and for pondering on the questions can also be taken by the respondents, which tends to lead to more accurate information.

16.6   Disadvantages

As discussed throughout this chapter, the key disadvantage of a questionnaire is in getting people to actually respond. This can be in-part due to the impersonal nature of the questionnaire and several strategies have been suggested to negate this (refer to the previous section on 'preparation'). Questionnaires also do not allow the researcher to ask follow-up questions at the time. This can lead to incomplete answers, or additional time requirements for further investigation from both the researcher and respondent.

16.7   What should I do now?

As with the section on interviews, to further develop your understanding of questionnaires, actually try developing one adhering to the guidance in this chapter. Identify key areas that you want to investigate through the questionnaire and how this relates to your objectives. Once this has been achieved, try different questions and question types to assess which would be the most appropriate for your research. Ensure that you limit the types of responses asked for, by avoiding too many different question and answer types.

Establish the logical order for the questions on the questionnaire and trial this with a pilot sample or your friends, taking feedback on whether any questions were ambiguous, whether the questionnaire was appealing, etc.

Once you are happy with the questionnaire, consider how you will distribute these and the necessary time and cost in implementing this. Do you have a back-up plan if you get little or no returns on your questionnaire?

A further consideration is in how you intend to process the questionnaires once you have them returned. Consider whether you will use simple or complex statistical tests and how you will reduce the data into a manageable format.

16.8   References to more information

The resources identified below would also be worth reading to obtain different views on how questionnaires can be prepared. They are listed in order of usefulness:

Briggs, A.R.J. and Coleman, M., eds (2007) *Research Methods in Educational Leadership and Management*, 2nd edn. London: Sage.

See Chapter 14.

Cohen, L., Manion, L. and Morrison, K. (2007) *Research Methods in Education*, 6th edn. Abingdon: Routledge.

See Chapter 15.

Denscombe, M. (2003) *The Good Research Guide for Small-Scale Social Research Projects*. Buckingham: Open University Press.

See Chapter 6.

Dillman, D.A. (2006) *Mail and Internet Surveys: The Tailored Design Method*, 2nd edn. Chichester: John Wiley & Sons Inc.

Fink, A. (2003) *How to Sample in Surveys*, Vol. 7 of The Survey Kit. Thousand Oaks: Sage.

Gillham, W.E. and William E.C. (2000) *Developing a Questionnaire*. London: Continuum.

MacNaughton, G., Rolfe, S.A. and Siraj-Blatchford, I. (2006) *Doing Early Childhood Research: International Perspectives on Theory and Practice*. Maidenhead: Open University Press.

See Chapter 10.

McNiff, J. Lomax, P. and Whitehead, J. (1996) *You and Your Action Research Project*. London: Routledge.

See Chapter 5.

Opie, C., ed (2004) *Doing Educational Research: A Guide to First Time Researchers*. London: Sage.

See Chapter 6.

Peterson, R.A. (2000) *Constructing Effective Questionnaires*. London: Sage.

Roberts-Holmes, G. (2005) *Doing Your Early Years Research Project: A Step by Step Guide*. London: Paul Chapman.

See Chapter 9.

Robson, C. (2002) *Real World Research: A Resource for Social Scientists and Practitioner-Researchers*, 2nd edn. Oxford: Blackwell.

See Chapter 8.

17 How Do I Undertake Effective Observations?

17.1 Introduction

So far, we have looked at collecting information through talking to people and assessing their thoughts and feelings through questionnaire and interview. Yet, what do people actually do when it comes down to it? Some people like chat shows, yet others like the reality shows ... observation allows the researcher to justify why they are addicted to such television shows as you cannot beat observing humans behaving as humans! This voyeuristic tendency has filled up the television listings increasingly over the last few years. Yet, what is it that makes such compulsive viewing? Take a moment to consider either why you like such shows, or why you think people like them (if you absolutely detest them!).

How does all this relate to your research? Needless to say, it is problematic practically and ethically to have a camera crew follow students around all day, or even positioning a series of cameras around the research setting. It may be possible to record certain aspects for your research with a video camera (of course, adhering to ethical issues!) although in the main, if conducting observation for your research, other methods will probably need to be employed. Yet, why choose observation as a method of data collection?

People can say one thing yet do something completely different. If a person is asked whether they are a safe driver, they are likely to respond positively as few people would admit to driving like a maniac. Yet, spending a day with the person behind the wheel may allow you to assess whether they are painting a better picture of themselves than one they would want to portray! The education setting is similar. You could for example ask children what they do at playtime, and the response may be 'not much!', yet if you actually observe the child at play, an awful lot more may be revealed! Another example could be watching teachers engaged in teaching to assess where they position themselves, if all learners are engaged, if different methods are used to ensure different learning styles are accounted for, etc.

Furthermore, observation is not limited to the visual sense. Any sense, for example smell, touch, hearing, can be involved although to a lesser extent in order to capture the ambiance of the situation. If you consider a school setting, there may be the smell of disinfectant, polish or school dinners; there may be an eerie silence in the evening, or sounds of children playing; the 'feel' of the place, whether it is hot or cold, warm and welcoming, etc. could also be noted.

Observation can at first appear daunting! What should you be looking for? Surely there is so much happening that it would be impossible to capture all of this? Where do you begin?

FIGURE 17.1 Observation can record whether people act different to what they say.

17.2 Preparation

What objective/s?

As with the other forms of data collection, it is first necessary to identify if observation is a suitable method in order to meet one (or more) of your objectives as these are central to your dissertation. Objectives lending themselves to observation may include a comparison between a certain exhibited procedure or behaviour. Examples of this could be comparing teaching styles, playground games played by various aged children, frequencies of children answering specific questions, etc.

Quantitative or qualitative?

As with the other forms of data collection, both quantitative and qualitative methods may be employed. If your research was assessing playground rituals, games, etc. you may want to employ a qualitative approach, where a rich description of events happening over the lunch hour could be recorded. As such, you are trying to 'make the familiar strange' – by this, exploring in detail aspects taken for granted by those within the setting by trying to see events as new experiences, perhaps through the eyes of a child first starting school, or a stranger from a completely different country. Alternatively, you could employ a quantitative method of data collection where you count the number of children playing a specific game or just talking, maybe working out the percentage of the playground used for different activities. For example, you could stipulate that 60 per cent of the playground is dominated by the 30 per cent of children who play football. Although such observation of playground games is only one example of where observation could be employed, this does demonstrate the diversity of aspects that could be observed.

Capturing the information

Before discussing this section, it is first necessary to identify what exactly you want to capture. What are you actually looking for in order to meet your research objectives? If we take the aforementioned example of playground activities how would you classify these? Perhaps you may be interested in the games being played, yet how is the term 'game' defined? Does this involve two or more children? How about the single child happily kicking a ball against the wall? Does a game have to have an element of competition or could children be working cooperatively? Furthermore, unfortunately you only have one pair of eyes, so can you realistically capture everything happening within the setting, thus would your data collection be both valid and reliable?

Consequently, a narrow observation focus is required, whether collecting quantitative or qualitative data. Continuing with the playground activity theme, you could make repeated observations of different parts of the playground on different days of the week, in order to provide a greater account of playground use. Perhaps you may just want to observe one-child's activities over a period of time. The key is to ensure that you have a narrow focus which ensures you are able to capture sufficient data to meet your research needs.

In relation to recording qualitative data, a note-book is a researcher's most useful tool where you can record events, noting the time and date of the event, before noting a brief description of what has been observed or of what you have heard. You may want to trial different note-books: if it is too small, you may be constantly turning the page while writing, if it is too big, it may become cumbersome for use in the setting furthermore being difficult to keep discrete while making your notes.

Only trial and error will help you identify what is useful and beneficial in making observation notes. At first you may question that what you are recording has little value, or continue questioning whether you are recording it in the right manner. Unfortunately, qualitative notes are unique to the researcher so it is a case of working out what is best for you. An example of an observation schedule has been provided which could be adapted for your purposes. Within the following example (Table 17.1), the notes/interpretation column is completed after the observation.

In relation to recording quantitative data, an observation schedule needs to be prepared in advance noting exactly what will be observed and how this will be recorded.

TABLE 17.1 Example of an observation schedule.

Date	5th May 2007
Time	1.50 p.m.
Lesson	Science
Group	Group: 6 children

Context	
The lesson was on floating and sinking. Previously, the class had identified which objects floated and sank. This was the second lesson out of the planned unit of work.	

The teacher asked the group to try and make a ball of plasticine float and from this try and work out what helps to make things float.

Water tanks were set up in two locations and children were working in pairs.

The group working on floating and sinking were working with the teacher in a separate room, while the teaching assistant (HLTA) led the rest of the class through a different set of activities. By the end of the afternoon, all of the class would have worked with the teacher on the activity.

Observation	Notes/Interpretation
The teacher gave very little input into the lesson apart from setting the objectives.	On discussion with the teacher, he wanted to ensure that children maximized time on the task while working in a constructivist manner without providing the children with too much guidance on what to try and what to expect.
1.55 p.m. The children try making different shapes, rolling the ball into a sausage shape or cone or making a cube.	At first it seemed there was little thought being put into the activity.
2.01 p.m. Child A and B flattened the ball. Child A said 'it took longer to sink than the ball'. Child A and B then flattened the shape further and noted again that it took even longer to sink.	The children seemed to be refining their previous attempt, noting that a flatter shape helped things to sink slower.
2.02 p.m. Child C overheard A and B and decided that she would make the plasticine as flat as possible. She tested it with Child D. Child D said 'it almost floated completely!'	Child C appeared to hypothesize that if a flatter shape made the plasticine sink slower, a very flat shape would appear to be better.
2.05 p.m. Child C and D note that the water seemed to come over the sides of the shape and start to roll the sides slightly before testing again. Child A asks the pair what they are doing. Child D tells him. Child A then works with Child B to try and make a similar shape.	The children appear to be learning from each other taking what has worked and then trying to incorporate this into their own designs. Although the children appeared to be competing at first, they seem to be cooperating and sharing their ideas more.
2.09 p.m. Both groups appear to have success with the task. It is not long before the third group also succeed.	—
2.12 p.m. The teacher brings the children back together and asks them what they have found out. Child D said 'Flat things float'. Child B said 'Only if they have sides on them'. Child E said 'The sides stop the water from coming in'. The teacher records these on the board. The teacher asks the children to consider what is different between the ball and their shape that floats. Child A said 'It is flatter … the plasticine weighs less as it is more spread out and lighter things float'. The other children agree with this. The teacher then asks the groups to see if they can use what they have found out to make different shapes.	Although the children note certain properties that help the plasticine float, their understanding as to why this happens is still limited, as demonstrated by Child A's comment. I asked the teacher why he didn't intervene with the correct explanation at this stage but he noted he wanted them to experiment more to see if they could come up with a better explanation through further exploration and discussion among themselves …

The schedule needs to be consistent from one observation to another in order to ensure that the same information is recorded for the same purpose, namely comparison.

Such quantitative recording could consist of a frequency count of a specific behaviour, for example, you may want to observe whether a behaviour intervention strategy works on a child interrupting a lesson by lessening the disruptive behaviour, or you may want to assess the time a child can maintain concentration while working independently. As with the qualitative form, the date, time, lesson context, etc. could all be recorded initially.

Although this chapter has so far noted recording observations as they happen, there are different forms of observation you may also want to consider.

Photographs 'A picture tells a thousand words': indeed, a photograph can capture a moment in time. The photograph could be of a lesson in process, children's work, the playground, resources, the list could go on! The photograph can then be interpreted for the reader, highlighting aspects of importance within the context. Remember to ensure that good ethical practice is maintained by referring back to Chapter 3.

Video The setting or events within the setting could be videoed. This allows analysis at a later stage and keeps an accurate, objective record of the events. Such events could be a lesson, a part of a lesson, how children use a play area creatively, a-day-in-the-life-of a specific child or group, etc. Again, the issues of ethical practice will need consideration.

Patterns of activity A sketch map of where a teacher walks in the room during a lesson can illustrate where their time is predominantly focussed. Such maps could also be used to record the conversations a child has with their peers, playground activity, etc.

From the examples of how observation could be recorded in different formats, hopefully you can see that the only limitation on how observation can be utilized is the imagination! Indeed you may consider many other applications not listed here.

Observation setting

Observation can take place in any setting: the only constraints are your access to the setting, ethical issues as applicable and whether your presence may impact on what is being observed. Take for an example an inspector walking into a classroom and sitting in the corner observing a lesson unfolding: the mere presence of another may make a teacher more nervous, or the teacher may become more animated. Similarly, the children may be interested in this other person and be distracted by the task at hand.

If it is clear that a respondent is being observed, they may act differently. Take the example where I could be working with a small group and observing every time Child A taps a pencil on the desk. If the child taps the pencil and I note this down, the child may pick up the pattern and tap the pencil again, seeing me make further notes. The child then becomes the researcher! This is known as research reflexivity, whereby the mere presence of the researcher impacts on the research setting.

17.3   Advantages

Observation can offer many advantages to the researcher, specifically capturing events as they happen in a natural setting. This can help the researcher gain new insight into the processes to which they may have become familiar, allowing the researcher to build up a better portrayal of how events unfold. Take, for example the qualitative lesson on floating and sinking: actually observing how children can create their own learning can allow the teacher to utilize similar methods for different lessons.

Observation also records whether people act differently to what they actually say they do. A respondent may tell you that they engage all learners in their lessons, including all children, yet upon observation, it may become clear that they predominantly ask questions to the children they know will answer correctly, or perhaps interact with one group of children more than another.

17.4   Disadvantages

It is important to keep in mind that observation and the associated data analysis is dependent on the perspective of the researcher, especially in such small-scale research. In other words, if two people observe an event, they may both see different aspects depending on where they are placed, their level of attention, what they are specifically looking for, etc. In a way, it is like looking at the Necker Cube (Illustration 17.1), whereby some people see the cube as if looking from above, others from below. (Other examples of such ambiguous illusions are included in Illustrations 17.2 and 17.3.) Attention can vary whereby you can see either but not at the same time!

Associated with this is whether you are able to observe all events simultaneously. You may note that a child has become very upset and assumed that this could be due to the work they have been set, yet what you may not have noted was that another child had kicked them under the table! Although you may record the resultant behaviour, you may not know what the antecedent was that initially caused this behaviour.

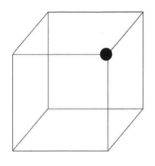

Look at the dot. Is it located in the upper right front or the upper right rear?

ILLUSTRATION 17.1   Necker Cube.

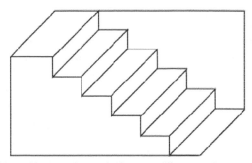

This ambiguous picture depicts two different staircases: one going up from the right to the left, the other turned upside down.

ILLUSTRATION 17.2   Schroeder Staircase.

Can you see a duck or a rabbit?

Can you see an Indian chief or a person in a winter coat facing the wall?

Can you see a woman's face or a saxophone player?

ILLUSTRATION 17.3   Perception.

Another problem with observation is the time factor. It can become difficult to try and ensure conditions are right for observation: for example if conducting a playground observation over a week, and for three of those days the children are inside due to inclement weather, the research may come to a standstill. Alternatively, so much can happen in a short period of time that it becomes impossible to observe and record everything.

Researcher reflexivity has previously been discussed, although this can become increasingly problematic should you wish to use visual recording devices for the observation. Watching a news reporter in the outside world can bring the unwanted attention of a passer-by 'playing to the camera', and this can certainly happen in an educational research setting. Increasingly, it is also becoming problematic due to child protection issues to record children using such devices and consent must be granted for all of those who may be recorded.

The role you adopt as an observer can also be problematic. If you are observing a group of children working with another person, what would happen if a child comes to you for assistance? Would you ignore them as your intervention could skew the data? Would you help them out, then realize that you have missed an important aspect that was happening?

17.5   What should I do now?

As with the previous data collection techniques, it is first necessary to establish whether observation would help you meet one (or more) of your objectives, and from this decide on what you actually want to observe, who, how, where and when.

In deciding what to observe, you are looking for behaviors that are indicative of your actual research intentions. It would be worth spending time in the research setting not making any notes initially and just absorbing what is happening, before trying to define too early on what to be attentive to. After this period 'in the field' you may be aware more precisely on what you want to find out. At this stage, try and develop an observation schedule. Again, play about with different formats and trial these through a pilot study to assess whether any changed need to be made.

Once you have an observation schedule you are happy with, who will you observe? Who would be representative within the whole population of the setting and do you have ethical permission to proceed? Establish also when the best time to observe could take place and allow for additional time in case the person is away, or another event happens.

The resources identified below would also be worth reading to obtain different views on how questionnaires can be prepared.

17.6   References to more information

You may want to start by referring to the following books to get an insight into observation.

Aubrey, C., David, T., Godfrey, R. and Thompson, L. (2000) *Early Childhood Educational Research*. London: Routledge.

Briggs, A.R.J. and Coleman, M., eds (2007) *Research Methods in Educational Leadership and Management*, 2nd edn. London: Sage.

See Chapter 15.

Cohen, L., Manion, L. and Morrison, K. (2007) *Research Methods in Education*, 6th edn. Abingdon: Routledge.

See Chapter 18.

Denscombe, M. (2003) *The Good Research Guide for Small-Scale Social Research Projects*. Buckingham: Open University Press.

See Chapter 8.

Foster, P. (1996) *Observing Schools: A Methodological Guide.* London: Paul Chapman.

Hopkins, D. (2002) *A Teacher's Guide to Classroom Research*, 3rd edn. Buckingham: Open University Press.

See Chapters 6 and 7.

MacNaughton, G., Rolfe, S.A. and Siraj-Blatchford, I. (2006) *Doing Early Childhood Research: International Perspectives on Theory and Practice.* Maidenhead: Open University Press.

See Chapter 15.

McNiff, J. Lomax, P. and Whitehead, J. (1996) *You and Your Action Research Project.* London: Routledge.

See Chapter 5.

Opie, C., ed. (2004) *Doing Educational Research: A Guide to First Time Researchers.* London: Sage.

See Chapter 6.

Roberts-Holmes, G. (2005) *Doing Your Early Years Research Project: A Step by Step Guide.* London: Paul Chapman.

See Chapters 6 and 8.

Robson, C. (2002) *Real World Research: A Resource for Social Scientists and Practitioner-Researchers*, 2nd edn. Oxford: Blackwell.

See Chapter 11.

Verma, G.K. and Mallick, K. (1999) *Researching Education: Perspectives and Techniques.* London: Falmer Press.

18 How Do I Write a Methodology Chapter?

18.1 What is methodology?

There is often confusion between the terms 'methodology' and 'methods'. The latter term concerns the data collection techniques you will use, whereas the former discusses a range of associated issues and considerations you will have to make which inform your research activities. Such considerations could include who you are going to research, where will the research take place, etc. Your methodology chapter therefore needs to consider the wider, associated issues around your research activities.

The methodology chapter is a discussion of the practical issues you need to resolve to ensure that you are able to gather the specific data you require. Furthermore, it also discusses the theoretical aspects of data collection and analysis.

18.2 Structure of the chapter

You completed the literature review by listing your research objectives, the objectives relating to the aim of your dissertation. The methodology chapter therefore uses these objectives as a starting point. Indeed, this chapter is really shedding light on how the objectives can be carried out.

The methodology chapter can be structured in a rather simple way. If you consider logistics, the management of planning, organization and control of the movement of 'goods' from place A to place B, the same applies to your research. The only difference is that the 'goods' in your dissertation consists of research data. So to re-phrase this, how can you ensure the effective planning, organization and control to ensure you get the required data from the field to the pages of your dissertation?

One way of considering this is by use of the acronym W5H1. Although at first this may strike fear in being a new strain of bird flu (that is H1N5), it is actually an acronym increasingly used in the field of business to remember the key question words: who, what, why, when, where, how.

Taking these key words, your methodology chapter can be structured in the way in which makes the most logical sense to you. Although I have proposed the following format, you may equally decide on a different structure.

Who

- Who will I use as research participants? Why?
- Who are the 'gatekeepers'? Why?
- Who do I need for consent? Why

What

- What stance are you taking as a researcher? Why?
- What data collection techniques are the most appropriate? Why?
- What are the strengths and limitations of the various data collection techniques? Why?
- What other data collection methods could I use? Why did I reject these?
- What ethical issues do I need to consider? Why?

Where

- Where will I conduct the research? Why?

When

- When will be the best time to conduct the research? Why?
- When will I know if I have enough data?

How

- How long do I have to conduct the research? Why?
- How will I record the data? Why?

- How did I select my research sample? Why?
- How will I ensure that my research has validity?
- How will I ensure that my research has reliability?
- How will I analyse the data? Why?

Why

- This has been kept separate as it can be tagged onto the end of each question above.

When it actually comes to writing the chapter, it would be best to avoid the questions as headings for the various subsections: instead they can be grouped and discussed under the following heading:

- General approach to your research (your research stance/philosophy)
- Selection and description of methods related to your objectives
- Selection of samples
- Ethical statement
- Discussion of how your research adheres to validity and reliability
- Method(s) of analysis and presentation of results (e.g. charts, graphs, diagrams, spreadsheets, statistics, coding systems, models, commentaries, etc.).

18.3   General approach to your research

The introduction to this chapter is based on positioning your research and yourself as a researcher. Your aim would previously have been outlined, yet different individuals could interpret these in different ways. For example, take an aim which states:

- An investigation of the problems of offering after-school provision at a large rural secondary school.

This could lead to different research projects depending on the researcher's point of view. One researcher could take a positivist approach by measuring and observing the provision offered, keeping a distance and assessing the views of other people on such provision. Another researcher could take the relativist approach, whereby they actually try and set up their own after-school activity, noting the issues that they face, thus being immersed in the research. There again, a third researcher could combine both of these and adopt the reconciliationist approach where they identify the problems as a detached observer and then as a participant, moving from a distance to being immersed in the research setting. Of course, it depends on how you view the world and how you attempt to deal with it. This was discussed in greater depth in Chapter 14.

This section of your chapter thus needs to discuss why you have adopted the philosophy you have selected. There is no right or wrong with this ... just that you need to let the reader know what you have adopted and why.

18.4 Selection and description of methods

This section of your methodology chapter naturally progresses from the discussion on your research stance, discussing the methods you have selected and providing a justification for these. From this, it is necessary to describe the relevant data collection methods you have employed. For example, you could discuss:

- What actually is an interview?
- What type of interview will you be conducting and why?
- How did you come up with your questions?

Once you have described the specific method and provided a suitable justification, you need to let the reader know that you are aware of the relative advantages of this method. For example, what does interviewing offer that a questionnaire or observation wouldn't? Why is this?

Needless to say, there will be limitations with whatever form of data collection you have selected. In order to demonstrate your awareness of these to the reader, it is necessary to discuss such limitations but more importantly, discuss how these limitations may in turn be reduced. What steps can you take in order to ensure such limitations do not become problematic? An example of this could be to discuss the problems of getting people to respond to questionnaires whereby you discuss the measures you have taken to maximize responses. This could be through including a return envelope, or personally distributing the questionnaire and a free pen to help the respondent reply immediately. For further information on research methods, refer to Chapters 15–17.

18.5 Selection of sample(s)

This section of your chapter needs to discuss who you have selected for your research and why they have been selected. Are they representative of a specific population, or are they unique and as such an interesting case? The sample need not necessarily apply just to people but could be on why a specific research setting was selected, etc. This would have been discussed briefly in your introductory chapter. For further information on sampling, refer to Chapter 13.

18.6 Ethical statement

It is important to discuss how and why you have adopted a specific ethical stance, thus demonstrating to the reader the issues you may have to contend with which in turn may inform them of certain problems you have faced and negated. Often this is written in a paragraph or two, yet personally I feel this needs to take greater prominence due to the rights of the individual and key policies that underlie everything within education (e.g. inclusion, Every Child Matters, etc.). A good discussion of the ethical issues demonstrates a level of empathy and the value you ascribe to those central within your dissertation. For further information on ethics, refer to Chapter 3.

18.7 Discussion how your research adheres to validity and reliability

This section of the chapter should address how trustworthy your data collection and interpretation will be. In other words, why should anyone believe what you have written? Who are you to make such claims?

At a basic level, trustworthiness can be ensured through validity and reliability:

- Validity refers to the accuracy of a result, whether the collected data is representative and illustrates the phenomenon. As such it is a level of 'trueness'.
- Reliability refers to the consistency of the data: if the same data collection methods were used with a similar sample, would similar results be obtained?

As Robson (2002: 101) notes, 'unless a measure is reliable, it cannot be valid. However, while reliability is necessary, it is not sufficient to ensure validity'. Thus, you can have one without the other, yet it may not actually measure what you want it to. An example of this is that I could collect information on effective teaching using a questionnaire aimed at practicing teacher, with one of the questions being, 'What attributes make a good teacher?' Although this question is likely to be reliable in capturing information on the issue, it may not necessarily be valid if I use this information to assess whether the teacher is actually effective his- or herself! It is one thing to know what makes a good teacher, another to actually being one!

Consequently, discussing how you have ensured that your research is both reliable and valid is a key element to this chapter.

For purely quantitative research, such reliability and validity can be obtained by discussing how the measures you have selected are appropriate, furthermore your statistical tests and interpretation from this. For qualitative research you could use triangulation whereby data is corroborated from one method to another, 'methodological triangulation' (i.e. interview responses are correlated with observation), or where different respondents' views are corroborated 'participant triangulation (i.e. where views from one person are compared with that of another).

18.8 Method(s) of analysis and presentation of results

Finally, your chapter should discuss what you will do with the data when it has been collected. How are you specifically going to analyse the information? You may want to describe the specific statistical test(s) you will utilize, providing a justification for this. Alternatively you could describe the coding system you will use for qualitative data, and discuss why this has been selected and how you intend to carry this out. It would be worth reading ahead to Chapters 19 and 20 as this discusses the processing of data in greater detail.

18.9   What should I do now?

Having waded through this rather long chapter, you will have got a good idea of what kinds of data there are and what your options are for getting hold of the necessary data required for your dissertation research. What you really need to decide now is just what data you will have to gather, and then to choose suitable collection methods. You will probably find that your project is not so simple as to require only one data collection method. In all cases, secondary data will be required, if only to provide some background information on which to base the research. You might need to use two or three different methods for data collection, one for each aspect of your investigations, or to triangulate the information on just one subject.

For example, if you were studying the effect of particular television programmes on children's play habits, you might want to make observations and set up questionnaires to get the children's and their parents' view; consult statistics about publicity and toy and video sales to get data about the promotion of the programmes; interview the programme makers; read previous research on the subject to find methodological approaches to studying this subject; and so on.

As usual, a good way to approach this is to ask yourself a series of questions, the answers to which should form a simple argument, for example:

*   Who/what/where are the different people/things/ phenomena that need to be investigated?
*   In each case, what sort of data are needed?
*   In each case, what is the best method for obtaining those data?

You should make a list of the answers to the above questions, and then see how you could organize the data collection in a manageable way. You will quickly see whether it is practicable to do everything on the list. Consider not only the amount of data you need to collect (e.g. how many questions you need to ask of how many people) but also the issues of where you have to go, and when and how you can get access to the information. Don't attempt too much – you will stress yourself out! Rather, narrow the scope of the research to ensure that it can be reasonably completed on time. For example, in the project above, you could restrict your investigations to the children's perspective, and avoid the commercial and production aspects.

The results of your deliberations can now be fed into your project plan, with allotted timing for each data collection task.

18.10   References to more information

There are hundreds of books written about data collection methods that go into greater detail than has been offered in this chapter. Some of these have been indicated in the reference section of the previous chapters. Consult your library catalogue using the search terms of 'interviews', 'observations', 'questionnaires', etc.

It would also be worth checking your library catalogue for previous dissertations that may have been completed in your subject area: this would provide you with examples of methodology chapters and associated data collection techniques for a research project that may have similarities to yours. When it comes to actually writing your chapter for the dissertation, the key books mentioned in Chapter 1 would be worth reviewing, for example:

Clough, P. and Nutbrown, C. (2002) *A Student's Guide to Methodology*. London: Sage.

Mounsey, C. (2002) *Essays and Dissertations*. Oxford: Oxford University Press.

Opie, C., ed. (2004) *Doing Educational Research: A Guide to First Time Researchers*. London: Sage.

See Chapter 2.

Rudestam, K.E. and Newton, R.R. (2001) *Surviving your Dissertation: A Comprehensive Guide to Content and Process*, 2nd edn. Thousand Oaks: Sage.

See Chapter 5.

Swetnam, D. (2000) *Writing Your Dissertation: How to Plan, Prepare and Present Successful Work*. Oxford: How To Books.

SECTION 5

The chapters in this section discuss in detail how to process your data once you have successfully collected it. Chapter 19 discusses how to analyse quantitative data, with Chapter 20 on analysing qualitative data. Both of these chapters similarly discuss how to draw conclusions from the analysis.

Chapter 21 subsequently discusses how to complete the discussion chapter: this chapter is where you start to bring your background reading, your data and your thoughts together. It could be considered the hardest chapter to write as you are 'juggling' with a number of different concepts; however, it is also one of the most therapeutic in that you are actually creating your views on what you have found. Indeed, you will find that from the outset of your dissertation you may have ideas jostling for your attention: this is where you can let them out to roam freely and explore, before trying to bring them back into order within the final stages of your dissertation.

19 How Do I Analyse Quantitative Data?

19.1 Raw data

The results of your survey, experiments, archival studies, or whatever methods you used to collect data about your chosen subject, are of little use to anyone if they are merely presented as raw data. It should not be the duty of the reader to try to make sense of them, and to relate them to your research questions or problems. It is up to you to use the information that you have collected to make a case for arriving at some conclusions. How exactly you do this depends on what kind of questions you raised at the beginning of the dissertation, and the directions you have taken in order to answer them.

The data you have collected might be recorded in different ways that are not easy to read or to summarize. Perhaps they are contained in numerous questionnaire responses, in handwritten laboratory reports, recorded speech, as a series of photographs or observations in a diary. It can be difficult for even you, who have done the collecting, to make sense of it all, let alone someone who has not been involved in the project.

The question now is how to grapple with the various forms of data so that you can present them in a clear and concise fashion, and how you can analyse the presented data to support an argument that leads to convincing conclusions. In order to do this you must be clear about what you are trying to achieve.

19.2   Refer to the research objectives

This is a very good time to return to your research proposal, and to any revisions you might have made in the interim, to refocus on exactly what you intended to do so many weeks/months ago. What are the burning issues that you wanted to tackle? What were the stated aims of your research? What specific questions or problems were raised? What sort of answers were you aiming at?

Now you can briefly review that information you have collected and assess whether you really have kept to the issues raised in the proposal. Are the data likely to produce the answers you were seeking? If you have not strayed from the intended route, then it is likely that you will be able to go on to analyse the data successfully as intended. But, what if you feel that as time went by you got diverted from your original intentions, that unexpected events occurred that led you to consider different, perhaps more important issues, or that your interests were drawn to aspects about which you were not aware before? Now is the time to consider the best way ahead in the light of changed circumstances.

Your original proposal was not written in stone! You based it on the knowledge and understanding you had at the time. The process of collecting data about your subject has put you in a much stronger position to know better about the important issues in your chosen field. In order to produce a good dissertation, you must now reconsider the main aims of the research and revise them on the basis of your new direction. I presume that the changes will not be huge, more a realignment than a new beginning. But what is important is that you redefine questions or problems so that you will be able to produce some answers or solutions based on the data that you have collected. It is best to actually formulate these questions or problems in writing; you will need to discuss them anyway at the beginning of your dissertation. If you have already written the first chapters, review these in the light of your most recent thoughts.

FIGURE 19.1   If you have not strayed from your intended route.

19.3 Analysis according to types of data

There are several reasons why you may want to analyse data. Some of these are the same as the reasons why you wanted to do the study in the first place. You can use analytical methods to:

- Measure
- Make comparisons
- Examine relationships
- Make forecasts
- Test hypotheses
- Construct concepts and theories
- Explore
- Control
- Explain

This book is much too short to be able to describe all the analytical methods possible. I can just review some of the main methods, and refer you to more specialized publications where you can get detailed instructions on how do the analysis.

The common way to categorize data for both collection and analysis is to distinguish between quantitative and qualitative data (see Chapter 13). You must have done this already when you did your data collection. However, life is rarely as tidy as theory. You possibly have some of both types of data – not a bad thing as they can provide different perspectives on a subject. In fact, some of the analytical methods can be used both quantitatively and qualitatively. These are mentioned where appropriate. As the subject of analysis is rather large and of essential importance to your dissertation, I have spread it over two chapters. This one continues with a discussion of quantitative analysis, and the next takes on the techniques of qualitative analysis.

19.4 Quantitative analysis

Quantitative analysis deals with numbers and uses mathematical operations to investigate the properties of data. The levels of measurement used in the collection of the data, i.e. nominal, ordinal, interval and ratio (see Chapter 13), are an important factor in choosing the type of analysis that is applicable, as is the numbers of cases involved. Statistics is the name given to this type of analysis, and is defined in this sense as:

> The science of collecting and analysing numerical data, especially in, or for, large quantities, and usually inferring proportions in a whole from proportions in a representative sample. (*Oxford Encyclopaedic Dictionary*).

Most surveys result in quantitative data, for example numbers of people who believed this or that, how many children of what age do which sports, levels of family income, etc. However, not all quantitative data originate from surveys. For example, content analysis is a specific method of examining records of all kinds (e.g. radio and TV programmes, films, etc.), documents or publications. A checklist is made to count how frequently certain ideas, words, phrases, images or scenes appear in order to be able to draw some conclusions from the frequency of their appearance (e.g. the perception of bullying in the media).

One of the primary purposes of doing research is to describe the data and to discover relationships among events in order to describe, explain, predict and possibly control their occurrence. Statistical methods are a valuable tool to enable you to present and describe the data and, if necessary, to discover and quantify relationships. And you do not even have to be a mathematician to use these techniques, as user-friendly computer packages (such as Microsoft Excel and Statistical Package for the Social Sciences, SPSS) will do all the presentation and calculations for you. However, you must be able to understand the relevance and function of the various displays and tests in relationship to your own sets of data and the kind of analysis required.

The most straightforward process is to describe the data in the form of tables, graphs and diagrams. For this, a spreadsheet program such as Excel is quite sufficient. This will order and display the data in a compact form so that you can make comparisons, detect trends and measure amounts and combinations of amounts. If you do not know how to use a spreadsheet for this, attend a course of instruction or find a handbook to guide you.

If you need to do more sophisticated analysis, then there is a wide range of statistical techniques that you can employ using SPSS. Many tests bear exotic names like Kruskal's gamma, Kendall's coefficient of concordance, Guttman's lambda, and chi-square (χ^2) and Kolmogorov-Smirnov tests. However, don't be put off by these, as you will only be required to use the most common ones and there are simple rules as to when and how they should be applied. Even so, it is always advisable to consult somebody with specialist statistical knowledge in order to check that you will be doing the right thing before you start. Also, attend a course, usually made available to you by your college or university, in the use of SPSS or any other program that is available to you.

FIGURE 19.2 Consult somebody with statistical knowledge.

Another factor to be taken into account when selecting suitable statistical tests, is the number of cases about which you have data. Generally, statistical tests are more reliable the greater the number of cases. Usually, more than about 30 cases are required to make any sense of the analysis, though some tests are designed to work with less.

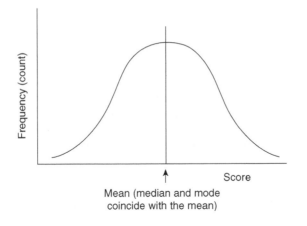

FIGURE 19.3   A Gaussian curve.

Always consult the instructions on this issue for the particular tests you want to use. It may affect your choice.

There is not space (or need) in this book to explain in detail the range of tests and their uses. There are many books that specialize in just this. It will, however, help your understanding if I give a general description of statistics and the various branches of the discipline.

19.5   Parametric and non-parametric statistics

The two major classes of statistics are parametric and non-parametric statistics. You need to understand the meaning of a parameter in order to appreciate the difference between these two types. A parameter of a population (i.e. the things or people you are surveying) is a constant feature that it shares with other populations. The most common one is the 'bell' or 'Gaussian' curve of a normal frequency distribution.

This parameter reveals that most populations display a large number of more or less 'average' cases with extreme cases tailing off at each end. For example, most people are of about average height, with those who are extremely tall or small being in a distinct minority. The distribution of people's heights shown on a graph would take the form of the normal distribution curve, or Gaussian curve (Figure 19.3).

Although the shape of this curve varies from case to case (e.g. flatter or steeper, lop-sided to the left or right), this feature is so common among populations that statisticians take it as a constant – a basic parameter. Calculations of parametric statistics are based on this feature.

Not all data are parametric, i.e. populations sometimes do not behave in the form of a Gaussian curve. Data measured by nominal and ordinal methods will not be orga-nized in a curve form. Nominal data tend to be in the dichotomous form of either/or (e.g. this is a cow or a sheep or neither), while ordinal data can be displayed in the form of a set of steps (e.g. the first, second and third positions on a winners' podium). For those cases where this parameter is absent, non-parametric statistics may be applicable.

Non-parametric statistical tests have been devised to recognize the particular characteristics of non-curve data and to take into account these singular characteristics by specialized methods. In general, these types of test are less sensitive and powerful than parametric tests; they need larger samples in order to generate the same level of significance.

19.6 Statistical tests: parametric

The two classes of parametric statistical tests are descriptive and inferential.

Descriptive statistics

Descriptive statistics provide a method of quantifying the characteristics of the data, where their centre is, how broadly they spread and how one aspect of the data relates to another aspect of the same data. The 'centre of gravity' of the data, their point of central tendency, can be determined by finding the 'mode' or the 'median' and any one of several 'means'. These measures have their own characteristics and applications and should be chosen with regard to the data being analysed.

The measure of the dispersion (or spread) of the data, how flat or steep the Gaussian curve appears, is an indication of how many of the data closely resemble the mean. The flatter the curve, the greater is the amount of data that deviate from the mean, i.e. the fewer that are close to the average. The horizontal length of the curve also gives an indication of the spread of values and the extent of the extremes represented in the data, while the occurrence of a non-symmetrical curve indicates a skewness in the data values.

Apart from examining the qualities of a single set of data, the main purpose of statistical analysis is to identify and quantify relationships between variables. This is the type of research called correlation research. But remember, the mere discovery and measurement of correlations is not sufficient on its own to provide research answers. It is the interpretation of these discoveries that provides the valuable knowledge that will give answers to your research question.

The technical term for the measure of correlation is the coefficient of correlation. There are many types of these, the Pearson r being the most common. It is possible to measure the correlation between more than two variables if you use the appropriate tests. However, be wary about assuming that, because a strong statistical correlation between variables can be demonstrated, there is necessarily a causal bond between the variables. It may be purely chance or the influence of other factors that, say, leads to areas of high-density development in cities having high crime rates. You must carefully question the assumptions on which such a causal assertion is made, and review the facts to examine if such causality is verifiable in other ways.

Inferential statistics

Inferential statistical tests go beyond describing the characteristics of data and the examination of correlations between variables. As the name implies, they are used to produce predictions through inference, based on the data analysed. This entails making predictions about the qualities of a total population on the basis of the qualities of a sample. This exercise is commonly carried out in quality control in production processes, where a sample of the production is tested in order to estimate the qualities of the total production. Three parameters (qualities) are commonly estimated: central tendency (proportion of products which are close to the norm, for example within permitted size tolerance); variability (e.g. range of sizes occurring) and probability (e.g. the proportion of acceptable products produced).

As with all predictions made from samples, the representative quality of the sample is crucial to accuracy, i.e. the sample must be as typical as possible of the whole.

19.7   Statistical tests: non-parametric

Statistical tests built around discovering the means, standard deviations, etc. of the typical characteristics of a Gaussian curve are clearly inappropriate for analysing non-parametric data. Hence, non-parametric data cannot be statistically tested in the above ways.

There are tests that can be used to compare the qualities of two or more groups or samples, to analyse the rankings made by different judges, or to compare the data from observed and theoretical sources. Detailed information about which tests to use for particular data sets can be obtained from specialized texts on statistics and your own expert statistical adviser. It is perhaps a good place to warn you that computer statistical packages (e.g. SPSS) will not distinguish between different types of parametric and non-parametric data.

In order to avoid producing reams of impressive looking, but meaningless analytical output, it is up to you to ensure that the tests are appropriate for the type of data you have.

19.8   Discussion of results

Both spreadsheets and statistical programs will produce very attractive results in the form of charts, graphs and tables that you can integrate into your dissertation to back up your argument. The important issue is that you have carried out the appropriate analysis related to what you want to demonstrate or test. Explain what data you have collected, perhaps supplying a sample to show their form (e.g. a questionnaire return), give the reasons for doing the particular tests for each section of the investigation, and then present the results of the tests.

Graphs, tables and other forms of presentation always need to be explained. Do not believe that the reader knows how to read them and that they are self-explanatory in relation to your argument. Spell out in words the main features of the results and

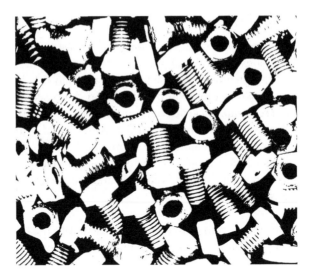

FIGURE 19.4   The sample must be as typical as possible of the whole.

explain how these relate to the parts of the objectives that you are addressing. Now draw conclusions. What implications do the results have? Are they conclusive or is there room for doubt? Mention the limitations that might affect the strength of the result, for example limited number of responses, possible bias or time constraints. Each conclusion will only form a small part of the overall argument, so you need to fit everything together like constructing a jigsaw puzzle. The full picture should clearly emerge at the end. It is best to devote one section or chapter to each of the objectives. Leave it to the final chapter to draw all the threads together in order to answer the main issue of the dissertation.

Computer programs provide you with enormous choice when it comes to presenting graphs and charts. It is best to experiment to see which kind of presentation is the clearest. Consider whether you will be printing in monochrome or colour, as different coloured graph lines will lose their distinctiveness when reduced to shades of grey. It is also a good idea to set up a style that you maintain throughout the dissertation.

19.9   What should I do now?

If you are not experienced in doing quantitative analysis and see the need to do it to analyse your findings, now is the time to learn. You will definitely need to go on a short course in using the relevant computer programs, such as spreadsheets and statistics. SPSS is the most commonly used statistical package, and has become very user friendly, so you should experience few practical problems. Find out from your computer centre or library when the course takes place, and book yourself in.

One of your first jobs will be to enter all the data onto a spreadsheet, for example all the answers to all the questions from the questionnaires. Before you embark on any actual analysis, first take time to examine the nature of your data and what kind of analysis you want to subject them to. Will you be measuring them, making comparisons, examining

FIGURE 19.5   Leave yourself plenty of time to discuss the results.

relationships, etc? Are the data parametric or non-parametric? If you are doing some statistical tests, you will have to ensure that you select the right ones. This will require some reading about statistical tests and possibly getting some advice from staff. Do not become too ambitious: keep it simple and within your level of understanding. It is quite easy to get carried away with doing grandiloquent sounding tests as they are carried out just as fast as any other; but could you really explain what they are about?

Leave yourself plenty of time to discuss the results in writing and to work on the conclusions. This is, of course, the whole point of gathering all the data in the first place and making the effort to test them. One of the commonest faults in undergraduate dissertations is that the impressive displays of graphs, tables, charts, etc. are left for the reader to interpret. So relate the conclusions directly back to the questions asked or problems posed at the beginning of the dissertation, and check that your overall argument is still sound. Then you will have achieved the purpose of all your research work.

19.10   References to more information

The following books contain an overview of quantitative analysis and introductory statistics.

Briggs, A.R.J. and Coleman, M., eds (2007) *Research Methods in Educational Leadership and Management*, 2nd edn. London: Sage.

See Chapter 19.

Cohen, L., Manion, L. and Morrison, K. (2007) *Research Methods in Education*, 6th edn. Abingdon: Routledge.

See Chapter 24.

Diamond, I. and Jeffries, J. (2000) *Beginning Statistics: An Introduction for Social Scientists*. London: Sage.

This book emphasizes description, examples, graphs and displays rather than statistical formula. A good guide to understanding the basic ideas of statistics.

Denscombe, M. (2003) *The Good Research Guide for Small-Scale Social Research Projects*. Buckingham: Open University Press.

See Chapter 10.

Huff, D. (2003) *How to Lie With Statistics*. London: W.W. Norton.

Preece, R. (1994) *Starting Research: An Introduction to Academic Research and Dissertation Writing*. London: Pinter.

See Chapter 7.

Robson, C. (2002) *Real World Research: A Resource for Social Scientists and Practitioner-Researchers*, 2nd edn. Oxford: Blackwell.

See Chapter 13.

Rumsey, D. (2000) *Statistics for Dummies*. Hoboken: Wiley.

As the title of the book implies, this is a good entry-level book on statistics.

Wright, D.B. (2002) *First Steps in Statistics*. London: Sage.

These books introduce one of the widely used statistical packages, SPSS.

Kerr, A., Hall, H. and Kozub, S. (2002) *Doing Statistics with SPSS*. London: Sage.

Kinnear, P.R. and Gray, C.D. (2006) *SPSS14 Made Simple*. Hove: Psychology Press.

This has a good introductory chapter on statistics. This develops into discussing the appropriate statistical method to use with SPSS, taking you through the program in detailed steps while explaining how to interpret the results.

Pallant, J. (2005) *SPSS Survival Manual: a step by step guide to data analysis using SPSS version 12*, 2nd edn. Maidenhead: Open University Press.

Although this book is based on an earlier version of SPSS, the differences between the programs are not too extensive. Again this book takes you through the process step-by-step with good explanation on the appropriate test to use and how to actually write the interpretation of results for your results chapter. Pallant's book is ring bound, thus useful for keeping the book open while working on the computer.

The list could go on for pages with ever increasing abstruseness. You could also have a browse through what is available on your library shelves to see if there are some simple guides there.

Byrne, D. (2002) *Interpreting Quantitative Data*. London: Sage.

Siegel, S. and Castellan, N.J. (1988) *Nonparametric Statistics for the Behavioural Sciences*. New York: McGraw-Hill.

Wasserman, L. (2005) *All of Nonparametric Statistics: A Concise Course in Nonparametric Statistical Inference*. New York: Springer-Verlag.

And for a good guide on how to interpret official statistics, look at Chapter 15 by Don Slater in the following book:

Searle, C., ed (2004) *Researching Society and Culture*. Thousand Oaks: Sage.

20 How Do I Analyse Qualitative Data?

20.1 Qualitative research

Doing research is not always a tidy process where every step is completed before moving on to the next. In fact, especially if you are doing it for the first time, you often need to go back and reconsider previous decisions, or adjust and elaborate on work as you gain more knowledge and acquire more skills. But there are also types of research in which there is an essential reciprocal process of data collection and data analysis.

Qualitative research is the main one of these. This does not involve counting and dealing with numbers but is based more on information expressed in words – descriptions, accounts, opinions, feelings, etc. This approach is common whenever people are the focus of the study, particularly small groups or individuals, but can also concentrate on more general beliefs or customs. Frequently, it is not possible to determine precisely what data should be collected as the situation or process is not sufficiently understood. Periodic analysis of collected data provides direction to further data collection. Adjustments to what is further looked at, what questions are asked and what actions are carried out are based on what has already been seen, answered and done. This emphasis on reiteration and interpretation is the hallmark of qualitative research.

20.2 Qualitative data collection and analysis

The essential difference between quantitative analysis and qualitative analysis is that with the former, you need to have completed your data collection before you can start analysis, while with the latter, analysis is carried out concurrently with data collection. With qualitative studies, there is a constant interplay between collection and analysis that produces a gradual growth of understanding. You collect information, review it, collect more data based on what you have discovered, then analyse again what you have found. This is quite a demanding and difficult process, and is prone to uncertainties and doubts. At the level of an undergraduate dissertation, you will have to be careful not to be too ambitious, as the restricted time you have does not allow for lengthy delving and pondering. Keep the study focused and limited in scope so that you can complete the process. The important criteria for the examiner will be whether you have correctly used the methods and whether your conclusions are based on evidence found in the data collected.

Bromley (1986: 26) provides a list of 10 steps in the process of qualitative research, summarized as follows:

- Clearly state the research issues or questions.
- Collect background information to help understand the relevant context, concepts and theories.
- Suggest several interpretations or answers to the research problems or questions based on this information.
- Use these to direct your search for evidence that might support or contradict these. Change the interpretations or answers if necessary.
- Continue looking for relevant evidence. Eliminate interpretations or answers that are contradicted, leaving, hopefully, one or more that are supported by the evidence.
- 'Cross-examine' the quality and sources of the evidence to ensure accuracy and consistency.
- Carefully check the logic and validity of the arguments leading to your conclusions.
- Select the strongest case in the event of more than one possible conclusion.
- If appropriate, suggest a plan of action in the light of this.
- Prepare your report as an account of your research; in this case present your dissertation.

According to Robson, 'the central requirement in qualitative analysis is clear thinking on the part of the analyst' (1993: 374), where the analyst is put to the test as much as the data! Although it has been the aim of many researchers to make qualitative analysis as systematic and as 'scientific' as possible, there is still an element of 'art' in dealing with qualitative data. However, in order to convince others of your conclusions, there must be a good argument to support them. A good argument requires high-quality evidence and sound logic. In fact, you will be acting rather like a lawyer presenting a case, using a quasi-judicial approach such as used in an enquiry into a disaster or scandal.

Qualitative data, represented in words, pictures and even sounds, cannot be analysed by mathematical means such as statistics. So how is it possible to organize all these data and be able to come to some conclusions about what they reveal? Unlike the well-established statistical methods of analysing quantitative data, qualitative data analysis is still in its early stages. The certainties of mathematical formulae and determinable levels of probability are not applicable to the 'soft' nature of qualitative data, which are inextricably bound up with human feelings, attitudes and judgements. Also, unlike the large amounts of data that are often collected for quantitative analysis which can readily be managed with the available standard statistical procedures conveniently incorporated in computer packages, there are no such standard procedures for codifying and analysing qualitative data.

However, there are some essential activities that are necessary in all qualitative data analysis. Miles and Huberman (1994: 10–12) suggested that there are three concurrent flows of action:

- Data reduction
- Data display
- Conclusion drawing/verification.

The activity of data display is important. The awkward mass of information that you will normally collect to provide the basis for analysis cannot be easily understood when presented as extended text, even when coded, clustered, summarized, etc. Information in text is dispersed, sequential rather than concurrent, bulky and difficult to structure. Our minds are not good at processing large amounts of information, preferring to simplify complex information into patterns and easily understood configurations. Consequently, if you use suitable methods to display the data in the form of matrices, graphs, charts and networks, you not only reduce and order the data, but also can analyse it.

20.3   Preliminary analysis during data collection

When you conduct field research it is important that you keep a critical attitude to the type and amount of data being collected, and the assumptions and thoughts that brought you to this stage. It is always easier to structure the information while the details are fresh in the mind, to identify gaps, to allow new ideas and hypotheses to develop, and to challenge your assumptions and biases. Raw field notes, often scribbled and full of abbreviations, and tapes of interviews or events need to be processed in order to make them useful. Much information will be lost if this task is left for long.

The process of data reduction and analysis should be a sequential and continuous procedure, simple in the beginning stages of the data collection, and becoming more complex as the project progresses. To begin with, one-page summaries can be made of the results of contacts, for example phone conversations, visits. A standardized set of headings will prompt the ordering of the information: contact details, main issues, summary of information acquired, interesting issues raised, new questions resulting from these. Similar one-page forms can be used to summarize the contents of documents.

20.4   Typologies and taxonomies

As the data accumulate, a valuable step is to organize the shapeless mass of data by building typologies and taxonomies. These are technical words for the nominal level of measurement (remember Chapter 13), i.e. ordering by type or properties, thereby forming subgroups within the general category.

Even the simplest classification can help to organize seemingly shapeless information and to identify differences in, say, behaviour or types of people. For example, children's behaviour in the playground could be divided into 'joiners' and 'loners', or people in the shopping centre into 'serious shoppers', 'window shoppers', 'passers through', 'loiterers', etc. This can help you to organize amorphous material and to identify patterns in the data. Then, noting the differences in terms of behaviour patterns between these categories can help you to generate the kinds of analysis that will form the basis for the development of explanations and conclusions.

This exercise in classification is the start of the development of a coding system, which is an important aspect of forming typologies. Codes are labels or tags used to allocate units of meaning to the collected data. Coding helps you to organize your piles of data (in the form of notes, observations, transcripts, documents, etc.) and to provide a first step in conceptualization, and helps to prevent 'data overload' resulting from mountains of unprocessed data in the form of ambiguous words.

Codes can be used to label different aspects of the subjects of study. Lofland (1971: 14–15), for example, devised six classes on which you could devise a coding scheme for 'social phenomena':

- Acts
- Activities
- Meanings
- Participation
- Relationships
- Settings.

The process of coding is analytical, and requires you to review, select, interpret and summarize the information without distorting it. Normally, you should compile a set of codes before doing the fieldwork, based on your background study, and then refine it during the data collection.

There are two essentially different types of coding, one that you can use for the retrieval of text sequences, the other devised for theory generation. The former refers to the process of cutting out and pasting sections of text from transcripts or notes under various headings. The latter is a more open coding system used as an index for your interpretive ideas – reflective notes or memos, rather than merely bits of text.

Several computer programs used for analysing qualitative data (such as Ethnograph and NUDIST) also have facilities for filing and retrieving coded information. They allow

FIGURE 20.1   Noting the differences in terms of behaviour patterns.

codes to be attached to the numbered lines of notes or transcripts of interviews, and for the source of the information/opinion to be noted. This enables a rapid retrieval of selected information from the mass of material collected. However, it does take quite some time to master the techniques involved, so take advice before contemplating the use of these programs.

20.5   Pattern coding, memoing and interim summary

The next stage of analysis requires you to begin to look for patterns and themes, and explanations of why and how these occur. This requires a method of pulling together the coded information into more compact and meaningful groupings. Pattern coding can do this by reducing the data into smaller analytical units such as themes, causes/explanations, relationships among people and emerging concepts, to allow you to develop a more integrated understanding of the situation studied, and to test the initial explanations or answers to the research issues or questions. This will generally help to focus later field-work and lay the foundations for cross-case analysis in multicase studies by identifying common themes and processes.

Miles and Huberman (1994: 70–1) describe three successive ways that pattern codes may be used:

• The newly developed codes are provisionally added to the existing list of codes and checked out in the next set of field notes to see whether they fit.

- Next, the most promising codes are written up in a memo (described below) to clarify and explain the concept so that it can be related to other data and cases.
- Finally, the new pattern codes are tested out in the next round of data collection.

Actually, you will find that generating pattern codes is surprisingly easy, as it is the way by which we habitually process information. However, it is important not to cling uncritically onto initially developed patterns, but to test and develop, and if necessary, reject them as your understanding of the data develops, and as new waves of data are produced.

Compiling memos is a good way to explore links between data and to record and develop intuitions and ideas. You can do this at any time – but it is best done when the idea is fresh! Remember that memos are written for yourself, so the length and style are not important, but it is necessary to label a memo so that it can be easily sorted and retrieved. You should continue the activity of memoing throughout the research project. You will find that the ideas become more stable with time until 'saturation' point, i.e. the point where you are satisfied with your understanding and explanation of the data, is achieved.

It is a very good idea, at probably about one-third way through the data collection, to take stock and seek to reassure yourself and your supervisors by checking:

- The quantity and quality of what you have found out so far
- Your confidence in the reliability of the data
- The presence and nature of any gaps or puzzles that have been revealed
- What still needs to be collected in relation to your time available.

This exercise should result in the production of an interim summary, a provisional report a few pages long. This report will be the first time that everything you know about a case will be summarized, and presents the first opportunity to make cross-case analyses in multicase studies and to review emergent explanatory variables.

Remember however, that the nature of the summary is provisional. Though it is perhaps sketchy and incomplete, it should be seen as a useful tool for you to reflect on the work done, for discussion with your colleagues and supervisors, and for indicating any changes that might be needed in the coding and in the subsequent data collection work. In order to check on the amount of data collected about each research question, you will find it useful to compile a data accounting sheet. This is a table that sets out the research questions and the amount of data collected from the different informants, settings, situations, etc. With this you will easily be able to identify any shortcomings.

20.6 Main analysis during and after data collection

Traditional text-based reports tend to be lengthy and cumbersome when presenting, analysing, interpreting and communicating the findings of a qualitative research project. Not only do they have to present the evidence and arguments sequentially, they also tend to be bulky and difficult to grasp quickly because information is dispersed over many pages.

This presents a problem for you, the writer, as well as for the final reader, who rarely has time to browse backwards and forwards through masses of text to gain full information. Graphical methods of data display and analysis can largely overcome these problems and are useful for exploring and describing as well as explaining and predicting phenomena. They can be used equally effectively for one case and cross-case analysis.

Graphical displays fall into two categories: matrices and networks.

Matrices or tables

The two-dimensional arrangement of rows and columns can summarize a substantial amount of information. You can easily produce these informally in a freehand fashion to explore aspects of the data, to any size. You can also use computer programs in the form of databases and spreadsheets

FIGURE 20.2 Traditional text-based reports tend to be lengthy and cumbersome.

to help in their production. You can use matrices to record variables such as time, levels of measurement, roles, clusters, outcomes and effects. If you want to get really sophisticated, latest developments allow you to formulate three-dimensional matrices.

Networks

A network is made up of blocks (nodes) connected by links. You can produce these maps and charts in a wide variety of formats, each with the capability of displaying different types of data:

- Flowcharts are useful for studying processes or procedures. Not only helpful for explanation, their development is a good device for creating understanding.
- Organization charts display relationships between variables and their nature, for example formal and informal hierarchies.
- Causal networks are used to examine and display the causal relationships between important independent and dependent variables, causes and effects.

These methods of displaying and analysing qualitative data are particularly useful when you compare the results of several case studies, as they permit a certain standardization of presentation, allowing comparisons to be made more easily across the cases.

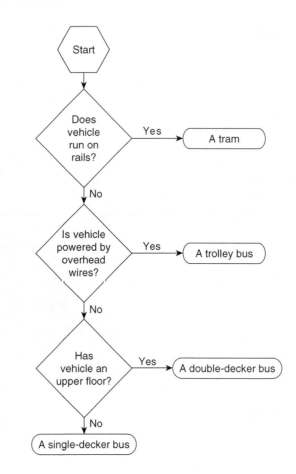

FIGURE 20.3   Example of a network: a flowchart sorting out public transport vehicles.

You can display the information in the form of text, codes, abbreviated notes, symbols, quotations or any other form that helps to communicate compactly. The detail and sophistication of the display can vary depending on its function and on the amount of information available. Displays are useful at any stage in the research process.

Ordering information in displays

The different types of display can be described by the way that information is ordered in them.

Time ordered displays   These record a sequence of events in relation to their chronology. A simple example of this is a project programme giving names, times and locations for tasks of different kinds. The scale and precision of timing can be suited to the subject. Events can be of various types, for example tasks, critical events, experiences, stages in a programme, activities, decisions, etc.

Some examples of types of time ordered displays are:

- Events lists or networks – showing a sequence of events, perhaps highlighting the critical ones, and perhaps including times and dates.
- Activity records – showing the sequential steps required to accomplish a task.
- Decision models – commonly used to analyse a course of action employing a matrix with yes/no routes from each decision taken.

Conceptually ordered displays　These concentrate on variables in the form of abstract concepts related to a theory and the relationships between these. Examples of such variables are motives, attitudes, expertise, barriers, coping strategies, etc. They can be shown as matrices or networks to illustrate taxonomies, content analysis, cognitive structures, relationships of cause and effect or influence.

Here is a selection of different types:

- Conceptually or thematically clustered matrix – helps to summarize the mass of data about numerous research questions by combining groups of questions that are connected, either from a theoretical point of view, or as a result of groupings that can be detected in the data.
- Taxonomy tree diagram – useful to break down concepts into their constituent parts or elements.
- Cognitive map – a descriptive diagrammatic plotting of a person's way of thinking about an issue, useful to understand somebody's way of thinking or to compare that of several people.
- Effects matrix – plots the observed effects of an action or intervention, a necessary precursor to explaining or predicting effects.
- Decision tree modelling – helps to make clear a sequence of decisions, by setting up a network of sequential yes/no response routes.
- Causal models – used in theory building to provide a testable set of propositions about a complete network of variables with causal and other relationships between them, based on a multicase situation. A preliminary stage in the development of a causal model is to develop causal chains, linear cause/effect lines.

Role ordered displays　These show people's roles and their relationships in formal and informal organizations or groups. A role defines a person's standing and position by assessing their behaviour and expectations within the group or organization. These may be conventionally recognized positions, for example judge, mother, machine operator; or more abstract and situation dependent, for example motivator, objector. People in different roles tend to see situations from different perspectives: a strike in a factory will be viewed very differently by the management and the workforce. A role ordered matrix will help to systematically display these differences or can be used to investigate whether people in the same roles are unified in their views.

Partially ordered displays　These are useful in analysing 'messy' situations without trying to impose too much internal order on them. For example a context chart can be designed

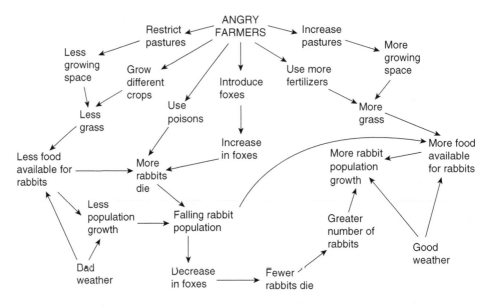

FIGURE 20.4   Example of a network: multiple-cause diagram of a rabbit control system.

to show, in the form of a network, the influences and pressures that bear on an individual from surrounding organizations and persons when making a decision to act. This will help to understand why a particular action was taken.

Case ordered displays   These show the data of cases arranged in some kind of order according to an important variable in the study. This allows you to compare cases and note their different features according to where they appear in the order.

If you are comparing several case studies, you can combine the above displays to make 'meta' displays that amalgamate and contrast the data from each case. For example, a case ordered meta-matrix does this by simply arranging case matrices next to each other in the chosen order to enable you to simply compare the data across the meta-matrix. The meta-matrix can initially be quite large if there are a number of cases. A function of the analysis will be to summarize the data in a smaller matrix, giving a summary of the significant issues discovered. Following this a contrast table can also be devised to display and compare how one or two variables perform in cases as ordered in the meta-matrix.

20.7   What should I do now?

After reading the above information about qualitative data collection and analysis, how do you think the different techniques could be used in your dissertation? If you are focusing your work on people in society, especially at the level of the individual or small groups, or on people's customs, beliefs, etc. you will not be able to do your research by analysing numbers, you will have to deal with lots of information in the form of written material. As you will probably have gathered, the process can be quite complicated and difficult to do for the first time. It is a great help if you can use a previous research programme as a model, perhaps to test out its methods and findings in a different context. For example, if you are interested in examining the factors that influence work motivation and productivity in an estate agent's office, perhaps a professional research project has already been done on these in a different office setting. This would provide useful guidelines on the main variables to examine, and practical techniques of data collection, display and analysis.

I suggest that you do the following things to get you on your way. Note how you will be building up an argument for doing your research the way you propose.

- Think carefully about your dissertation topic and ask yourself: what is the nature of what you are going to investigate? Are the variables readily recognizable and easily measurable, and are there more than 20 or 30 cases in your study? If so, a quantitative approach is more suitable. Are the variables open to interpretation, difficult to measure, and are there only a few cases to examine? If yes, then you have to use qualitative research methods to examine these. Note that there may be aspects of your dissertation topic that fall into each of these categories. No problem: you will just have to use whichever type of method is appropriate for each of the aspects.
- If you think that a qualitative approach is appropriate for all or some of your research, examine what are the main factors at play. How are they described, for example jealousy, belief, loyalty, tradition?
- From your background reading, look for writings that specifically describe and explain investigations dealing with these factors, particularly those that were in your area of study. Examine these to see if there are methods used that you could adapt for your own work to get the answers that you are aiming at.
- Set up a plan of work to describe the sequence of data gathering and analysis, the types of activities you will undertake at each step, together with timing. This will help to ensure that you will not bite off more than you can chew. Obviously, there will be some uncertainties: point these out. If there are too many, the project could get horribly out of hand, so alter the setting, eliminate problem areas, find other more familiar ways, or even adjust the research questions to make the work more practicable and less chancy.

If you can, it is really worth talking to your supervisor about your plan to discuss the practical and skill issues. Obviously, the clearer you can draw it up, the more use it will be. The main questions to ask are:

- Is the plan practically possible with your time, skills and access to your objects of study?
- Will it produce the answers to the questions posed by your project?
- Will the project fulfil the requirements of the dissertation assignment?

If the answers are all 'Yes' to the above questions, then things are looking good. If you managed to get some feedback from your supervisor, make sure that you understood what he/she advised, and reflect how this advice might alter your work. Check again against the questions after you have made any alterations.

20.8   References to more information

As you would expect with this big and complex subject, there are a myriad of books dedicated to explaining all aspects. In the list below, I have tried to explain a bit about each individual book and how it may be of use to you. I have ordered them in what I think is going from simplest to most sophisticated.

Briggs, A.R.J. and Coleman, M., eds (2007) *Research Methods in Educational Leadership and Management*, 2nd edn. London: Sage.

See Chapter 20.

Denscombe, M. (2003) *The Good Research Guide for Small-Scale Social Research Projects*. Buckingham: Open University Press.

See Chapter 11.

Flick, U. (2006) *An Introduction to Qualitative Research*, 3rd revised edn. London: Sage.

Parts 3 and 4 of the book is dedicated to analysing verbal and visual data, with practical advice on documentation, coding, interpretation and analysis. Be selective in picking out what is relevant to you, as a lot of it will not be.

Robson, C. (2002) *Real World Research: A Resource for Social Scientists and Practitioner-Researchers*, 2nd edn. Oxford: Blackwell.

See Chapter 14.

Seale, C., ed. (2004) *Researching Society and Culture*, 2nd edn. Thousand Oaks: Sage.

This edited book has chapters by various authors, each on one aspect of research. Specifically look at the chapters on qualitative analysis, choosing whatever is appropriate for your study.

For a really comprehensive though incredibly dense and rather technical guide to qualitative data analysis, refer to:

Miles, M.B. and Huberman, A.M. (1994*) Qualitative Data Analysis: An Expanded Sourcebook*, 2nd revised edn. Thousand Oaks: Sage.

This has a lot of examples of displays that help to explain how they work, but is technically sophisticated so you might find it difficult to understand the terminology in the examples.

And a few more books if you don't find what you want in the above. Your library catalogue will list many more. Try a search using key words, such as 'data analysis', with 'management', 'education' or whatever your particular subject is, to see if there are specific books dedicated to your particular interest.

Coffey, A. and Atkinson, P. (1996) *Making Sense of Qualitative Data: Complementary Research Strategies*. London: Sage.

Holliday, A. (2006) *Doing and Writing Qualitative Research*. London: Sage.

A general guide to writing qualitative research aimed at students of sociology, applied linguistics, management and education.

Schwandt, T. (2007) *The Sage Dictionary of Qualitative Inquiry*, 3rd edn. London: Sage.

To help you understand all the technical jargon.

Silverman, D. (2006*) Interpreting Qualitative Data: Methods for Analysing Talk, Text and Interaction*, 3rd edn. London: Sage.

21 How Do I Write a Discussion Chapter?

21.1   A word of warning

You would have already provided your results and some interpretation but as yet you would not have actually discussed the implications of the data, instead saving it for this chapter. The chapter is sometime referred to as the evaluation chapter as it evaluates the data in light of your aim and objectives.

From the outset of your research, you would have had thoughts about what to include in this chapter, issues that have arisen which will inform your work. The important thing to keep in mind is that anything you discuss in this chapter needs to be supported with evidence from the information you have previously collected and presented opposed to issues that may be implied. As such, your dissertation is making an argument founded on the information you provide and not conjecture (a guess made about the appearance of a situation without proof).

The discussion chapter can make or break the dissertation. If you have invested time and effort into establishing the focus and collecting your data, a rushed discussion can lead the reader to consider that the whole dissertation is slightly disjointed or has an unfinished feel. The key to success in this chapter is to ensure that you allow sufficient time to do justice to the time and effort you have previously invested.

Indeed, the trouble with this part of the dissertation is that it inevitably comes near the end of your project, when you are probably tired from all the work you have already done, when your time is running out, when you have pressures from other commitments such as revision and exams – let alone all the other things you want to get in before your undergraduate days are over.

To compound it all, the coming to conclusions is a quite demanding and creative process that requires a lot of clear thinking, perception and meticulous care. All the previous work will be devalued if you do not sufficiently draw out the implications of your analysis and capitalize on the insights that it affords. You cannot rely on the reader to make inferences from your results. It really is up to you to vividly explain how the results of your analysis provide evidence for new insight into your chosen subject, and to give answers to the particular research questions that you posed at the beginning of the dissertation. The main point I want to make is that you should programme some time for this process, and not underestimate its importance.

As long as you have kept to the advice in this book, you should find this the easiest chapter to write. You would have completed all of your reading for the literature review, completed your data collection and analysis and by now have a good insight into the focus of your dissertation, consequently there is little to do except review what you have written so far and consider it carefully.

This chapter should not include data from the research but it should comment on what the data actually means to the focus of your work. Furthermore, although you can use literature in this chapter, using new sources that are not cited in your literature review will cause the reader to question why such a key source was not included in the first instance.

21.2   Structure of the chapter

The discussion chapter can be written adhering to the subheadings listed below. The subsequent points indicate areas that could be included within each subheading.

Introduction

As with the previous chapters, you should indicate to the reader how your chapter will unfold, detailing the structure of the chapter and providing a rationale for this. You will need to relate this to your overall dissertation and the focus to provide some sort of context for the chapter, so for example, you would explain how you will start by examining your research to identify trends and how this relates to your objective, while also referring back to literature from your literature review, discussing whether there are any parallels. From this you may describe how, in light of your findings, this all relates back to practice, examining the impact of your work on the research participants and on a larger scale. A discussion of the methodology you used and lessons learnt from this demonstrate a reflective approach to your work. It would also highlight issues for others interested in conducting similar research. You may then direct the reader to a series of recommendations based on your research before summarizing briefly your whole dissertation in the conclusion.

Impact of findings

Your objectives have been the scaffolding for your dissertation and as a result, you need to discuss these in turn in order to inform the reader of the impact of the findings. This will explain to the reader the extent to which you have been successful in achieving the ultimate aim you previously established. Even if you were unable to complete one of your objectives to a satisfactory standard, you could explain why this may have occurred and the lessons derived from this. This would demonstrate your ability to be reflective, a key aspect for any professional to see what they are doing right but also to learn from their mistakes. Your examiner will not fail you because of this but if anything, acknowledging areas for improvement will demonstrate your insight into the process.

An example of how you could present this is as follows:

Objective 1

- To assess the impact of sleep on concentration through a structured observation.
  - From the data analysis, it would appear that 70 per cent of Year 6 students who had at least 8 hours sleep each night, were able to maintain sustained concentration on a creative writing task for at least 10 minutes. Conversely, 80 per cent of students who had less than 8 hours had difficulty in sustaining concentration for the same duration. These results appear to support the findings by Walliman and Buckler (2006) [e.g.] who examined a larger sample of Year 9 students, although their findings measured concentration over engagement with mathematical tasks. Consequently, from the findings in this dissertation and through the work of previous researchers, students who average at least 8 hours of sleep appear to have sustained periods of concentration.

It must, however, be noted that there may well be numerous factors that affect concentration on a day-to-day basis, for example the state of health (e.g. if they have a cold) or sate of mind (e.g. if a student is worrying about a forthcoming dental appointment). As a future direction for research, a questionnaire could be used to measure such affective factors on concentration.

Each of the objectives could be addressed in a similar manner, before drawing these together in a discussion of how the objectives inform the aim. From this the aim can be discussed in a similar manner, in terms of exploring how well the research has informed this, which ultimately relates back to your initial research problem.

In summary this chapter covers the following areas:

- A review of the objectives in light of your findings
- A review of how the objectives inform the aim
- Have the objectives been accomplished? If not, why not?

Impact on practice

As has been mentioned several times, you have invested a considerable amount of time and effort into completing your dissertation. Will your dissertation just sit on your shelf once it has been completed, locked away from the world, or will your findings be put into practice? I often question whether this collective pool of stagnating information, sitting lonely and forgotten, could be used to radically shake up the education system for the better. Consequently, what is the impact of your research on the education system?

There are different layers of answering this, looking at the micro- and macroscopic impacts. The microscopic assesses how your research impacts on those who you have directly worked with: the research participants. If you have found that eight hours of sleep are beneficial for sustained concentration, will you keep this to yourself, or will you actually inform the students and their parents? If your research has discovered that a specific learning strategy works wonders, will you inform the other teachers or staff within the setting?

In this part of your discussion, discuss how realistically you could ensure that your work is utilized effectively, that your research is of importance and why it is significant for the research participants, parents, colleagues or indeed anyone who has come into contact with your research.

The other aspect to discuss is the macrosopic level, or how your research could impact on a wider scale. To this extent, you could comment on the impact of your research on a broader context than just the research participants, for example, at a local level, could your research inform a number of schools in a cluster group? Perhaps your research could inform organizations nationally, or internationally. For example perhaps your findings could be disseminated through a professional magazine or journal, or that you contribute to a conference.

Although this discussion may seem nauseatingly twee and somewhat removed from the reality of submitting your dissertation on time alongside other pressing concerns (perhaps finding employment after completing your degree, etc.) you should take a pride in your hard work. Indeed, Chapter 26 will discuss in greater detail how your work could be disseminated and you are left with time on your hands. As such, ideas that change the world need to come from somewhere ... and why shouldn't they be yours? Thus discussing the anticipated impact of your research on the educational, social, political or the economic context would demonstrate how you could take your research forwards.

Taking the example of sleep on concentration, educationally students may achieve higher grades, socially the impact could be greater tolerance for one another, economically less energy would be used on lighting, etc. yet politically could such legislation be bought in through a national policy? For fear that this discussion of sleep may be making you drowsy, let's move on to the next section ... Recommendations for Action.

In summary, this section deals with the impact on the microscopic and macroscopic and the discussion should cover:

Microscopic

- A review on how your research will impact on a micro scale
- Students/parents/colleagues
- Learners
- Is there evidence to substantiate impact? How?
- Better learners? Better behaviour?

Macroscopic

- A review of how your research will impact on a macro scale
- Anticipated impact
- Has a key policy been reviewed?
- Effect on the staff/setting/wider focus
- Your research in view of the wider context – local/national/international policy
- Political/economic and social context

Recommendations for action

Although in the previous section you have discussed the potential impact of your research, the recommendations you are making should discuss how your findings will specifically be put into action, predominantly on the microscopic level although may well include the macroscopic depending on your focus and your role as a professional.

This is a relatively brief section and could be presented as a series of bullet points outlining

- Short-term goals
- Medium-term goals
- Long-term goals

Within each of these, it would be worth noting the anticipated impact of your recommendations along with resourcing implications, whether these are human or material costs.

An example of a short-term goal could be:

- To prepare a leaflet for parents informing them of the importance of sleep on concentration for their child.
  - This would contain a summary of key findings from this dissertation with practical techniques on ensuring routine. Although some parents may not take any notice of the leaflet, it will provide information as there appears to be little advice for parents on this issue and the potential benefits. The leaflet would not take much time to produce and the only cost would be for copying.

In summary, this section should discuss:

- How findings might be translated into practice
- Short term/medium term/ long term goals
- Resourcing issues – human and material.

Impact of methodology

We live in the real world, and seldom does it run smoothly. In Chapter 1, the 'research roller coaster' was raised and if, when you get to writing this part of your dissertation can you put your hand on your heart and say that everything went according to plan, then I will buy you a coffee. The research process is an unfolding journey, the only destination being the submission deadline, as such how did the journey go, my intrepid explorer? What were the highs and lows of the journey, what would you avoid next time, did you take the appropriate route? What advice can you provide for fellow travellers?

This section thus needs to discuss these aspects highlighting what worked well and why and what didn't go according to plan and why. As mentioned above, you will not loose marks for being honest as this will demonstrate your ability to be reflective.

This section of the chapter should cover:

- A review of the research as a process
- A review of your methodology
- Were your methods appropriate?
- Were there any problems in collecting research? If so, what did you do?
- What surprised you?
- What would you do differently next time?

Impact on you

You have been central to the research, telling the story of your research journey according to your reality. Yet, how has this shaped you as a researcher but also as a professional? What do you know that you didn't before you set off? How has your research changed your perspective, whether as a result of your research aim, or as the result of some other associated aspect of your dissertation? Perhaps your research has led you into a new direction personally or professionally … if so, explain how and why this has happened and what you will do as a result.

Ultimately this section should provide:

- A review of your role as a researcher
- A discussion of how the research has contributed to your professional development,
- Comment on what you will do as a result of your research.

Conclusion

The conclusion provides a summary of your argument and the main themes from your dissertation as discussed so far in this chapter. It is basically a very brief overview, a couple of paragraphs long with the last sentence summarizing your argument and linking back to the title of your dissertation.

Sometimes the conclusion is written as a separate chapter after the discussion: sometimes it is included within the discussion chapter as suggested here. This will either make your dissertation five or six chapters long and you may want to check with your supervisor as to the preference at your institution.

21.3   What should I do now?

By this chapter, you should have a clear idea of where the dissertation journey has taken you and where you are heading. From the outset, everything you have worked on in your dissertation has led to this chapter and you may well have had ideas developing that you have wanted to discuss from the first word you wrote. There is nothing stopping you making notes on ideas as they come to you throughout the whole process as the dissertation is seldom conducted in the neat, specified manner outlined in your final draft.

You may want to develop a mind-map/concept-map of the different elements that need to be placed in this chapter, noting how one aspect links to another and why this link is important and logical. A number of these maps could be prepared for the different sections so that you can bring order to what may be a wealth of ideas you have buzzing around.

From these maps, you should be able to identify trends of associated ideas and you can start grouping these under different headings: these headings will help serve as a paragraph plan for your chapter. As with the different sections of the literature review, you may want to restructure these to see what order tells the best story before you finally write these up.

The key aspect within this chapter is to ensure that you have related your discussion back to your research aim and objectives as these are central to the whole process. If you mentioned in the earlier chapters that you were going to investigate one specific phenomenon, but in the discussion chapter get side-tracked discussing something partially related, the whole dissertation will appear disjointed. It is your responsibility to try and ensure that there are no surprises for the reader; that they do not end up reading a thriller with lots of twists and turns! Consequently you may want to get a willing friend to read your dissertation through, while you return the favour for them … and don't hold back on the criticism! Have an honest and open discussion as criticism can only improve on your dissertation.

21.4   References to more information

Your final chapter is unique. It is predominantly based on what you have researched, the information you have collected, also on the literature you have previously cited. Although this chapter has discussed the key issues to include in your discussion and conclusion, it would be worth reading other dissertations to see how other people have structured their chapters. Again, you may also want to refer to other books on the dissertation process to gain insight into different ways the discussion could be structured, for example:

Hart, C. (2004) *Doing Your Masters Dissertation (Essential Study Skills)*. London: Sage.

Mounsey, C. (2002) *Essays and Dissertations*. Oxford: Oxford University Press.

Redman, P. (2005) *Good Essay Writing*. London: Sage.

   See Chapter 8.

Roberts-Holmes, G. (2005) *Doing Your Early Years Research Project: A Step by Step Guide*. London: Paul Chapman.

   See Chapter 10.

Rudestam, K.E. and Newton, R.R. (2001) *Surviving your Dissertation: A Comprehensive Guide to Content and Process*, 2nd edn. Thousand Oaks: Sage.

   See Chapter 7.

SECTION 6

This last section contains a number of chapters to help you over the dissertation process and beyond. For simplicity, it could be referred to as the 'hints and tips' section, or the 'how do I cope?' section.

Chapter 22 raises a number of issues in establishing a good working rapport with your supervisor and how to ensure you get the best quality supervision.

Chapters 23–25 discuss the writing process. This may well be the first time you have written such a lengthy piece of work and these chapters explore how to make this a pleasurable experience opposed to an onerous chore.

The final chapter discusses what you can do with your dissertation once it has been completed. The general consensus may be to never see it again, however, with the time and effort invested into your work, it would be a pity if you didn't reap some potential rewards from it!

22 How Can I Work Effectively with My Supervisor?

22.1 Introduction

At the start of the dissertation phase you should be allocated a specific tutor or supervisor, responsible for ensuring you are guided through to completion. Unlike most other modules you may have taken, the dissertation is unique in that there are seldom any taught lectures: instead you have the benefit of working on a one-to-one basis. Although you may have attended tutorials before, it is often the final year, during the dissertation phase, that many students start to utilize the tutorial process to full effect. This chapter will therefore outline a range of issues to maximize your working relationship with your supervisor through discussing a number of issues that will positively impact on your dissertation.

22.2 What is the role of the supervisor?

Prior to starting the dissertation phase, you may well have completed a research methods module or equivalent that culminated in the submission of a proposal. The focus of the proposal would have been used to help allocate a tutor or supervisor to mentor your dissertation. Your supervisor will have some experience in your field although they may not necessarily be an expert in your refined area. Fundamentally however, is that your supervisor has had a range of research experience related to your area, and they are aware of what works, what could be improved and what to avoid.

The allocation of your supervisor depends partly on how supervision is arranged at your institution. Generally, a supervisor is provided with a set time allocation for supervising dissertation students, yet how this time is allocated can vary substantially. It would be great to think that your supervisor can solely devote their time to your work, yet in reality some supervisors may receive as little as four hours to supervise a student, other institutions may provide more time. The time that each supervisor is allocated is divided between different aspects of the dissertation process, for example tutorials, answering e-mails or phone calls, reading and commenting on draft work, marking and moderation of the final submission, also attendance at exam boards.

Furthermore, the working pattern adopted by supervisors may differ between institutions. Some supervisors may conduct individual tutorials at the student's discretion, others may only be available for a limited time period each week. Group tutorials may be used where students are working on a similar theme throughout the process, other supervisors may conduct a mix of group and individual tutorials. A further factor to note is that depending on your choice of topic, you may be allocated two supervisors, both of whom may have different working patterns.

Ultimately, whatever structure is in place at your institution the important aspect to note is that time for supervision is limited and this may be further impacted on by the way in which this time is allocated. Thankfully, most supervisors dedicate substantially more time to students than allocated, due to their professional pride in ensuring students present a quality dissertation that may well be read by other students and academics at the institution and beyond. The reason for highlighting the limitation of hours is to ensure how the supervisor's time can be maximized for successful completion.

Fundamentally, the role of the supervisor is to ensure that the student succeeds through guiding the student's proposal to a completed dissertation. Yet what is meant by 'guidance' and how is such support provided? How much help and guidance can you ask for during the process?

There is a continuum between absolutely no supervisory support and your supervisor writing the dissertation for you. Both are obviously extremes yet where is the balance between how much you contribute to your dissertation and how much your supervisor contributes? You could always ask … although the following should provide some useful pointers. What is important to note is that the dissertation is a two-way process: you provide the work which in turn is structured by the supervisor.

22.3   Professional limits of your supervisor

There are professional limits to the amount of support a supervisor can offer. You can expect your supervisor to be knowledgeable about the focus of your dissertation and the methodology employed to investigate the area. Furthermore, you can expect your supervisor to provide appropriate support and advice throughout the process, with direct and reliable comments about your work. A direct and reliable comment about your work may improve your overall grade, yet if your work is currently around the D minus range, such comments may progress your work to a C minus yet not an A plus.

The dissertation is a two-way process, thus you would be expected to act upon your supervisor's comments, addressing the points raised while being aware of what the impact of these are. One comment that most supervisors find difficult to deal with is 'What do I need to do to get an A grade for my dissertation?' This question undermines the professional relationship between you and your supervisor. It also implies that you are unsure of your own abilities and that you have not utilized advice from your previous assignments.

A further limit of your supervisor is that of their time: in an ideal world, they would be there to support you continually throughout the process, answering your requests as they arise. Unfortunately, with many competing demands, supervisors may not be there as and when you want them. As such, it is necessary to ensure that you are aware of when they are available and the best way to contact them, also whether they have any leave or forthcoming absence.

22.4 Making use of a critical friend

Your supervisor is there to provide guidance on the academic content of your work, your focus and methodology opposed to being a proofreader in correcting spellings, grammatical and typographical errors. As such, draft work submitted to your supervisor should be beyond that of etched notes. This is where use of a 'critical friend' would be of immense benefit. Such a friend could be a peer on the same course as you: through reading each others work and providing critical comment on style, referencing, spelling, etc. you would both benefit from sharing ideas and writing styles.

22.5 Issues and resolutions with your supervisor

There may well be times when things do not appear to be going too well with your supervisor for a number of reasons. Most problems are easily resolved and are generally due to miscommunication between one or both parties. It must be noted that the relationship between a supervisor and student is somewhat different to that normally experienced on modules. For example, on some modules, you may be taught by one or more tutors in a large group size, where direct lectures are the predominant learning experience. This can make such modules impersonal, yet for the dissertation phase, you are working generally on a one-to-one basis. No matter how well you know your supervisor, or how approachable and open they may appear, the issue of power balance can be seen as a hindrance: your supervisor already has their degree and most likely a higher degree. Furthermore, they would have had established practical experience within an educational setting. Consequently, it can sometimes feel difficult not to accept every piece of advice unquestioningly let alone query the supervision process. However, this is your dissertation and you need to ensure you can get the best quality service as possible, especially when there is a problem.

Problems do occur. Listed below are some common issues that may arise with suggestions as to how to negate these. Although not an exhaustive list for every eventuality, the issues discussed should help provide you with some guidance that can be adapted for other circumstances.

They are never there when you try and find them

Your supervisor may well have an office although the door always seems shut. Supervisors may well have a number of different roles they fulfil, from lecturing other year groups and other courses, through to supervising students on practice, alongside numerous meetings, marking, etc. It is possible for your supervisor to be on campus yet not in their office for most of the working week.

Your supervisor may have a timetable on their door where students can sign up for tutorials which is an obvious solution: if however, they do not, try e-mailing or leaving a telephone message outlining your name, contact number, that they are your allocated supervisor for your dissertation and that you would like to arrange a tutorial. E-mails are generally a favoured way of contacting supervisors: where a supervisor may be working away from campus and thus not able to access their phone messages, they are more likely to check their e-mails more regularly. Of course, you could try both methods, as it is known for e-mails not to get through.

Your supervisor is hard to get hold of or does not return your calls/e-mails

Following on from the last point, how long is it courteous to wait for a response to a message? A day? Two days? A week? Without wanting to pressurize your supervisor, you may never get a response, possibly due to the failings of technology or that they are away at a conference. As a general rule, for a phone message, five working days should be sufficient: for e-mails, a couple of days. If the response is longer than this, try again. If you still do not have any luck, it would be worth contacting the course administrator or the course leader in case your supervisor is absent for some reason.

From the outset, it would be worth establishing the best way to contact your supervisor and when they are likely to be able to respond to work: if your supervisor is only on campus for a couple of days a week, what days are these? Similarly, when is the best time to meet for a tutorial?

Your supervisor is ill/away

Unfortunately, your supervisor may be away for a period of time, either through illness or through leave. Although illness cannot be planned for, if you find that you are not getting any responses to your messages, take the action suggested in the last point.

It would be worth asking your supervisor at the outset as to when they may be away on leave or when they may have excessive demands on their time, so that you can arrange mutually convenient tutorials. No doubt your tutor will take leave around major holidays and they are likely to be busy at the start of a new semester or when assignments are due for marking. With these dates known in advance, you can ensure that you maximize the time available.

Supervisor talks off track

Just as an artist likes to paint, a supervisor likes to talk! (I am putting myself on the line here!) Tutorial time is limited from the outset and unless focussed, can result in you leaving without any additional benefit. Generally, your supervisor will keep to the point but they may elaborate on irrelevant issues. Try to steer your supervisor towards your immediate needs.

During the dissertation process, the amount of discussion from your supervisor will change: at the outset, they are likely to talk more about providing advice to help start you on the process. In the latter stages, it is more likely that you will take the lead, discussing the issues raised from your reading, patterns and generalizations from your research, etc.

One way of ensuring that you can maximize the potential from your tutorial is to define from the outset the focus for the tutorial: what is it you actually want to discuss? This will be elaborated further in this chapter under the tutorial section.

They want to change the focus of your work or suggest something you are not happy with

From the outset of your dissertation, you will have had an idea that has been lingering for a lengthy period, something that interests you, something you are passionate about. Yet in the space of a couple of minutes, your supervisor can shatter this focus by telling you it is unmanageable, or that you should focus on a different aspect.

As noted earlier, your supervisor would have been allocated due to their expertise in your area and that they would have conducted research previously. Furthermore, they are likely to have supervised a number of dissertations to completion already, thus aware of specific issues that can be problematic. This can result in good advice by your supervisor about your focus yet it can also deflate your aspirations about what you want to research. The last thing your supervisor wants to do is to shatter your confidence and motivation.

Consequently, it is important to consider why such suggestions have been made and the impact of this on your work.

In the initial stages of your dissertation, you would have submitted a proposal outlining your focus and suggested methodology. This should have provided a sufficient argument as to what you wanted to investigate and why. You may want to reiterate why you feel that this is an important area to investigate while asking them for the reasons as to why they suggest such changes. You could also ask what may happen if you do not accept their advice in terms of negative impacts on your research or your dissertation.

It is unlikely that your supervisor will ask you to completely reconsider your focus but will help to provide a better framework if necessary to structure your dissertation. One of the most common aspects students may find is that their focus it too broad or too ambitious. For example, a focus of 'What makes a good reader?' is very general. What is actually meant by this? Is a 'good reader' one who can decode words, one who understands the text, or one who does both? What is the measure of 'goodness' – is this a child who reads at their expected age, or one who reads six months in advance? What age are we measuring when we try to find out what makes a good reader – a specific year, key stage, or across the key stages? Is a 'good reader' a child who takes their book home every night? Is a 'good reader' a child who like both fiction and non-fiction? What parental influences affect reading ability? Is a child a 'good reader' if they are exposed to many different types of texts at home? Perhaps a 'good reader' is a child who sits quietly with a book … but are they necessarily reading? Is a 'good reader' a child who can use a range of strategies to work out meaning, or do they rely on just one strategy … what strategy is best?

Needless to say, within the proposed title 'What makes a good reader?' are a number of diverse issues. This could be refocused in different ways, for example:

- 'What are the predominant reading strategies among Year 3 children who are reading at six months higher than their chronological age?'
- 'An investigation into Year 2 children and their views on what makes a good reader'.

Pause for a moment and consider an alternate investigation to 'What makes a good reader?'

Dealing with criticism

After devoting several weeks to the initial chapters of your dissertation, you submit your work to your supervisor … and wait. You attend a tutorial for feedback awaiting the praise and adulation for your efforts, telling you what a delightful piece of research you have submitted. And you wait … yet no such praise is forthcoming. All your supervisor seems to say is what could be improved, that your paragraphing needs addressing, that it could be better structured if such a section is moved to here, and so on. How do you feel post-tutorial – disillusioned, deflated, dejected and discouraged?

It is only natural to feel that criticism, no matter how small, can have a negative impact, especially as this is your seminal piece of work which may make the difference between a first and a two-one. People deal with criticism in different ways, some using it as a fuel to ignite further work, others as a sign to stop everything and devote their efforts to the part-time job that has supplemented the student fees for the last couple of years. Needless to say, look at any critical comment as a positive remark in that it will help your work improve culminating in a quality dissertation you will be proud of.

Two supervisors

Depending on the nature of you dissertation, you may have two supervisors allocated, especially if your focus covers two areas (e.g. ICT in education). Your supervisors may know each other well, there again they may be in different areas altogether. This can result in not knowing who to ask for advice, or who to submit work to, furthermore each supervisor may only comment on the part of the dissertation relating to their field ... there again, they may not provide too much comment as they feel the other supervisor will! In order to resolve this, it is necessary to ensure that you meet with both supervisors at the same time. Obviously this magnifies the difficulty of trying to ensure both can coordinate times with you, especially if, as outlined above one (or both) are problematic to find.

Meeting with both supervisors can therefore ensure that they negotiate who provides what support and when, how work is submitted and whether they both meet to share their feedback before passing this onto you.

22.6   Making the most of tutorials

Using tutorials effectively in the dissertation stage is imperative. This is the opportunity where you can get quality time, guidance and feedback with your supervisor. The onus on acquiring a quality tutorial is not, as you may expect, with your supervisor but on the time and effort you put in to prepare. It may be helpful to consider a tutorial as a polished mirror, reflecting exactly what you put in. I have had students coming for a tutorial with nothing prepared to discuss with no plan of action, thus the thirty to forty minutes set aside are often reduced while the student waits for me to impart some useful nugget of information which will suddenly bring their dissertation to life. Alas this seldom happens. As I have noted in the introduction to this chapter, the dissertation is a two-way process, a give and take of ideas.

So how can tutorials be utilized for your advantage? Perhaps the most important aspect is to actually see your supervisor and attend tutorials. Even if you have nothing prepared, an initial discussion can point you in the right direction. From the outset, ensure you make contact with your supervisor, let them know who you are (up to the moment you first meet, you may have just been a name on an e-mail or class list). If you can, arrange to see your supervisor before the summer holidays to discuss your proposal so that you can actually spend time working on, or just thinking about your dissertation over the summer. Try also to get a couple of dates for future tutorials in the diary. This is useful in that it establishes a pattern and sets a deadline in order to prepare some work.

In terms of the practical side of tutorials, you can establish how your supervisor is best contacted (i.e. signing up for a tutorial, phoning or e-mailing), and how much time they will need to go through any draft work you submit (whether a couple of days or a week). It would also be worth discussing the major milestones of your dissertation and arranging tutorials to coincide: by this, when do you plan to collect your data? Ensuring you have a tutorial before you collect data to ensure that your data collection is practical, capturing the data you want to address your objectives may be useful, alongside a tutorial midway through data collection to discuss any issues.

It would also be worth trying to negotiate working deadlines. You could start from the submission date and work backwards: when does your supervisor want a final draft so that they can comment and allow you time to action any points? When would they like to see your literature review to ensure that there is sufficient scope for your focus? From these rough deadlines, you have a target for which to work towards.

Pre-tutorial

Ensure that you actually plan for the tutorial otherwise you may find your time and that of your supervisor, wasted. In terms of planning, this may include ensuring that you have submitted work with sufficient time for your supervisor to comment on your work. Furthermore, you may also want to note down some specific questions or areas to discuss to help you with the next stage of your dissertation. Such areas could be on practical issues (i.e. data collection), theoretical issues (i.e. ensuring you have understood a concept correctly from your literature review) or pragmatic issues (i.e. negotiating access to a research setting).

You may wish to e-mail your questions prior to the tutorial to your supervisor. This will allow them time to consider their response while also indicating the direction you wish the tutorial to take. Needless to say, this is probably best discussed with your supervisor from the outset to ensure that they are happy with this process. A final piece of advice is to get to your tutorial on time, perhaps with sufficient time to spare. If you are delayed, this may result in a shorter tutorial than you require as your supervisor may have other students waiting, or may have a meeting or lecture to attend. To the same courteous extent, you should expect that your supervisor is there on time and is not running late, or that if they are, you are provided with sufficient time to respond to your queries.

Even if you do not have pages of completed work to submit, you may want to submit a skeleton plan of a chapter, indicating the main themes you are likely to discuss: this will allow your supervisor to see what you are aiming towards and allow some discussion on the process.

During the tutorial

Assuming that you have tracked down your supervisor, ensured that they can meet you at a specific time, that you have submitted some work, that you have both turned up on time and you have your list of questions ready, the tutorial should be a positive experience.

However, there are some other aspects to keep in mind, for example, ensuring you have paper and pens to make notes of what your supervisor says.

Often in a tutorial, your supervisor may scribble on pieces of paper, jotting ideas, diagrams, etc. I sometimes provide students with four sheets of scribbles. Having looked at these pages in due course, I often wonder whether the student can understand what the tutorial was about if I can barely decode my jottings. Consequently, it is imperative that you make your own notes to supplement those of your supervisor. You could negotiate with your supervisor if they would be happy for you to record the tutorial using a voice recorder, although not every supervisor may be open to this … there is no harm in asking though.

It is also important to ask your supervisor if you are unsure of something they have written or have said. Without such clarification, you may find that you are facing greater problems as time passes.

Ensure that you date your notes, numbering any pages and providing a title so that what may look like an innocent piece of paper which could easily be thrown away is filed accurately. For this purpose, some students prefer to keep a notebook, jotting ideas, tutorial notes, etc. as the dissertation progresses.

During the tutorial, be honest about the progress you are making. If you genuinely have achieved little since the last tutorial, highlight this to your supervisor. They may be able to work out why you are stuck and provide strategies for moving forwards. Finally, at the end of the tutorial, ensure that you have agreed future targets and a date to meet.

Post-tutorial

Check through the notes you have made and any notes your supervisor has provided you with. You may want to annotate these further so that they make sense the next time you look at these.

Contacting your supervisor outside of tutorials

There may be incidences when you wish to contact your supervisor and when you are unable to make a tutorial. This may be for any number of reasons, however, ensure that you do make contact.

Be explicit about the nature of your query … for this reason, it is preferable to e-mail your supervisor so that you can ask a specific question and receive a specific answer. This also avoids the game of 'telephone tag', where you leave a message for your supervisor, they leave a message for you, and so on.

When composing an e-mail, ensure that the subject line is explicit: writing 'Hi!' is perhaps not going to grab the attention of your supervisor in the same way as writing 'Dissertation query: skeleton plan of literature review'. Furthermore, keep niceties to a minimum.

Questioning the state of health of your supervisor, whether they had a good weekend, what they think about the weather, etc. then asking your specific question can waste time.

If you are contacting your supervisor by telephone, if (on the rare occasion) they are actually in their office, it is courteous to ask whether they have time to speak currently (they may be just off out of the door or with another student). If they have time to speak, great, if not, ask what time would be convenient to call back.

22.7   Summary of the key points

- Your supervisor's time is limited. Ensure you use their time wisely.
- The dissertation is a two-way process.
- Make contact with your supervisor.
- Make use of a critical friend.
- Establish a pattern for tutorials.
- Prepare for tutorials, noting specific questions or areas to discuss.
- Make notes during the tutorial.
- E-mails are preferable to phone calls.

22.8   What should I do now?

You should know who your supervisor is, however, do not expect them to come looking for you! You need to be proactive with this. E-mail, telephone or visit them in person to arrange your first tutorial. If the person is somebody you have never met, remember the importance of good first impressions. It would also be beneficial to supply your supervisor with your research proposal prior to the first tutorial so that they actually know what you intend to investigate.

Establish your plan of action for the dissertation and share this with your supervisor. Establish whether they will be around for the duration of your research, or whether there will be times when they may be off work for holidays or research purposes.

22.9   References to more information

There is very little that has been written on working effectively with your supervisor at undergraduate or postgraduate level. It would be worth contacting your academic department to find out what support is provided and how this is accessed. The following books do, however, provide some further guidance:

Cottrell, S. (2003) *The Study Skills Handbook*, 2nd edn. Basingstoke: Palgrave Macmillan.

Roberts-Holmes, G. (2005) *Doing Your Early Years Research Project: A Step by Step Guide*. London: Paul Chapman.

See p 14.

23 What About Working and Planning My Time?

23.1   Motivation and discipline

This chapter is in danger of sounding patronizing in places, partly because it sometimes states the obvious, and partly because the idea of discipline evokes the picture of someone talking from on high and wagging a finger at you. But I know only too well (from writing this book) that motivation and discipline are two factors that play an important part in helping to actually get the work done. It is after all self-motivation and self-discipline that are the issue, not something imposed by a higher authority. So, to become aware of a few techniques which help to make life easier is no bad thing.

Ideally, if you have enough motivation, you are unlikely to need to impose much onerous discipline on yourself. In order to be motivated, it is pretty important that the project you have chosen really interests you. When you think of it, this is probably the first opportunity you have had since beginning your education to choose yourself what you will study for the next few months, so you should seize the opportunity to select something that will make this exercise enjoyable and rewarding. This point has already been more fully made in Chapters 4 and 5.

Even so, not every task can be interesting, and there are so many other enjoyable things to do and other deadlines to meet. There will also be several new skills to learn and others to develop, both of which require energy and dedication. You are only human, so it is worth considering how your efforts can be optimized by being in tune with your personality and mental and physical characteristics. Below are some ideas of how you can achieve this.

23.2   Moods

No one can be upbeat and raring to go all of the time. We are all subject to moods that have an important influence on our ability to concentrate and be creative. Davies (2001: 15) mentions two sets of opposite conditions – energetic/tired and calm/tense – which can be understood to contain a range of moods from mild to extreme. One cannot simply equate one or other state with being conducive to hard work or concentrated effort. It depends on your personality how you react to these moods. What is useful though is to be aware of how you are feeling, and also what sort of activities you can do best in which mood. For instance, some people need the tension of working to a deadline to get going, while others are only productive when they can mull over their work in a peaceful setting.

It is well known that people's mood varies during the course of the day. But they are not all the same: some are 'morning people', others 'evening people', while some fall between the two, or are even 'night people'. Take note of how you feel during the day. Do you find working easiest during the morning, or do you only get going in the evening hours? This is not just a psychological phenomenon, but also a physiologi-cal one (something to do with body temperature at different times of the day). If you can detect a pattern, then plan your activities to suit. For example, I find I can con-centrate best from 4 a.m. (yes…4 a.m.!) through to 11 a.m., then I slump but pick up again around 4 p.m. for another couple of hours. Everyone is different – whether you are an early-morning lark or a night owl. Not all that you need to do requires intense concentration, so you can reserve the less demanding tasks for your 'weaker' periods.

Moods are also a form of information or feedback about your biomedical condition. Healthy living in the form of plenty of exercise, a balanced diet, and regular and sufficient rest, promote an upbeat mood. Conversely, a lack of sleep, poor diet, too much drink and smoking, and lack of exercise will tend to depress your mood. However a good meal and a night's sleep will actually make working easier.

You can also do things to influence your mood. To avoid getting stuck in a boring and depressing routine, why not organize a shift of scene? Work somewhere different, visit different libraries, choose case studies or do other field research in different locations. Although you might not be in a position to make a study of exotic butterflies in the Amazon jungle, visits to new places can be a stimulating experience.

Ruminating about a subject for a long time can be a 'downer'. There is only so much that one can resolve in one's head. Thinking too long around a problem, without getting it down on paper or discussing it with someone, tends to lead to circular thinking and the feeling of being stuck. Only when the problem gets clearly laid out can you find ways to grapple with it, or even to let your subconscious work on it.

Make the best of when you are feeling great. At these times you will feel inspired, ideas will tumble into your head, you will see connections and have insights and have a strong urge to get it all down onto paper. Avoid getting interrupted, as it is difficult to pick up from where you left off. Put off other commitments and savour the moments: this is when you will be at your most productive. There are other times when you feel that you are running at half speed. Make use of these times for more menial tasks, such as tidying up, sorting out notes, drawing or scanning illustrations, making graphs and figures. You can also catch up on your reading.

Sometimes, having worked for some time you can get stuck, fed up or just tired. Woods (1999: 19–21) has collected a few ploys that he and other well-known writers have used to reinvigorate themselves. Spend some time gazing out of the window (at a panoramic vista if there is one), drink numerous cups of coffee, pace the room, listen to the birds singing or to a piece of music, examine what is going on in the neighbourhood with a pair

FIGURE 23.1   It depends on your personality how you react to these moods.

of binoculars, give an imaginary speech or hold a conversation with yourself, take a walk or go for a run, play the violin or a computer game or a game of snooker, go out and do some sport.

23.3   Being creative

One of the main points of getting you to do a dissertation is to force you to work independently, and this requires a certain creativity. Although you will get a certain level of support, it is really up to you to work things out and find solutions, and even to discover problems that need solving. Understanding complex situations also needs an open-minded approach. Creative thinking helps you to break out from habitual thought patterns and to explore a wider range of possibilities. There are several easy-to-use techniques that can help you to think creatively. Here are a few exercises you might find useful.

Brainstorming

(This term is commonly being replaced with other politically correct terms like 'thought-shower', etc.)

You need a group of people for this (though you can do it on your own; it is then called brainwriting). First clearly define a particular problem you want to solve. List as many ideas as come into your heads of how to solve the problem. In a group, you can also feed off other people's suggestions, combine ideas and extrapolate or modify them. The main rule is not to criticize, however, bizarre or ridiculous the suggestions may be. The evaluation of the ideas comes later. A typical brainstorming may produce about 50 different ideas (probably rather less for brainwriting) for solutions to a particular problem. These can then be classified and evaluated.

Checklists

A bit like a shopping list. Make lists of things you need to consider, difficulties you might encounter, tasks you need to do, information you need to collect, etc. Again, you need to focus on one aspect of your project for useful results. You can also use checklists to look at alternative ways of doing things by using trigger words, for example combine solutions, reverse the problem (see it from a different perspective). Other trigger words are adapt, rearrange, substitute, magnify, minify, modify, put to other uses.

Analogies

You can often draw parallels between two different problems or situations, where knowledge about one can help to explain or solve the other. This is quite a natural process, a way of learning from experience. Put to more deliberate use, it can help to obtain new insights and perspectives. For example, the techniques your favourite chat show hosts use to prise information out of their guests could be used in your own interviews; or analysis of dynamics among a group of people could be compared with that of an extended family or a small business.

Immersion in the problem

This takes time, and is a good reason for defining a problem at an early stage. Once you are aware of the problem, be it of a practical or a theoretical nature, think about it for a bit, and then just 'forget' it for a few days and allow your subconscious to work on it. You might just jump out of the bath shouting 'eureka' as a solution presents itself out of the blue.

Discussion

A problem shared is a problem halved, so they say. It is best if you talk with people who share similar problems, and especially those who have found good solutions!

Systems thinking

There is a range of ways of looking at systems, i.e. a complex of interrelated things or events such as machines, organizations, social groups or natural phenomena. You can draw a diagram to explore the sequences of cause and effect, or of the influence that factors

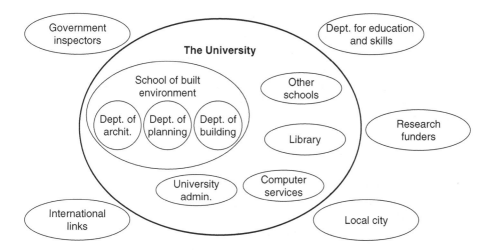

FIGURE 23.2   Systems map of the university (very simplified).

have on one another. Other types of diagram are organization diagrams, cognitive maps, flowcharts and decision trees.

You will probably find it necessary to spend plenty of time by yourself in order to get yourself going. Having the TV on in the background is a real concentration killer. I find even having music on is a distraction – I keep wanting to listen.

23.4   All the things you need to do

A dissertation is probably the biggest academic project that you have ever undertaken. The worst aspect of this is not that the task seems impossibly complex and lengthy, but that there are so many unknowns that it will be very difficult to plan for a successful and timely completion.

In order to remove some of the mystique, here is a list of the tasks that you will (or in some cases, might) need to undertake, in a typical order. This list, tailored to the requirements of your type of study, will help you to work out a sequence of activities, make an estimate of how long each activity might take, and thus give you the information to set up a programme of work. You can then use this both to assure yourself that you can complete on time, and to check that you are not falling behind too much in your rate of work. It will also ensure that you do not spend too long on any aspect of the work, thus avoiding last minute panics. You can get some idea of what is involved in each task by scanning through the chapters mentioned.

- Decide on a subject and type of investigation and, if possible, get it provisionally approved by your supervisor (see Chapters 4 and 5).
- Investigate the subject so that you have enough information to write the proposal (see Chapter 6).

- Write a proposal explaining the subject of your research and giving some indication of how you will do it (see Chapter 6). It is a good idea to discuss your proposal with your supervisor, as it represents the foundation of your efforts over the next months.
- Organize your note taking and your archiving system (see Chapter 9).
- Carry out background research through study of the literature to determine what has been done already in the subject (see Chapter 8) in order to see where your study fits into current and past work.
- Investigate methods of data collection and analysis which have been used to do similar studies to your own, and the practical aspects of doing them, for example observations, interviews, questionnaires, etc. (see Chapters 13–17). This will help you to decide just how you do your investigation and enable you to make estimates of what will be involved in time, expense, organization and perhaps getting permissions and access to sources of information.
- Work out a structure for the dissertation (i.e. chapter headings and short lists of contents for each) and write a draft of your preliminary chapter(s) (see Chapters 1 and 7).
- Start writing. It is a good idea to start writing the introductory chapter(s) quite early on while you are immersed in the literature review. Do not try to perfect it – even blocks of notes will be a useful start.
- Plan your project work, i.e. the part of the research that will generate new information (e.g. fieldwork, experiments, trials, archive searches, textual analyses, etc.). This might entail getting permissions for access to institutions, selecting case studies, obtaining documents for analysis, setting up questionnaires, etc. (see Chapters 3 and 8).
- Carry out the project work as planned above. Take into account time required for travel, waiting for responses to questionnaires, getting appointments with people, etc. (see Chapters 15, 16 and 17).
- Sort and analyse the collected information. In some cases, you may need to take some time to learn computer programs to help with the analysis (see Chapters 19 and 20).
- Write up the results of your analysis, devising graphs, diagrams and illustrations to help explain the data.
- Write up how you did the research (easier to do this after you have done it, though it should appear earlier in the dissertation), and write conclusions based on what you have found out (see Chapter 18).
- Prepare a final draft. This is the time to pull all the written work together in a structured form. Check that the length complies with the requirements, ensure that chapters or sections follow a good sequence, and assess the need for illustrations, graphs and diagrams, etc. You can experiment with layout designs at this stage (see Chapter 25).
- Write up the final version based on the final draft. This will also involve inserting illustrations, graphs and diagrams, lists of references, contents and finally setting out the layout and page numberings.

23.5   Setting up a programme

At the beginning of a project, when there seems to be loads of time to complete it, it is easy to sit back and believe that planning can be done later, when time starts to run out. After all, there is no need to be all organized when time is not an issue, is there? The trouble is, until you actually assess how much work is involved in writing your dissertation, it is quite difficult to judge whether there actually is loads of time. For this reason, it is a good idea to devise a simple programme early on so that you can reassure yourself that you will not get into a desperate panic later.

In order to be of any real use, a programme should be realistic in its aims. It is easy to plan out a timetable of work that should be done, ignoring all the obstacles that might get in the way. For this reason it is important to include in your timing any other commitments you may have, for example holidays, sport, other assignments and exam dates. If the objectives are realistic, then you may actually keep referring to the programme that you have spent time devising in order to check on your progress and to plan your next moves.

It helps to break up your project into stages. Give yourself deadlines to complete aspects of the work. This is a common requirement of professional research projects, where intermediate reports are required to check up on the progress of the work. You are unlikely to have to submit your work in stages like this, but the satisfaction and comfort of consciously getting parts of the project out of the way are worth the effort. The other advantage of splitting the work into sections is that you set limited goals, ones that you can see that you can achieve without being daunted. In addition, having some intermediate deadlines will stop you getting carried away or dithering on any one aspect of the work and spending far too much time on it.

The easiest way to devise a programme is to set up a table, with a list of tasks on the left-hand side, and the time in weeks along the top. It is best to use the table facility in your word processor or a spreadsheet program for ease of adjustment and neat presentation. If you like, you can include your other activities to make sure that there are no clashes in timing. Try to be realistic, or the programme will become obsolete within a few weeks.

FIGURE 23.3   Ignoring all the obstacles that might get in the way.

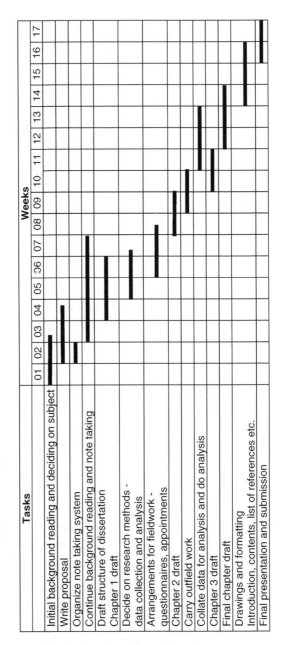

FIGURE 23.4   Programme of work.

If you cannot fit the necessary work into the time available, then reduce the scope to the work.

Your programme will help to motivate you, as you will easily be able to see that whatever you are doing in your list of tasks, the job is useful and a necessary part of the sequence. And the task will also have a defined and meaningful end. You will also be able to check that you are not drifting by spending too much time on particular aspects of the work, and that you allow enough time for the latter stages. Seeing that you will manage to complete on time is a great comfort. If the work does slip in relation to the programme, you will be able to adjust it so that you still find time (even if it is somewhat reduced) for all the essential tasks.

23.6 Starting to write

Even professional writers state what a pain it is to write, and how they need to be a bit insane in order to do it. However, you can take comfort in the fact that you are not writing a novel or some poetry – totally dependent on your own resources. The content of your writing will be based on other people's publications and your own collection of information and observations. You will have plenty of raw materials, so the page will not need to be blank for long!

Perhaps the most difficult step is to start writing. You might feel that you have nothing to write about until you have done all the reading and research. In fact, through just thinking about what you want to do for your dissertation you already know quite a lot. At the start of any project, there has to be some writing done to explain to other people what you intend to do. So this is a good time to start.

At this early stage, you can afford to be uncertain about matters; raise them anyway as points for further investigation. For example, you can start with describing what area of study you want to pursue (e.g. primary education, adult education, management), and exploring some of the situations where you could concentrate your investigation (e.g. in relation to the above, a specific curriculum area, teaching and learning processes, staff deployment). What you write is not chiselled into stone, so just let your thoughts get onto paper (or the computer screen) without being too critical. Once ideas are written, then you can play around with them, and add, cut, and adjust them. You cannot do this all in your head, so the process of writing it down will actually help you to think about it, and to make decisions about what you really want to do.

As you get more into your subject, a good way to get something onto paper without even having to form sentences is to make a list. This can be of things to do, topics to investigate, or headings of subjects you want to write about. Once you have a basic list, you can add some subheadings to the items that expand on these. Before long, perhaps after doing some reading, you will be able to add a few sentences under the subheadings. You can first concentrate on the bits that are easy. Later, when you already have a body of text, you will be more confident to tackle the harder aspects that require more thought and knowledge.

Later on in the project, when the real bulk of writing needs to be done, the pressure and difficulty will be at their greatest. This is where the creative and original work is produced. Woods (1999: 15–18) describes how he needs to 'crank himself up' before he starts writing up his research. Analysis and presentation of the information you have collected is a multifaceted task that is quite painful and demanding work. A few tentative starts are to be expected as you 'psych yourself up'. People often remark on how they become unsociable when they are involved in creative work: you need to be concentrated on yourself and your own thinking in quite a selfish way. However, do switch off in between your working sessions. If you are quite strict with your timing and set yourself realistic goals (e.g. so many words per day), then you can feel you have really earned your time off. Most professional writers work regular office hours – whether they are inspired or not.

This is a good place to remind you that you must save and back up your work regularly. Computers are notoriously fickle and can ruin your day if your work gets lost or deleted by accident or failure. Keep all your writing recorded in at least two – better three, different formats – floppy disk, hard drive, your home directory on the university intranet. Make a habit of saving your work manually every 10–15 minutes, and set the program to make auto-recover files every few minutes. I have heard some tragic true stories of work getting 'lost' – perhaps one of the most infuriating and disappointing things that can happen to one's hard-won writing efforts.

23.7 Stress

To round off this chapter, one final aspect will be looked at: stress. If all of the advice in this chapter (and the book) is followed, you should avoid feeling any stress about your dissertation. Yet, stress, however, is becoming more prevalent especially when balancing competing demands such as: other assignments, looking for a graduate job, part-time work, financial pressures, health issues, relationships, interests, social life, etc. Admittedly, some people thrive on a challenge, yet when the challenge becomes too great, it is easy to feel a loss of control. This is what stress is – the inability to cope with excessive pressure.

In order to deal with stress, it is important to recognize the source of stress before making attempts to resolve it. If you feel that stress is becoming excessive and you are unable to cope, you should seek medical advice. There are, however, a few stress management strategies that you could try.

Stress management for the mind

Being in the present   We tend to live our lives by concentrating on past events, or future concerns, yet seldom do we concentrate on being here and now. No doubt as you are reading this paragraph, the mind has wandered between one or more alternate things. As such, the mind needs to be trained to keep still and stop chattering away. This can be achieved by practicing calming the mind through meditation.

What is 'meditation'? Although many definitions could be forwarded, the simplest is concentrating on one thing, and one thing only. Although there is a wealth of esoteric practices, finding something where you can stop and concentrate on one task for a period of time is the key. Such activities can vary from person to person, but ultimately it is about being in the present.

Examples of 'meditation' include:

- Concentrating on your breathing (as discussed later in this chapter)
- Listening to relaxing music
- Listening to guided meditation tapes
- Gardening
- Saying a phrase repeated time and time again, or a positive affirmation you wish to bring about, for example 'I will get my dissertation completed on time and enjoy the process!'
- Exercising in a non-competitive and relaxed manner. Walking, jogging, swimming and cycling with full attention can be deemed to be meditative. Please note that a steady pace needs to be maintained: it is hard to keep the mind focussed on the activity while walking down a busy street!

Basically try and avoid competitive activities or activities that over-stimulate the mind (television and computer games are not forms of meditation …) while trying to fully be in the moment with the activity you have selected.

Stress management for the body

Exercise   As a paradox, exercising can actually cause the body to relax. The body is mechanically designed to be active, yet our modern lifestyle tends to make life all too convenient and automated. It is easier to e-mail or text a friend than to actually visit them.

Through exercise, endorphins can be released that make the body feel good. Such endorphin release can be mimicked through the use of other substances (alcohol, caffeine, smoking, etc.) yet exercise is relatively inexpensive and has more positive, health-producing effects.

Exercise does not necessarily mean heading down to the local gym for a work out: instead, anything that raises the heart rate to a specific level is beneficial. There are many different types of exercise you could try and it would be useful if you can take this up with a friend so that you can both motivate each other. Ensure, however, that you seek your doctor's permission first.

Breathing

> 'You can live two months without food and two weeks without water, but only a few minutes without air'. Master Hung Yi Hsiang (courtesy of www.wingchun.co.uk)

One of the simplest ways of controlling stress and slowing down the pace of life is to stop … and breathe! This may sound strange, surely we breathe 'naturally' and have done it ever since we first came into existence. However, concentrate on your breathing now … how are you doing it?

Our lungs are like big bellows, yet we tend to breathe using the top half of the lungs, taking shallow breaths. Diaphragmatic breathing utilizes the whole of the lungs, whereby you concentrate on breathing by visualizing the breath being drawn into the stomach.

This causes the stomach to expand (by the diaphragm pulling downwards), allowing your lungs to be completely filled with air. This is the most natural way to breathe, yet pressure and tension cause us to breathe incorrectly, keeping a lot of stress in the chest.

Although there are many forms of breathing within yoga, Asian martial and medical systems, one of the simplest breathing exercises is outlined below. Try it now!

In order to breathe correctly:

- Sit or stand using good posture. Imagine that your entire body is being hung from a thread at the top of your head. This will help straighten the spine … no slouching.
- Relax the body. Scan it to ensure there is no unnecessary tension in any of the major muscle groups, or your face muscles, etc.
- Inhale slowly and deeply through your nose while pushing the stomach out.
- Hold the breath for a few seconds.
- Exhale controlled and slowly through the mouth, at the same time pulling the stomach in.
- Complete nine breathes like this every time you need to 'take a breather!'.
- During the course of the day, from time to time concentrate on your breathing. Aim to complete at least four cycles as described above.

Breathing like this is great if it can be practised in the air outside, especially first thing in the morning or last thing at night, although this is not an excuse not to practice such breathing at any time in the day.

Diet   There is some truth in the cliché 'you are what you eat'. You wouldn't choose to drink stagnant water, or continue to breathe in a polluted environment, therefore why shouldn't you pay the same attention to the food you consume?

Try to eat a balanced diet rich in fruit and vegetables (a palm-sized serving of five different types) each day, while allowing sufficient time to eat each meal. Ensure that your food is eaten slowly, chewing thoroughly before swallowing to ensure that all of the goodness from the food is released.

There is plenty of advice on healthy eating on the Internet, yet knowing what we should eat is different from actually choosing to eat properly. Habits can be hard to break.

Pressure points   Use of pressure points, or finger-tip massage can provide some instant relief from stress. A couple of easy and safe techniques are outlined here, however, visiting a qualified acupressure or reflexology practitioner is fundamental should you wish to explore this further.

Two key points that are easy to find and safe to use are:

1   The point located above the bridge of the nose between the eyebrows. Gentle fingertip pressure applied in either a circular motion or pumping in and out of the point, for about two minutes will help.

2   The point located on the palm side of the hand, on the wrist crease, directly below the little finger. There is a bony protrusion and the point is next to that, in a small indentation. Press for 30 seconds with moderate to firm pressure, gradually releasing the pressure.

23.8   What should I do now?

Whatever stage you are at in your project, if you have not done so yet, set up a programme of work. Try to be realistic and take into account your preferred method of working and also your other commitments. It is usually difficult to judge just how long each task will take (usually longer than you think). However, as time will always be a limiting factor you will often have to cut the work to fit the time – a reasonable justification for limiting the scope of your work. The main thing is to get the proportions between the various stages of the work to be reasonable.

FIGURE 23.5   You may be faced with a combination of problems.

Start writing something. If you are still at the beginning, outline the area of your study, bringing in any information or quotations from things you have read. Try to define a focus for your project in the form of questions or aims. If you are further on, you could make a start on your background chapter, using the notes you have made from your reading in order to set the scene for your individual work. You could also write out a structure for your dissertation in the form of a list of headings and subheadings.

If you are unclear of what you want to do, or of how to progress, define the problem as you see it, and try out one or more of the ideas-generating techniques above. You may be faced with a combination of problems that make you feel helpless and lost. Try to break them down into different aspects and tackle each one in turn. Once you have found solutions, start by putting them down in writing and listing what actions you want to take. Even if you don't start working on them straight away, at least you have a record to fall back on.

23.9   References to more information

Adair, J. (2007) *The Art of Creative Thinking: How to be Innovative and Develop Great Ideas*. London: Kogan Page.

Buzan, T. (2006) *The Buzan Study Skills Handbooks: The Shortcut to Success in Your Studies with Mind Mapping, Speed Reading and Winning Memory Techniques*. London: BBC Active.

Cottrell, S. (2005) *Critical Thinking Skills: Developing Effective Analysis and Argument*. Basingstoke: Palgrave Macmillan.

Davies, P. (2001) *Get Up and Grow: How to Motivate Yourself and Everybody Else Too*. London: Hodder and Stoughton.

Michalko, M. (2006) *Thinkertoys: A Handbook of Creative-Thinking Techniques*, 2nd edn. Berkeley: Ten Speed Press.

There are many books on creative thinking. De Bono became a creative thinking guru in the 1970 and 1980s with a string of books and public appearances. Here are some of his most popular – and easy to read – books.

De Bono, E. (1995) *Serious Creativity: Using the Power of Lateral Thinking to Create New Ideas*. London: Harper Collins.

De Bono, E. (1996) *Teach Yourself to Think*. Harmondsworth: Penguin.

De Bono, E. (2006) *De Bono's Thinking Course: Powerful Tools to Transform Your Thinking*. London: BBC Active.

De Bono, E. (2007) *How to Have Creative Ideas: 62 Exercises to Develop the Mind*. London: Vermilion.

I found a few more on thinking creatively and problem solving – worth delving into.

Bransford, J.D. (1993) *The Ideal Problem Solver: A Guide for Improving Thinking, Learning, and Creativity*, 2nd edn. New York: Freeman.

Smith, F. (1992) *To Think: In Language, Learning and Education*. London: Routledge.

Gilhooly, K.J. (1996) *Thinking: Directed, Undirected and Creative*, 3rd edn. London: Academic.

These books offer lots of advice on writing. I have put them in order of accessibility and level of academic stage aimed at.

Clanchy, J. and Ballard, B. (1998) *How to Write Essays: A Practical Guide for Students*, 3rd edn. Melbourne: Longman.

Pirie, D.B. (1985) *How to Write Critical Essays: A Guide for Students of Literature*. London: Routledge.

Bowden, J. (2004) *How to Write a Report: How to Prepare, Write and Present Effective Reports*, 7th edn. Plymouth: How To Books.

Murray, R. (2002) *How to Write a Thesis*. Buckingham: Open University Press.

Berry, R. (2004) *The Research Project: How to Write It*, 5th edn. London: Routledge.

Woods, P. (2005) *Successful Writing for Qualitative Researchers*. London: Taylor and Francis.

Finally, some books on stress:

Carlson, R. (1997) *Don't Sweat the Small Stuff ... and It's All Small Stuff: Simple Ways to Keep the Little Things from Taking Over Your Life*. London: Hodder and Stoughton.

Davis, M., Eshelman, E.R. and McKay, M. (2000) *The Relaxation and Stress Reduction Workbook*, 5th edn. Oakland: New Harbinger Publications.

Elkin, A. (1999) *Stress Management for Dummies*. Hoboken: Wiley.

24 How Can I Manage a Long Piece of Writing?

24.1 When to start writing up

To sit down in front of a blank computer monitor with the task of writing a lengthy dissertation is a daunting prospect and one to be avoided. You can easily arrange that you will not be faced with this situation. The trick is to gradually amass a collection of notes, observations and data on the issues relevant to your study, which you can then use as a basis for your first draft. This way, you will have started writing your dissertation without even realizing it! If you have followed the advice in Chapter 9 about organizing your note-taking system, you should have little problem in retrieving the notes in an orderly fashion.

To lessen the anguish of starting to write up later on in the programme, it helps to build up your first draft from an early stage. To be able to do this, you will need to prepare a structure for the dissertation as soon as you are clear what you will be doing. You can devise this in outline after you have done some background reading and completed your proposal. The structure will then provide a framework into which you can insert your text. Don't expect either the framework or the text to be the final version. Both will need refining and revising as your work and understanding progress. Luckily, word processors make revision very quick and easy.

The issue of writing style should be considered at this point. As a dissertation is an academic piece of work, generally a more formal style is adopted. At its extreme, this avoids the personal pronoun 'I' altogether although for some research projects this may not be the case. It is a good idea to raise the issue of style when you discuss your work with your tutor. There may be some indications given in the assignment details: you should read these carefully anyway for instructions on what is expected of you.

24.2 Frame and fill

FIGURE 24.1 A more formal style is adopted.

You may want to return to Chapter 1 to look at the framework of the dissertation and the component chapters generally used. Alternatively you can create a framework for your dissertation by making a list of possible chapter or section headings. Consult your proposal and plan of work for indications of what these may be. At the very simplest level the divisions may be like this:

- Introduction
- Literature review (background of the subject)
- Methodology
- Results
- Discussion
- Conclusions

This assumes that you will use the background reading to clarify the main issues of your research; that you will use one or several research methods to delve more deeply into these issues; that this will produce some data or results that you will present and analyse; and that you will be able to draw some conclusions from this analysis in relation to the main issues. This is a conventional format and can be applied to a study in almost any subject. There are other, unconventional, ways of organizing a dissertation. If you do want to use an unusual structure or even want to develop your own, it is best to discuss this with your supervisor to check that it will be acceptable. The main thing is that you can set up a convincing overall argument that leads from your intentions to your conclusions.

Once you have the main framework, you can elaborate on the contents of each section by inserting subheadings indicating the aspects that you want to cover in each. Just use your current knowledge and a bit of imagination at first to suggest relevant subheadings. This will help to establish the thread of your argument as discussed in Chapter 11. You will be able to reorder, expand or change these as you progress.

Although each section of this book concludes with a suggestion about how each of the dissertation chapters could be structured, a summary is provided here. However, remember that you can adapt and amend this according to your preferences and the way your dissertation unfolds.

Introduction (refer to Chapter 7)

- Define the focus of your research
  - A short summary of the context of the study
  - The main problems or issues to be investigated
  - The overall approach to the project
- The environmental issues of your research
- Research aim and objectives
- Signposting your research.

Literature review (refer to Chapter 12)

- Introduction
- Development
  - Aspects of the subject investigated
  - Historical and current context
  - Evidence of problems or contentious issues
  - Current debate – comparison of different opinions or approaches
- Conclusion
  - Shortcomings in the level of knowledge.

Methodology (refer to Chapter 18)

- General approach to your research (your research stance/philosophy)
- Selection and description of methods related to your objectives
- Selection of samples
- Ethical statement
- Discussion of how your research adheres to validity and reliability
- Method(s) of analysis and presentation of results (e.g. charts, graphs, diagrams, spreadsheets, statistics, coding systems, models, commentaries, etc.).

Results (refer to Chapters 19 and 20)

- Charts, graphs, diagrams, etc. with annotation and interpretation.

Discussion (refer to Chapter 21)

- Introduction
- Impact of findings
- Impact on practice
- Recommendations for action
- Impact of methodology
- Impact on you.

Conclusions

- Conclusions drawn from sets of data in relation to the main issues (this can be separated into sections for each objective).
- Overall conclusions of the dissertation.

FIGURE 24.2 Once you have the main framework, you can elaborate on the contents.

I have kept the subheadings as general as possible so that you can possibly apply these or something equivalent in the context of your subject. You will have to use your imagination and judgement to assess if this arrangement actually suits what you want to do. Devise your own sequence if you like, but note the overall pattern of identifying issues from background study, the definition of how you will investigate these, and how you will present the information gained and how this will be analysed to enable you to come to conclusions.

You do not have to start writing your text at the beginning and continue to the end. Use what notes you have got so far and insert them where they are relevant in order to fill in the framework. If you have the notes already written on computer, then you can simply copy and paste them in a rough order under the appropriate headings and subheadings. If you have recorded them on paper, now is the time to transfer them into the word processor. You will thus quickly have several pages of (very) rough draft.

However, be warned. Even though it might look pretty impressive, the text will be no more than a series of raw notes, completely unedited, disjointed and incomplete. But it will provide a solid basis for working on to produce a first draft.

24.3 Marshalling your notes and drafting your text

You will probably be told what the overall length of your dissertation is required to be. If not, find out by asking your tutor, or consult previous dissertations written in your course. You need to know this in order to determine how long each section should be to get a balanced result. As a guide, 5000 words are equivalent to about 25 pages of double-space type. Taking the above six-chapter arrangement, a balanced proportion of

FIGURE 24.3   Use what notes you have got so far.

content might be as follows:

- Introduction, 5 per cent. This serves as a guide to the dissertation for the reader.
- Literature review, 20 per cent. A review of the literature and information about the context of the study.
- Methodology, 20 per cent. A description of the steps you will take and techniques you will use to actually investigate the main issues. Reasons for using these methods must also be included.
- Results, 15 per cent. A record of what you did and what results came out of your investigations. You might split this into two or three sections if you are investigating two or three different issues.
- Discussion, 30 per cent. A detailed discussion of the impact of your results and how these relate to the research issue. Further discussion of the research process and future recommendations may also be included.
- Conclusions, 10 per cent. An interpretation of the results in light of the main issues.

Now you will be ready to start inserting your notes into your structure. How do you get the right notes in the right place? This is where your retrieval techniques will be put to the test. Assuming that your framework gives you enough indication of what you are looking for, search through your notes by key word or subject. If you do this on the computer, you will be shown a selection of relevant notes, from which you can choose what you think is suitable for that section. You can do this manually with notes on paper. Other useful search parameters may be date or author.

For the introduction, just insert your proposal for now. You will be able to use this, suitably edited, when you have finished the rest of the writing, to explain the nature of the dissertation. More will be added later to explain the structure of the dissertation.

Your proposal will indicate the sort of areas that your background study will need to cover. There are likely to be several aspects of the subject that need looking at, for example historical precedents, conflicting opinions, political, financial, organizational and social aspects, etc. At this stage you will need to clearly define the limits of your study: you only have a short time to complete it, so keep it manageable.

24.4 Revisions

The nice thing about using a word processor is that you can easily change things after you have written them. This takes off the pressure of getting everything right first time – something that is impossible to do anyway. Once your work is on paper, then you can review it, get a second opinion on it, and discuss it. You cannot do these if it is still all in your head. Hence the importance of getting on with writing as soon as possible. Regard the making of revisions as an integral part of the process of doing a dissertation. You will of course have to include some time for this in your time plan.

You do not have to finish the dissertation or even a section of it before you revise it. You can use the process to accumulate your written material, adding to the latest version as the information comes in or as you get the writing bug. Regularly reviewing what you have done so far and to what quality will keep you aware of how far you have progressed and what still needs to be done. It also enables you to break down the work into small sections, revising, altering and expanding sections as your understanding develops. The text will thus evolve as a series of small steps that should need no drastic revision at the last moment.

Revising can be done at different levels. The more general levels are concerned with getting the structure and sequence right. Revision might entail moving around headings and blocks of text. Apart from the content of the text, you may want to try out different page layouts and formatting. At a more detailed level, you might look at the sequence of paragraphs: does each concentrate on one point, do they follow each other in the right sequence? At the most detailed level you will be looking at grammar, punctuation, vocabulary and spelling.

I find that it is much easier to review what I have written when it is printed out on paper rather than still on screen, I can get a better overview of the layout, length of sections, and line of the argument. If your eyesight is good, change the font to really small (perhaps 8 point) before printing, both to save paper and to make it easier to have an overall view of the work. You will quickly spot gaps, dislocations in the sequence and imbalances in the length of sections. Alternatively, reduce the line spacing instead of the font size in order to maintain the line justification and familiar appearance of the script. Do remember though, that you are only doing these adjustments to make it easier to review your draft. Normally, the final version must not be submitted in less than 11 or 12 point font size (check with the submission details for your dissertation, see Chapter 25).

It is important to keep track of your revisions: make sure you know what the latest one is! The best way is to save each revision as a new file, clearly labelled with a revision number

FIGURE 24.4   Getting everything right first time.

(e.g. Chapter 3/1, 3/2, etc.) You will thus be able to go back to a previous revision if you change your mind or want to check on some detail. Most word processing programs also provide a facility for keeping track of revisions.

24.5   Tops and tails

Particularly if you write your dissertation over a longish period and produce sections based on your notes, thoughts, blocks of data, etc. it is difficult to get smooth continuity in the text. This is really needed in order to make the dissertation clear and easy to read. You cannot usually do this completely as you are building up the text, so one aspect of your revisions should be to check this. As is usual with most things, continuity can be considered at different scales. You can check on the following aspects in scales of descending order.

Scale of the whole dissertation

- Introduction – gives a brief guide to the reader about the content and structure of the whole work. It should be a separate chapter or section at the beginning of the dissertation.
- Conclusions – the finale of your dissertation. One should be able to read this section separately as a full account of the results of your investigations.
- Links and cross-referencing – the issues studied should arise out of the background; the methods used in the investigation should relate to the types of questions/issues studied; the actual fieldwork or personal research work should follow the methods described; the

data should arise from the fieldwork or personal research; the conclusions should be produced from the data and encapsulate the answers to the questions or issues raised at the beginning of the work. In this way, you will complete the circle: problems raised, answers found.

Scale of the chapters or sections

- Introduction – a few paragraphs provide a lead-in to the subject of the chapter.
- Conclusion or summary – draws together the main results of the discussion in the chapter.
- Links and cross-referencing – the introduction might usefully refer to the main issues/problems dealt with in the chapter; a final sentence or two form a bridge to the next chapter; sometimes cross-references are usefully added to linked information in other chapters.

Scale of the paragraphs and sentences

- Paragraphs – make one overall point or deal with one topic. First sentence introduces this, subsequent sentences develop this, the final sentence possibly forms a conclusion and leads to the next paragraph.
- Sentences – best to keep short and clear.
- Links and cross-referencing – consistent use of terminology. Define terms and abbreviations the first time they are used.

24.6   Grammar

The principles of English grammar are too complicated to outline here. If you have forgotten the principles of grammar, or never learned them, don't worry. Use your own 'voice' as you write, and explain everything as clearly as you would if you were talking to someone. However, do make sure about any particular requirements of academic writing style; certain subjects may demand this. Generally, as long as you are consistent in developing your argument by using straightforward sentences to build up well-formed paragraphs (as explained above) you will be able to communicate effectively. If you are writing in a foreign language, it is worth getting a native speaking colleague to check through a section of your work to see if you are making any recurring mistakes.

Your word processor program (in this case Microsoft Word) will indicate any gross grammatical errors if you use the grammar check facility in the tools menu. Check the settings of the spelling and grammar options in the tools menu to see what is actually being checked: you can tick the option boxes for different features. Similar features will be available in most word processing programs.

24.7   Spelling

Spelling can be checked with the spell check facility. Make sure that the language is correctly stipulated (again, find this in the tools menu). Because of the ease of use of this facility, it is no longer acceptable to submit work with typographical errors. Spell checkers are not infallible, however. They will not detect a typing mistake that forms a recognizable – albeit a wrong – word (e.g. their or there; lose or loose; place or plaice!). If, for reasons of presentation, you are handwriting some parts of your work, after checking the spelling yourself, get someone else to read the text. It is surprising how blind one gets to one's own mistakes.

24.8   Punctuation

Punctuation can also be checked automatically. There is some flexibility here. A good guide to the use of punctuation is to read the text aloud, and fit the punctuation in where the natural pauses occur in speech, for example: commas for short pauses, semicolons for greater divisions, colons preceding lists. Commas or spaced dashes (often typed as spaced hyphens) should be used both before and after an aside or additional piece of information within a sentence, just as you would with brackets. Direct quotations must always be within quotation marks (now usually only single inverted commas), unless they are lengthy, in which case they are best presented as indented paragraphs.

One of the most common punctuation errors concerns the apostrophe with 's' when noting possession, for example 'the animal's face'. With 'it', only use the apostrophe when you can read 'it's' as 'it is'; for the possessive, for example 'its face', no apostrophe is needed. As the style of writing a dissertation should not be too conversational, it is better anyway to avoid using abbreviations such as 'it's', 'don't', 'couldn't'.

24.9   What should I do now?

Get started, is the simple message! If you have not yet formulated an outline of your dissertation, then this is probably the best place to start. This framework will allow you to painlessly insert any notes you have, thus providing a first body of written work.

It is worth checking your word processing program for the spelling and grammar features mentioned above. They may need to be activated in order to work.

If you feel that there is not enough information or prompts in the text above, read other books that are more specialized on aspects of dissertation production, such as the process of writing, specific subject-oriented dissertation guides and study guides. See the references below for some suggestions.

24.10   References to more information

Here are three books that deal exhaustively with the art of writing, both the technique and practice.

Briggs, A.R.J. and Coleman, M., eds (2007) *Research Methods in Educational Leadership and Management*, 2nd edn. London: Sage.

See Chapter 21.

DuPre, L. (1998) *Bugs in Writing: A Guide to Debugging Your Prose*, Reading: Addison-Wesley.

Gilbert, N., ed. (2001) *Researching Social Life*, 2nd edn. London: Sage.

   See Chapter 21.

Jay, R. (1999) *How to Write Proposals and Reports That Get Results*. London: Prentice Hall.

   Really aimed at managers, but we all have to manage! Good practical advice on all aspects of writing.

Mounsey, C. (2002) *Essays and Dissertations*. Oxford: Oxford University Press.

   A compact, easy-to-read guide to writing; in the 'One Step Ahead' series.

Other titles in the same series might also be useful: *Editing and Revising* by Jo Billingham, *Punctuation and Spelling* by Robert Allen, and *Words and Writing Reports* by John Seely.

Opie, C., ed. (2004) *Doing Educational Research: A Guide to First Time Researchers*. London: Sage.

   See Chapter 3.

Redman, P. (2005) *Good Essay Writing*. London: Sage.

Rudestam, K.E. and Newton, R.R. (2001) *Surviving your Dissertation: A Comprehensive Guide to Content and Process*, 2nd edn. Thousand Oaks: Sage.

   See Chapter 9.

Woods, P. (2005) *Successful Writing for Qualitative Researchers*. London: Taylor and Francis.

   Really thorough on all aspects of writing – getting started and keeping going, organization, alternative forms of writing, style, editing, etc.

25 How Can I Make My Work Look Interesting and Easy to Read?

25.1   Presentation ideas

Unless you are particularly design oriented, you have probably not spent much time thinking about just what your dissertation will look like. After all, there are many more important things to occupy your time while trying to get it finished. However, a dissertation is as much an exercise in communication as one in research, so time spent in production design pays good dividends. When your examiner is faced with a pile of dissertations to mark, it is obviously those that are attractive, clear and easy to read that will be the most welcomed. Although there are many possible styles of presentation, a few basic guidelines should be followed. These relate to the actual design of the publication as well as the organization of the material contained within it. The best way to success is to devote some time in forethought and preparation, as it is very frustrating, time consuming and risky to work by trial and error.

As you will be only one of many students at the university or college with the same deadline for submission, the pressure on printing and binding facilities will become greater as the date approaches. Delays will increase just as you are running out of time. I know it is easy to say 'get your work finished early' but you will be doing your-self a favour not to have to join in the last minute scramble. In fact, giving yourself enough time can result in you actually enjoying putting the finishing touches to your 'masterpiece'.

25.2   Cover design and binding

Let us start with the first impressions from the outside. Ideally, you should keep the whole work in one volume. This may be difficult if you are, say, presenting large format graphical work as well as written text. Although A4 size is the most common for text-based dissertations, if your subject demands considerable graphic work, consider A3 size. You can still easily and economically photocopy in this format, and computer printers coping with this format are not uncommon. Text can also be comfortably integrated in columns on the page. The larger formats tend to be more expensive to reproduce and it is difficult to design the text elements in such a way that they are comfortable to read. If you do have to produce your work in two sizes, it is worth devising a way of connecting the two physically, so they do not drift apart – a common source of problems. If only a few large pages are needed, perhaps you can stay with the A4 or A3 format and arrange the larger sheets to fold out.

There are several ways of binding your work. Important is that pages cannot become separated, so a folder of loose sheets or slide-on plastic holders will not do. Even the clip-type ring binders are vulnerable to coming undone or the pages being pulled out, with disastrous results. Ring binding with plastic 'comb' rings can cope with almost any number of pages, and also allows the pages to be opened right up so that they lay flat. You need to have access to a special machine for slotting your paper and inserting the binder; these should be available to you somewhere in your department, so it is worth finding out in good time.

The cover should have the title of the dissertation, your name, a date and details of the module or course number. Check with the official instruction for any stipu-lations on this. Get some good quality coloured card for the front and back covers. You can print on these to good effect. For an even more glossy finish, you can add a piece of transparent plastic front and back. Especially if there is a design element in your course, it is worth spending some effort in making the cover distinctive, particularly if the result can be related to the contents of the dissertation. Even if you keep it very simple, ensure that the typography is well arranged and easy to read.

What does 'well arranged' mean? There are no hard and fast rules on this: you will need to rely on your aesthetic sense and on any ideas gleaned from the layout of other publications that you admire. Aim to get a certain logic and consistency in the layout, so that it expresses a distinct style. Decide whether you want to centre the text, or if you want to align it to the left or right. Usually, it is wise to keep to the same typeface, altering the size to suit the importance of the text. Using a large font for the main title

FIGURE 25.1   What does 'well arranged' mean?

aids legibility, as does leaving plenty of empty space around the lettering. Avoid having a strong picture as a background to the text.

25.3   Title

The title of your dissertation has undoubtedly been the focus of your work for many weeks or even months, but now that you have virtually completed the dissertation, it is worth reviewing it in the light of what you have actually done. Does it still accurately and succinctly sum up the nature of your study? As briefly stated in Chapter 3, the title must contain the crucial terms related to the work; after all, this is what will be listed in any reference to it. Keep it as short as possible.

A useful way to review your title is to check the following points:

- Are the one, two, or perhaps three main concepts or issues mentioned? For example: sport and fitness; learning difficulties; behaviour strategies.
- Are these then located into a context to focus and limit the study? The context might be sector of society, time period, location, etc., for example sport and fitness for sixth form girls; learning difficulties for those deemed to have special educational needs.
- An indication of the main methodology or philosophical stance might also be usefully added, for example a case study approach, a feminist perspective, an archival analysis, etc.

A common way of forming the title is to state the main concepts, then add the detail as a subsidiary phrase, for example 'Learning styles: facilitating inclusion in geography for a variety of Year 3 children'. Beginning phrases like 'A study of' or 'A comparison between' can generally be omitted.

On the title page, you should also add your name and the date. You might also add a description of what course or module the dissertation is set to fulfil. Check the assignment details for any specific instructions.

25.4   Acknowledgements

These are short expressions of thanks to people or organizations that have been particularly helpful in your work. The relatively small scale of an undergraduate dissertation makes this an optional feature, but you may feel particular gratitude that you want to express to someone. If you have been funded by an organization, you may be obliged to acknowledge this by the terms of the agreement.

25.5   Abstract

You have probably realized by now that you do not have time to read whole books or even journal articles in order to find out if they are of interest to you. You have also probably noticed how useful the abstract, list of contents and introduction are as shortcuts to finding out the content of the text. The index is also useful in this respect. In order to provide a guide to the reader of your dissertation, you should also provide these features. Seeing it from the point of view of the reader will help you to make these features really useful.

The abstract (or résumé, often called the executive summary in reports) is a compact summary of the whole dissertation, usually not more than 150–200 words long. It is placed right at the beginning of the dissertation, usually after the acknowledgements (if any) and before the list of contents. Despite it being at the beginning of your document, you can only write it, for obvious reasons, when you have completed the rest. This will be at a time when you are under stress to complete, so it is worth allotting some time for its production in your programme. It should not take too long, but is really worth the effort from the point of view of impressing your marker. Because it must be so short, it is not so very easy to write: you will need all your skills in summation to make it read well (this paragraph is already 150 words long!).

Start with a statement of the main aims of the project. Then add a bit of background to give the context in which it was carried out. Follow with the specific questions or problems that you posed, and then with the principal methods you used to investigate them. End with the main conclusions and perhaps a note about their significance.

For examples of abstracts, see any thesis, journal paper, conference paper, or a journal of abstracts.

25.6   Contents list

The list of contents is much easier to devise. All you have to do is make a list of all your chapter headings, subheadings, and even sub-subheadings, together with their page numbers. Put this just before the main text. You can automatically generate the list of contents with your word processing program if you do not want to do it manually. To be really professional, you can also add lists of figures, charts and illustrations, either separately or all together on one list. Just make a list of the titles and page numbers in order of appearance. Insert this after the list of contents, starting on a separate page. A list of appendices, if you have any, should also be added.

25.7   Introduction

The subject matter of the introduction has been mentioned in the previous chapter. Just to remind you, here it is again: the main aims of the dissertation, a short summary of the context of the study, the main problems or issues to be investigated, the overall approach to the project, and a short description of the structure of the dissertation. This lead-in to the main body of the work will be just a short chapter, the main function of which is to provide a guide to the reader about the subject and structure of the dissertation, and to point out its main features. It should whet the reader's appetite to read on, but not give away the conclusions – just as a detective novel will create a certain suspense from the start but not say 'whodunnit'. As your work is unlikely to go exactly as originally planned, it is not feasible to complete the introduction before the main part of the study is completed. Hence, allow yourself some time near the end of your program for finishing this writing.

25.8   References and bibliography

What is the difference between these two? A list of references mentions all the publications that have been referred to in the text, but nothing else. A bibliography lists also other publications that are useful or related to the subjects covered.

You definitely need to include a list of references. Normally, and most conveniently, the list is put at the end of the dissertation. Alternative locations, which are more difficult for your marker to review, are at the end of each chapter, or as footnotes to the relevant pages. If you are using the British Standard (numeric) system (see Chapter 10), make sure that the numbers follow correctly in sequence and tally with the references. These may have been shifted when you made revisions to the text. If you are using the Harvard (author/date) system, check that the references are in alphabetical order. You should also scan through all the citations in the text to ensure that they are detailed on the reference list – a tedious task, but one that can save you losing marks.

The order and punctuation in each reference should accord with the standard requirements and be consistent throughout. Mistakes are easily made here, so a thorough check

FIGURE 25.2   Unlikely to go exactly as planned.

is required. You will save yourself time and trouble if you have used a bibliographic database program, as the list can be generated automatically. Even if you have not, you have probably made a list of references as you went along, so paste this in and revise it rather than attempt to type it all out again from scratch.

25.9   Appendices

These are additional sections added at the end to supplement the main text, and are generally to be avoided. The main argument for this is that either the information is relevant to the subject and therefore should be included in the main text, or it is not directly relevant and should therefore not be added at all.

I believe that there are certain exceptions to this. If you have done a survey, a copy of the questionnaire or interview questions should be included as an appendix, perhaps also with a copy of a typical response. Similarly, a typical data sheet of observations could be shown. Copies of letters of permission or other crucial correspondence might also be included. Other bits of information that will illustrate how you did the work might also be usefully added, if these are really informative, but would disrupt the flow of the main text. You should refer to the appendices where appropriate in the main text.

To be avoided is inclusion of lengthy articles on related subjects, full survey responses, elaboration or discussion of important issues, etc. What is certain is that you will not get

FIGURE 25.3   The list can be generated automatically.

extra marks by padding out your dissertation with sundry additional information added as appendices.

25.10   Internal layout and design

Typographic design and layout is a profession of its own. But even without the help of an expert, it is possible to produce really smart results with a computer.

There will probably be stipulations about font choice, minimum font size, line spacing and margins, etc. in the instructions for your dissertation, so it is worth checking before you spend much time experimenting.

I will explain first the design issues that you need to face, then afterwards go into details on how you may achieve these using the computer (based on Microsoft Word).

Page layout and margins

A bit of design input should be used here. The page layout and margins determine the overall appearance of the content of the dissertation. You only have to look at a few books of different types, for example art books, novels, textbooks, etc. to see what a range of options there are. Once you have set up a page layout style, make sure that you are consistent in its application. One choice is whether to mirror the layout of left and right pages, or to keep the design the same orientation on all pages. If you are only allowed to print on one side of the paper, which is normally the case, this problem does not occur. As with most issues of design, a few experiments to try out and compare different options will help you to make decisions.

A balance should be achieved between white paper and printed areas; very full pages are tedious to read. Wide margins, as well as being left blank, can be used as an area to place key words, and small illustrations or diagrams. Leave plenty of space at the hinge side of the pages, especially if the pages cannot be folded flat when opened. If you are using A3 format you will almost certainly need to set your text in columns. You can determine the position and width of these.

Word processor tips

- File/Page Setup – start here to determine how the layout of all the pages will look
- Adjust the Margins, Paper Size, Paper Source, Page Layout as desired
- View/Page Layout – to see the appearance of your page while writing
- Try also File/Print Preview to see how it will look when printed
- Format/Columns – to set out your text in columns.

Typography

FIGURE 25.4 Very full pages are tedious to read.

Here you have a range of choices to make. First, you should decide on the typeface (font). There is a wide choice of these with a range of fanciful names but even among the 'standard' fonts there is quite a choice. The main distinction is between 'serif' and 'sans serif' designs. Serif designs have the little tails at the ends of the lines, derived from the stonemasons having to start the incision when carving the letters. Times New Roman is one of those. Sans serif fonts, without these tails, look more modern. Arial is one of those. Funnily enough, it is not always the simplest font that is easiest to read – perhaps because the lack of subtlety makes letters and words less instantly recognizable. The choice of font will determine the overall stylistic appearance of your text. It is easy to try out different ones to see what they look like and to pick an easily readable one.

Word processor tips

- Format/Font determines what font will be used from where you have the cursor onwards. For altering the font in all the text, go first to Edit/Select All to highlight the entire document. You can see in the window what the different fonts on the list look like. Normally you should keep to Regular Style. For Size, see below. You should not need to alter the

Character Spacing. The animations, though fun, are not really suitable for use in an academic work: they don't print out well anyway.

- Format Toolbar is a useful shortcut to formatting features. If it is not visible then go to View/Toolbars and tick the Formatting box.

Font sizes

- For easy legibility use a font size of 11 or 12 point for the general text. Large fonts make reading slower and take up lots of room (this can be used to your advantage if your content is rather meagre). Normally, keep to one font for the text. Exceptions can be for quotations, headings, labelling of diagrams and tables, etc. If the text is divided to serve two different purposes, for example as an extract from literature and as a commentary on that extract, then you could use two different fonts to make this obvious.

Word processor tips

- Format/Font/Size.

Line spacing

- A normal requirement for work that is marked is that the lines should be double-spaced. This provides room for the marker to add comments and corrections. Check on any official requirement in this respect. If you need to stretch your work a bit, then increase the spacing marginally. Quotations, if in a separate paragraph, are normally single-spaced (i.e. should not need correcting).

Word processor tips

- Format/Paragraph/Line Spacing controls only the appearance of the current and subsequent paragraphs. Highlight the whole text (Edit/Select All) in order to adjust the whole document.

Paragraphs

You have the choice of indenting the first line to show the beginning of each paragraph. However, this is not necessary if you leave a blank line between paragraphs.

Word processor tips

- Format/Paragraph/Indents – note the previous tip about what this controls.

Bold, italics and underlining

These should be used sparingly within the text. They can be used to good effect to accentuate particular words when they are used for the first time (e.g. specialist terminology), and to highlight crucial sentences (e.g. statement of the main research problem). Be consistent in their use, and it is best not to combine styles

FIGURE 25.5   Not to get too complicated.

(e.g. underlined italics). Another common use of a style change is italicized quotations within the text, and within the references in the list of references and bibliography.

Word processor tips

- Format/Font/Font Style, or use the 'buttons' on the Format Toolbar.

Headings

This is where a change of font, size and/or style can be used to emphasize the different levels of heading. The most important thing is not to get too complicated and to be consistent – not always easy in a long text. The placing of headings on the page can be varied. Normal is to keep them aligned to the left. Centred headings tend to look very formal and dated and headings aligned to the right are rather modern. Indenting subheadings is common.

Word processor tips

- Format/Font, etc. or use the Format Toolbar to do this manually.
- The Format Toolbar also has a Style section with a dropdown menu of automatic headings and other styles. Click on the desired heading level. You can alter these to your desire in Format/Style/Modify/Format.

Section numbering

Section numbering helps the reader to navigate the dissertation, so it should be consistent and easy to follow. The features that need numbering are: chapters, sections, possibly subsections, figures, diagrams, charts, tables, graphs, appendices and, most important of all, pages.

There are several styles of numbering of chapters and sections, all of which you can generate automatically using the word processing program. However, these formatting aids are not foolproof and sometimes come up with unexpected results, so checking is always necessary. Consistency is what is looked for. The simplest form of numbering and the most commonly used for lengthy reports is that each chapter is numbered in succession (1, 2, 3, etc.), each main section of the chapters is numbered within that Chapter (1.1, 1.2, 1.3, etc.). Subsequent subsections follow the same pattern within the main sections (1.1.1, 1.1.2, 1.1.3, etc.). Three levels of numbering are usually quite sufficient; you may find that two is enough. Make sure that the table of contents corresponds with the actual numbering in the text.

Bullets can be used when you are providing a list where the sequence of items is not significant. Bullets can be generated automatically.

Numbering of illustrations is a normal feature of academic writing. You will have to decide whether to make no differentiation between your different graphical additions, or to categorize them, with each category numbered separately. The simplest is to label them all figures and number them consecutively in each chapter (Figure 1.1, Figure 1.2, etc.). If there are many illustrations you could divide them into figures (pictures, drawings, cartoons, maps, etc.), charts (graphs, bar charts, pie charts, diagrams, etc.) or illustrations, and tables (tables and matrices). There are no established rules about this categorization; however, each type should be numbered separately in each chapter (Illustration 1.1, Illustration 1.2, Table 1.1, Table 1.2, etc.). An index of the illustrations at the beginning of the dissertation might be a useful feature. In all cases, use your judgement to provide maximum clarity and ease in navigation.

Word processor tips

- Select Numbering or Bullets on the Format Toolbar. To format these select Format/Bullets and Numbering.

Page numbering

This is an essential feature. If you have saved your text as several different files, you will have to ensure that, once combined, the page numbers follow through correctly from beginning to end. There is a choice about the location and style of page numbers that will be dictated by your overall presentation. Choose what you think is the best position for your page layout (top, bottom; centre, left or right), making the numbers easy to find when flicking through the pages. To aid easy finding, keep the numbers near the outside edge of the pages rather than in the centre. Automatic page numbering is a standard feature of word processors.

Word processor tips

- Insert/Page Numbers. To format these go to Format in this last window. If the numbers appear on the Print View but do not print, it might be because the header or footer margins are not big enough. Go to File/Page Setup/Margins to alter these.

Headers and footers

These are the zones at the top and bottom of the page that are repeated on every page, often containing the page number, chapter heading, dissertation title, etc. The headers and footers should be generated using the tool in the word processor; do not try to type them out on each page. The program will ensure that any changes to the length of the text on the page, an increase in page numbers, etc. will automatically be catered for. You can use different text in the left and right page headers, for example the dissertation title on the left, and the current chapter title on the right. You can insert a line to separate the headers and footers from the main text.

Word processor tips

- View/Header and Footer. Write in the box whatever text you want. Use the normal text Align Left/Centre/Right tools from the Format Toolbar to position the chosen headings. If the Header/Footer margins are not big enough to contain your text, etc. increase the margins in File/Page Setup/Margins.

Illustrations/figures

These can vary so much in size, shape and complexity that you need to make your own judgements as to how you will present them. Colour illustrations require lots of memory, and, of course, colour printing. Scanning in the pictures requires a bit of practice to get the best results. Ensure that you select a compressed file format (e.g. 'tif' for black and white, 'jpg' for colour) to ensure the file sizes do not become unwieldy. Don't forget to acknowledge the source of the illustrations.

Word processor tips

- Insert/Picture/From file. You can then locate the file of your illustration. Some clip art illustrations are also provided; most are rather banal, but they might be useful to highlight a point (see example below). Once inserted, you can change the size and position as required.

Graphical work

Graphs, charts and tables can easily be inserted, especially from associated programs (such as Microsoft Excel and Access in the case of Word). Most programs are interlinked through Windows.

Word processor tips

- Insert/Object or File. If you want to set up a table or worksheet from scratch, use the tools on the Standard Toolbar.

Text boxes

These can be used to separate sections of text in the form of vignettes, excerpts, lists, etc.

Word processor tips

- Insert/Text Box, then click on the place where you want it in your script. It can be sized to your requirements, and the font and layout of the text can be determined separately from the normal text. You can also fill the box with colour or shading, alter the frame lines, etc. and determine how the surrounding text reacts to it, all by clicking on the box and then Format/Text Box.

25.11   Advanced tips and tricks with the computer

Word processing programs bristle with features to help you write and compile reports (and dissertations) so that they are clear and easy to read. I will be referring to the Microsoft Word program in this section. However, similar features are provided by other word processing programs.

Spelling, grammar and language

Not really advanced, as checking spelling and grammar is a pretty basic task. You can set the program to check as you go along and alert you of any mistakes, with red or green underlines. If it does not do this, go to Tools/Options/Spelling and Grammar to alter the settings. But do remember to check what language is set (Tools/Set Language), as there are several types of English available. Highlight the whole document before you reset this (Edit/Select All).

Find and change

Sometimes you want to find a particular word in your document, or need to change a word whenever it appears. To save time go to Edit/Find, which will help you do both. Even bits of words, punctuation and other features can be found (look under Special).

Auto formatting

The Style Gallery tool in the Format menu gives a choice of instantly formatted styles. These arrange the margins, fonts, heading styles and indents to suit a wide range of different types of documents. If you apply one of the options to text that is already written, it shows you instantly in a window just what it will look like. The Auto Formatting tool gives you the full range of options on all aspects of formatting, and will apply your choices throughout the document.

Table of contents

This can be generated automatically if you have used the Style facility when setting your text. The Style is on the Formatting toolbar and gives a range of choices of text style, for example normal, Heading 1, Heading 2, etc. These will be picked up when you use the Insert/Index and Tables/Table of Contents facility. You will see that an Index, a Table of Figures and a Table of Authorities can also be generated this way. Consult the Help advice for details of how to mark the text correctly for these.

Readability

Readability scores can give an indication of how easy your style of writing is to read. When you finish checking spelling and grammar, information about the reading level of the document, including the following readability scores, is displayed. Each readability score bases its rating on the average number of syllables per word and words per sentence. The Flesch Reading Ease score rates text on a 100-point scale: the higher the score, the easier it is to understand the document. For most standard documents, aim for a score of approximately 60–70. The Flesch–Kincaid Grade Level score rates text on a US grade-school level. For example, a score of 8.0 means that an eighth grader can understand the document. For most standard documents, aim for a score of approximately 7.0–8.0.

Other word processing programs are likely have a similar readability check, and there are also other programs that are entirely dedicated to evaluating writing styles. Check on your university intranet for these.

Despite this kind of technological wizardry, it is difficult to beat personal judgement. Try to get one of your colleagues or relatives to read a section (or all, if you can persuade them) of your text and ask them whether it is easy to read, is clear and informative, and provides a convincing argument. Take a practical approach to any comments made; ask for suggestions on how any shortcomings could be remedied.

25.12   Avoid the production blues

Take some good advice on organizing your computer-based work.

Saving and backing up

You will be storing months of work on bits of vulnerable magnetic film, so easily corrupted or damaged beyond repair. Ensure against disaster by saving your work regularly and by making backups. Copy your work to two, or better, three different media, for example CD Rom, computer hard drive, memory stick and your institution's intranet home directory (if available). It is also a good idea to print out what you have done so far; if all else fails, you can scan this with a character/text recognition program. While you are writing, make a habit of saving your work every 10 or 15 minutes, so you do not lose too much if the computer crashes. You can instruct your program to make recovery and backup saves itself automatically at regular intervals (Tools/Options/Save/Autorecover every x minutes).

Printing

Dissertations can be quite complicated to print. It may take some time to get what you see on the screen to print correctly. Different printers have different printable areas, so your

FIGURE 25.6   Try to avoid the rush of the last few days.

carefully arranged pages may not appear as desired. Before printing, check all the pages on the Print Preview (File/Print Preview, or 'button' on the Format Toolbar). Colour illustrations and other graphic work may need colour printing, perhaps on different size paper. Tables and diagrams might need to be in landscape format, or perhaps you might want to print certain pages on acetate. This all needs some thought and time in order to get it right.

Timing

Remember that you will be one of many who want to use the computers and printers before the submission date, so try to avoid the rush of the last few days. Other equipment, such as scanners and binders, will also be in great demand during this time. If you have problems, even the help desk is likely to be subject to long queues.

25.13   What should I do now?

Make sure that all your work is adequately backed up. One way to preserve your text against all disasters is to print it out. To do this economically, temporarily reduce the font to 8 point, single-line spacing, when you print it. Not only do you save paper, but it is much easier to swiftly review what you have written, and to check the sequence of subheadings and numberings.

See what others have done in the past. You have surely by now looked at examples of successful dissertations from previous years. Now compare a few, looking at the presentation. You will soon see what is attractive, easy to read and professional looking. Consider the cover design, type of binding, and size of paper. Then look at the internal layout and design, use of illustrations and figures. What about the typeface and font size? You will have to make notes and even perhaps sketches of what you think is the most attractive and effective.

This is a good time to check with the official requirements. Is the minimum font size stipulated? Are there instructions about margins, paper size, line spacing, binding, etc?

If you cannot find the requirements, ask your supervisor for another copy. Better be safe than sorry!

Play a formatting game. Save one of your chapter drafts to a new file and give it a new label (safest for playing around with) and, with the cursor at the beginning, try out different styles in the style gallery in the format menu. You can also see examples of reports, etc. with full formatting. This not only will give you ideas on presentation but can provide a shortcut to the whole formatting process. Do check through afterwards to make sure that the formatting is as you wish throughout.

You can also experiment with generating the contents, fixing the headers and footers, aligning text around illustrations and text boxes, and all the other word processing tricks. Once you have decided what you want and determined how it works, then you can apply it to your proper text.

25.14 References to more information

The first port of call for questions about any aspect of word processing is the help facility in your program. This should answer questions about how to do things, and perhaps suggest things that you had not thought about or did not know. Although time consuming, just exploring all the menus of any computer program is a good way of learning how they work. As you probably will be short of time at this stage of the project, using an explanatory handbook about the program is another option that might be useful. See what is available in your library and your computer centre.

There is no point, I think, in my recommending here lots of books about typography, publishing design, layouts, etc. as you are unlikely to want to spend the time now in learning about these subjects in detail. If you are studying an arts subject that involves design issues, then use what you have learned to apply to your presentation work. However, here are a few books that might be useful:

The following book is highly recommended for presenting your work.

Allison, B. and Race, P. (2004) *The Student's Guide to Preparing Dissertations and Theses*, 2nd edn. Milton Park: Routledge Falmer.

These other books are also worth a look:

Hudson, D. (1998) *Designing for Desktop Publishing: How to Create Clear and Effective Documents*. Oxford: How To Books.

Lumgair, C. (2003) *Desktop Publishing*. London: Teach Yourself.

Parker, R.C. (2005) *Looking Good in Print*, 6th edn. Scottsdale: Paraglyph.

Redman, P. (2005) *Good Essay Writing*. London: Sage.

See Chapters 9 and 10.

26 Who Else Might Be Interested in My Writing?

26.1 Don't waste all your hard work: make it work for you!

As soon as you have submitted your dissertation, I am sure you will sigh with relief and be keen to get on with doing other things. But don't forget, your submission has been the result of a great deal of hard work and has taken up lots of your time. Perhaps you can wring more use out of it than just a mark from the examiners. It is therefore a very good idea to make a copy of your dissertation for your own use, as in most courses you will not receive it back. It will go into the dissertation collection that you consulted so many weeks ago (well, that is a good start to widening its readership!). Anyway, you will have probably (and should have) saved an electronic version onto disk.

So what can you do with it so that it produces some more advantages for you? Whatever you do will take time and effort, so it is only worth doing if you get some benefits. Consider the following possibilities. You could:

- Develop good contacts for possible future employment
- Get yourself known as an 'expert' on an aspect of your favourite pastime

- Create a stir in the press
- Appear on the radio or the TV
- Build up additional academic credibility to help your future career
- Put yourself on the Web
- Speak at a conference or workshop or society meeting
- Receive some funds to follow-up issues and activities that interest you
- Go on to do a research degree
- Set up a profit making business.

It is pretty obvious from this list that you might get several benefits at once if you work things out in the right way. So, how can you go about it? For a start, in order to be motivated and successful, you need to remain really interested in the subject of your dissertation, as you will have to spend some time revising the length and format of what you have written. If you chose your title wisely right at the beginning, you might have developed even more interest now that you know so much more about your subject.

I suggest below the different formats suitable for the different beneficial goals listed above.

26.2   Feedback to subjects and participants

If you have used a real-life situation for your dissertation research, for example in case studies or surveys, you have probably received plenty of help from several people. These may be managers, organizers, specialists, etc. If you were finding out about aspects of their organization, they may be very interested to know what you wrote. They are unlikely to want to read your whole dissertation, but the parts that deal particularly with their organization, perhaps in comparison with others, and the conclusions you have drawn, will certainly be of interest to them. You could cut and paste sections of your work to provide them with a short report, tailored to their particular interests. You could also investigate whether they have an in-house newsletter to which you could contribute a short article.

This will certainly get you noticed; your following up will impress both for the gratitude that you show and for the perhaps useful feedback that is usually the reason for getting involved in a research project. Not only does this provide a nice 'thank you' for their help, it might also be a good step towards getting some work in their organization, if that is what interests you. Even if you are not angling for a job, having contact with the movers and shakers in your particular field of interest is an asset that may be useful in the future.

It is more difficult, and probably not worth your effort, to provide feedback to a large number of interviewees or respondents to questionnaires. However, if you were investigating a community or some kind of an interest group, their leaders might appreciate it if you gave a short presentation of your study at one of their meetings. You might be treading on delicate ground, so make sure that the leaders are aware of the contents of your presentation. Assess how this exercise might be useful to you. It will certainly be a plus for your CV and might also lead to useful contacts and recommendations. It also might be a stimulating experience and end up in a lively discussion. If a face-to-face session rather daunts you, see if they produce a newsletter or discussion board, perhaps even a website to which you could contribute.

26.3 Newspapers, journals and magazines

Getting into print is always a good idea, though quite a challenge. You will be well aware of the huge variety of daily, weekly and monthly periodicals on offer at newsagents. Every one of them must fill their paper with articles and advertisements, so they are always looking for material. However, they must be selective – and therefore so must you! How do you target the right publication? It depends on what you write about. Consider the nature of the report you could submit.

If your research has come up with really surprising results, that could have a serious or wide significance, i.e. something that could be considered newsworthy in a general sense, either locally or nationally, then you could devise a press release and submit it to the local or national paper. A press release is only two or three paragraphs long and provides the essential details of the 'story', the what, where, how, when, who information. Address it to the editor and don't forget to add the date and your contact details. If someone on the editorial team is interested, they will contact you for more information. Obviously, local newspapers are easier to get into, particularly if the story is based in their area. Something along the lines of 'A study at our local university has recently revealed that…' might be a good way to start. The national tabloid press will be most interested in sensational (and bad) news – but don't get carried away. You could land yourself in hot water if you exaggerate or falsify your report.

FIGURE 26.1   A good step towards getting some work in their organization.

If your research is of interest only to a specialist readership because of its particular subject, then you should look for publications that are focused on this subject and cater for the people with this interest. Niche market magazines have proliferated in recent years, not only those that are publicly available at the newsagents, but also subscription magazines and professional papers and journals. You will probably be already aware of those catering for your particular interest. If there are several publications catering for the same interest, note that each will have its own character, and aim at a particular level of understanding. Gauge the level at which you will be most comfortable: will it be a more popular article for the interested, or a technically detailed one for the experts? Make your choice, keeping in mind the motivation for writing the article in the first place. You normally have to write the whole article first and then submit it to the editor of the chosen publication for consideration. Even so, it is a good idea to make a preliminary enquiry first by telephone to find out what they prefer and what your chances are of being accepted.

26.4   Radio and television

Some people will do anything to get onto television! You won't have to, as you have already chosen your own reason for appearing on the radio or television. How you persuade the programme makers is another question. And what advantages you will get from being successful you will have to ask yourself. Let us consider radio first.

The advantage of radio is that there is a multiplicity of stations ranging from the local hospital radio to national networks. My local area has at least three radio stations that feature all sorts of local news, characters and events. Listen in on the programmes for a few days, if you haven't already, and you should soon see whether you could compile something that would interest one of them. Obviously, if your work has revealed some attention-grabbing information about the locality, you will have a good chance of being asked to make an appearance – vocally, that is. National radio is a different matter. Apart from taking part in a phone-in discussion, many of which are of questionable quality and will definitely not get you any kudos, you will probably struggle to find acceptance. Only if your dissertation has produced really important or surprising information on a topic of national concern will you have a chance of interesting programme makers on national radio. Again, you need to be familiar with the format of the station output to spot the chance of getting on. Some stations do rely on audience input in some of their programmes.

Local television, apart from the regional news, is virtually non-existent, so you need to try a different approach. You are far more likely to appear on the television if you have committed 'an 'orrible murder' and got caught than if you have done sterling work to help your community! I have been invited several times to appear in top entertainment programmes just because I featured in a small book about weird hobbies, as someone who played the Swiss Alphorn. No one ever asked me to talk about my research projects! So unless your findings are shocking, amazing, amusing or damning, you will have difficulty in making your break on the small screen. Look out for feature programmes that draw on local knowledge or specialist expertise. One problem is that most serious programmes are planned well in advance, so you do not know what is being

FIGURE 26.2   Some people will do anything to get onto TV.

looked for. Personal contacts in the television world will be an invaluable asset in this respect.

26.5   Conference papers and poster presentations

There are numerous conferences that are organized for information, training and mutual contact on every subject and at every level of sophistication. There are some that are specifically aimed at the student level, while others sometimes have a student section in them. Find out from your institution's department and your older student friends what is on offer. Some conferences are an annual event and it is likely that previous students have contributed a paper or poster presentation at one of them. One thing is certain, you will not be paid for doing these.

A paper is presented as a short talk of about 15–20 minutes, usually supported by some visual matter on overheads, slides or Powerpoint presentation. A poster is an information panel about your work that is hung up in the conference area. You will normally have to respond to a call for papers by sending in a short summary (abstract) of your intended paper or poster months before the planned event. If accepted, you may have to submit the full paper or poster shortly before. If the conference is far away, perhaps even abroad, see if you can get some financial support for travel and accommodation from your university; they usually have a fund for this. Your presentation at a conference will be a good addition to your CV particulars.

26.6   Grants, awards and prizes

There are several schemes and competitions that give awards on the basis of undergraduate and postgraduate dissertations. If you have done particularly well you might have a chance to cash in on your work. Again, you will have to find out what is offered in your particular subject. Ask your supervisor, your department and your institution's information centre. The scheme may be awarded by your university, a professional body, a commercial company or another institution. You could win a grant to travel and widen your studies, win a cash award or prize, or win a place for work experience at a specialist institution or a foreign university. Whatever it is, it will be another good addition to your list of achievements on your CV, as well as an enjoyable reward for all your hard work.

26.7   Publishing on the Internet

Anyone can put up a Web page or add to information on the Internet. What good it will do is another question. But perhaps I am being cynical. It really depends on just how you design and locate your presence on the Web. Make a search to see what there is on your subject interest; you have probably done this already during your background research. The main question to ask, whatever you do, is: how will it benefit you?

Having a personal website has advantages if you have something to sell or you need to provide information about yourself and your activities. The contents of your dissertation are unlikely to be an important element of this. However, you might be able to use your newfound knowledge and skills to contribute to existing sites on your subject, or if you are particularly impassioned, to set up a new site dedicated to your interest. The main advantage of doing either of these is that you will be able to network with others with similar interests. Make sure there is a facility to contact you or contribute to a discussion forum on your site. There is plenty of advice available about how to set up and design Web pages: see in your library and at magazines in your newsagents. You will also be able to use computer programs at your college or university to do the work while you are still there.

26.8   Setting up your own business

This is probably a long shot in this context. But setting up a business does not necessarily mean hiring a suite of offices and getting yourself a PA. You may be able to exploit your acquired knowledge or skills to earn a bit of money in a more informal way. It is pointless for me to write here loads of advice about what kinds of business you could start and how it is done; the possible options are too wide. (Suffice to say, one education studies student I had the pleasure of mentoring has just turned her first million in providing corporate training, being recognized as business-woman of the year in her county.) But do spend some time considering whether you could offer some kind of a service that you could charge for. Has your added knowledge and skills in research and writing provided you with something other people need? If so, is there a way that you can convince them it is worth hiring you to do the work? Using personal contacts will inevitably be the

FIGURE 26.3   An enjoyable reward for all your hard work.

easiest way to find work of this kind. You will probably have made quite a few during your dissertation work and also have found out what the needs are. All it needs is some thought and imagination, then some skills of presentation and persuasion, and then some sound work to deliver the goods in order to earn perhaps a very useful addition to your income.

26.9   Ethics reminder

It is particularly important when you publicize your research work in any form, that you carefully follow the ethical guidelines. Make sure that where confidentiality has been assured, it is strictly adhered to. The last thing you will want is to cause damage to people or organizations, or get yourself landed in legal troubles.

The two main aspects you should consider are privacy and commercial/organizational sensitivity. Just because people have been willing to provide you with personal and company/organizational information for your university study, it does not mean that they would be happy to see that information in the public domain. Get specific written permission from the sources of information to ensure probity. If you are at all uncertain about any aspect of this, get advice from your supervisor, the ethics experts in the university, or in really delicate situations, legal specialists.

Watch out too for copyright issues on illustrations and copies of newspaper articles or headlines. Any pictures, diagrams, graphs, tables, etc. copied from published sources are covered by copyright. You need to have written permission from the copyright holder to reproduce them, and they sometimes charge for this. Look at the publishing details at the beginning of the book or journal to find out whom to apply to. Alternatively, only use your own figures and illustrations.

You should also be careful not to make claims that you cannot back up with sufficient evidence. You might not automatically get enough feedback from the marking of your dissertation to see if your arguments were really convincingly based on the supporting data. If in any doubt, you should consult with your supervisor, and even better, the internal examiner who marked your dissertation, and raise the relevant issues to gain his/her opinion.

26.10   What should I do now?

FIGURE 26.4   It does not mean that they would be happy.

Only go back to exploiting your dissertation work when you feel ready and motivated. I hope that this chapter has given you some interesting ideas of what you can do. As any of these options requires quite a bit of time and effort, make sure that you have clear reasons for doing what you have chosen and that you will reap sufficient benefits.

Most research work gets quickly out of date, so the longer you leave it the more difficult it will be to successfully exploit your work. Also, you will quickly lose contact with people you have consulted during the process and you yourself will have moved onto doing other things. So, strike while the iron is hot, make hay when the sun shines, and … well, you can probably think of a few more proverbs in this vein.

26.11   References to more information

I should think that the last thing you want to do now is to read more books. However, you may need to get some advice on writing press releases, articles and papers or designing a website. Here are some suggestions on different aspects of getting published – the titles speak for themselves:

Bartram, P. (1999) *Writing a Press Release: How to Get the Right Kind of Publicity and News Coverage*. Oxford: How To Books.

Baverstock, A. (2006) *Is There a Book in You?* London: A & C Black.

Baverstock, A. (2002) *One Step Ahead: Publicity, Newsletters, and Press Releases*. Oxford: Oxford University Press.

Chapman, N. and Chapman, J. (2006) *Web Design: A Complete Introduction*. Chichester: Wiley.

Croft, A. (2007) *The Freelance Writer's Handbook: How to Make Money and Enjoy Your Life,* 3rd edn. London: Piatkus Books.

Kogan (1998) *500 Tips for Getting Published: A Guide for Educators, Researchers and Professionals*. London: Kogan Page.

McNiff, J. Lomax, P. and Whitehead, J. (1996) *You and Your Action Research Project*. London: Routledge.

See Chapter 7.

Robbins, J.N. (2007) *Learning Web Design*, 3rd edn. Farnham: O'Reilly.

Wellington, J. (2003) *Getting Published: A Guide for Lecturers and Researchers*. London: Routledge Falmer.

References

Bartlett, S., Burton, D. and Peim, N. (2001) *Introduction to Education Studies*. London: Sage.

Bassey, M. (1990) 'On the nature of research in education', Part 2, *Research Intelligence* 37: 39–44.

Bromley, D.B. (1986) *The Case-Study Method in Psychology and Related Disciplines*. Chichester: Wiley.

Clark, C. (2005) 'The structure of educational research', *British Educational Research Journal* 31(3): 289–308.

Collier, A. (1994) *Critical Realism: An Introduction to Roy Bhaskhar's Philosophy*. London: Verso.

Copi, I.M. (1982) *Introduction to Logic*, 6th edn. New York: Macmillan.

Davies, P. (2001) *Get Up and Grow: How to Motivate Yourself and Everybody Else Too*. London: Hodder and Stoughton.

Freeman, R. and Meed, J. (1993) *How to Study Effectively*. London: Collins Educational.

Husserl, E. (1964) *The Idea of Phenomenology*, W. Alston and G. Nakhnikian (trans). The Hague: Martinus Nijhoff.

Kerlinger, F.N. (1970) *Foundations of Behavioral Research*. New York: Holt, Rinehart and Winston.

Lofland, J. (1971) *Analysing Social Settings: A Guide to Qualitative Observation and Analysis*. Belmont, CA: Wadsworth.

MacNaughton, G., Rolfe, S.A. and Siraj-Blatchford, I. (2006) *Doing Early Childhood Research: International Perspectives on Theory and Practice*. Maidenhead: Open University Press.

Matheson, D., ed. (2004) *An Introduction to the Study of Education*, 2nd edn. London: David Fulton Publishers.

Matthews, E. (1996) *Twentieth Century French Philosophy*. Oxford: Oxford University Press.

Miles, M.B. and Huberman, A.M. (1994) *Qualitative Data Analysis: An Expanded Sourcebook*. London: Sage.

Nisbet, J. (2005) 'What is educational research? Changing perspectives through the 20th century', *Research Papers in Education* 20(1): 25–44.

Oliver, P. (2004) *Writing Your Thesis*. London: Sage.

Opie, C., ed. (2004) *Doing Educational Research: A Guide to First Time Researchers*. London: Sage.

Pinter, H. (1998) *Various Voices: Prose, Poetry Politics 1948–1998*. London: Faber and Faber.

Preece, R. (1994) *Starting Research: An Introduction to Academic Research and Dissertation Writing*. London: Pinter.

Reynolds, P.D. (1977) *A Primer in Theory Construction*. Indianapolis: Bobbs Merrill Educational.

Robson, C. (1993) Real World Research: A Resource for Social Scientists and Practitioner-Researchers. Oxford: Blackwell

Robson, C. (2002) *Real World Research*, 2nd edn. Oxford: Blackwell.

Rudestam, K.E. and Newton, R.R. (2001) *Surviving your Dissertation: A Comprehensive Guide to Content and Process*, 2nd edn. London: Sage.

Taylor, G. (1989) *The Student's Writing Guide for the Arts and Social Sciences*. Cambridge: Cambridge University Press.

Verma, G.K. and Mallick, K. (1999) *Researching Education: Perspectives and Techniques*. London: Falmer Press.

Weston, A. (2000) *A Rulebook for Arguments*, 3rd edn. Indianapolis: Hackett.

Woods, P. (1999) *Successful Writing for Qualitative Researchers*. London: Routledge.

Index